ORGANIZING SOCIETIES FOR WAR

ORGANIZING SOCIETIES FOR WAR

The Process and Consequences of Societal Militarization

Patrick M. Regan

PRAEGER

Westport, Connecticut
London

Library of Congress Cataloging-in-Publication Data

Regan, Patrick M.
    Organizing societies for war : the process and consequences of
societal militarization / Patrick M. Regan.
        p.   cm.
    Includes bibliographical references (p.   ) and index.
    ISBN 0–275–94670–3 (alk. paper)
    1. Militarism.   I. Title.
U21.2.R43   1994
355.02′13—dc20   93–8621

British Library Cataloguing in Publication Data is available.

Library of Congress Catalog Card Number: 93–8621
ISBN: 0–275–94670–3

First published in 1994

Praeger Publishers, 88 Post Road West, Westport, CT 06881
An imprint of Greenwood Publishing Group, Inc.

Printed in the United States of America

The paper used in this book complies with the
Permanent Paper Standard issued by the National
Information Standards Organization (Z39.48–1984).

10 9 8 7 6 5 4 3 2 1

For Meg and Shane

Contents

Figures and Tables   ix

Preface   xiii

1   The Militarization of Societies   1

2   Identifying the Militarization Process:
The First Half of the Puzzle   27

3   Accounting for Violent Foreign Policy:
The Second Half of the Puzzle   59

4   The Feedback between Societal Militarization and
Violent Foreign Policy: Merging the Two Halves   77

5   Societal Symbols and Societal Militarization   95

6   In Search of Generalizations: The Case of Brazil   119

7   Conclusion   143

Appendix 1:   Coding Rules for the Manipulation of
the Perception of a Threat   157

Appendix 2:   Coding Rules for Counting War Toys   161

Appendix 3:   Coding Rules for Counting War Movies   163

Appendix 4:   Notes on the Coding of Data for the
               Militarization Index   165

Notes   169

References   173

Index   185

Figures and Tables

FIGURES

2.1 A Hypothetical Distribution along Industrialization
and Militarization Axes   34

2.2 Ratio of Military to Civilian Participation in Military
Mobilization, 1900-1985 (U.S.)   36

2.3 Ratio of Military to Civilian Participation in Military
Mobilization, 1900-1985 (U.K.)   37

2.4 Militarization Index, 1900-1985 (U.S.)   48

2.5 Militarization Index, 1900-1985 (U.K.)   49

2.6 Categorical Analysis of Disputes and Militarization in the
United States   53

4.1 Simultaneous Equation Model of the Feedback between
Militarization and Violent Foreign Policy   85

4.2 Results of Two-Stage Least Squares Estimation (U.S.)   88

4.3 Results of Two-Stage Least Squares Estimation (U.K.)   89

5.1 Militarization and Societal Symbols with
Patriotic Themes, United States, 1900-1985   111

5.2   Maintenance of the Perception of a Threat (U.S.)   112

5.3   U.S. Attitudes Regarding Future Wars and Societal Symbols
      with a Patriotic Theme   113

5.4   U.S. Attitudes toward Military Spending   114

5.5   Militarization and Societal Symbols with Patriotic Themes,
      Great Britain, 1930-1985   115

TABLES

2.1   Regression Results (U.S.): Outcome Variable, Militarization   50

2.2   Regression Results (U.K.): Outcome Variable, Militarization   51

2.3   Regression Results, Revised Model (U.S.): Outcome
      Variable, Militarization   54

2.4   Regression Results, Revised Model (U.K.): Outcome
      Variable, Militarization   55

3.1   Regression Results (U.S.): Outcome Variable, Disputes   70

3.2   Regression Results (U.K.): Outcome Variable, Disputes   71

3.3   Regression Results, Revised Model (U.S.): Outcome
      Variable, Disputes   72

3.4   Regression Results, Revised Model (U.K.): Outcome
      Variable, Disputes   73

3.5   Regression Results, Excluding War Years (1942 and 1945)
      (U.S.): Outcome Variable, Disputes   73

3.6   Regression Results, Excluding War Years (1915, 1917, 1940-45)
      (U.K.): Outcome Variable, Disputes   74

5.1   Bivariate Correlations between Societal Symbols and
      Militarization, Unlagged Models (U.S.)   108

5.2   Bivariate Correlations between Societal Symbols and
        Militarization, Unlagged Models (U.K.)   109

5.3   Bivariate Correlations between Societal Symbols and
        Militarization, Lagged Models (U.S.)   109

5.4   Bivariate Correlations between Societal Symbols and
        Militarization, Lagged Models (U.K.)   110

Preface

Between 1985, when Mikhail Gorbachev came to power in the Soviet Union, and 1993, there have been vast changes in the international environment. The Soviet Union has dissolved, various other countries that once appeared stable are in a state of disarray, parts of the nuclear arsenals in the United States and the former USSR have been dismantled, and the influence of the United Nations seems to be on the ascendency. To many students of international relations, we are undergoing a "natural experiment" in which the ordering in the international system is changing just as we sit back to ponder the effect of system hierarchy on such things as internation conflict. So much has changed in fact that it is sometimes difficult to focus on how much remains the same. For instance, military budgets are generally being reduced, but at a much slower rate than international threats seem to be dissipating; international conflict is still quite prevalent, possibly even on the increase, though the Cold War dynamics of it appears to have waned; and the veiled warnings of future doom can still be heard from the various quarters of the private and public sectors.

But even if the global village is in a period of uncertainty, we do stand poised to take advantage of an opportunity that may come along only once in a lifetime. For the first time in over three generations there is the real potential for serious reductions in the size and scope of the world's military forces, though that possibility seems to rest on a very shaky foundation. Many argue that a headlong rush to do away with "things military" would be destabilizing and ultimately threaten the fragile flowers of peace that are pushing up through the virgin soil. They may very well be right. But it seems clear that part of the key to successfully demilitarizing the world is in knowing how to do so, knowing how such policies can be carried out in a controlled and sustainable manner. This is an area for which we have a quite limited knowledge base and only a meager repertoire of proposals on which to draw.

Very few, if any, of the current cadre of policymakers have had experience in large-scale demobilizations of society's military forces, and the social science community has done little to help inform those policy practitioners of the attributes and behaviors that contribute to the militarization process. Expecting the political leadership to be successful at such a monumental task while groping in the dark for policies or solutions is asking too much. There appear to be too many short-term interests, too many international suspicions, and too many societal attributes all working toward a continuation of the status quo for any political coalition to proceed without a blueprint. This research is one attempt to develop the outlines of that blueprint.

Two years ago when I started this research I was warned by a colleague not to engage in an exercise in political history. Societal militarization, he said, was a thing of the past. Soon countries would be so determined to reduce the size of their militaries that in short order the whole topic would be relegated to the role of history. Never mind that we have a very weak grasp of the processes by which we arrived at this uneasy state of affairs over the past forty five years; there is such a public will to undo what has been done that the process will be painless, the resistance minimal, and the chances of success virtually assured. Hmmm. I was not sold on his interpretation.

I continued on with the project somewhat weary of my colleague's advice. But as I delved deeper into the search for evidence to test what seemed like a strong theoretical argument, I became convinced that we know far too little about how we reached this point of a world armed and poised for global destruction. I also came to realize that the resistance was going to be strong, that if attempts at demilitarization were to be successful, certain attributes of society, as well as behaviors of various individuals and groups, would have to be reevaluated. In short, there was still very good reason to believe that we lack the systematic knowledge necessary to make this transformation somewhat complete, but surely controlled. More important, it became clear that there was not one culprit at which the finger could be pointed, for instance a Military-Industrial Complex that stood at the forefront of resistance movements.

No, militarization is a process that involves nearly the whole of society. It is you and me and our neighbors. We are taught from a very early age that the military plays a virtuous role in society, that questioning that virtue is unpatriotic, and that those who direct the use of the military do so with nothing but the preservation of our sovereignty and security in mind. The mechanisms that lead to such a state of acquiescence are obscure: we watch war on television, we play with the toys that not only condone but reify the military, we grow up to be good journalists, academics, business people, and parents all somehow attached with short or long tentacles to this system that seeks to protect us. We would have it no other way. International politics, of course, fuels the militarization process, but international threats are not necessary to sustain it.

Many of our interests, not to mention incomes, are tied to the continued preparations for that war we hope never comes. And when there is talk of reducing the size of the military or scaling back on military contracts, it is not the Military-Industrial Complex that is at the heart of the resistance. It is you and me, the soldier, the sailor, the defense worker, the gas-station owner or barber near a military base. We put pressure on the politicians to cut defense, but in somebody else's backyard. This complex web of attitudes, perceptions, interests, international politics, and historical precedents makes the process of demilitarizing a rather tenuous affair and minimizes the chances for success. The greatest risk, of course, is to that of world peace and security--the very things that we are told the military is meant to ensure.

So in rejecting my colleague's advice to steer clear of a "dying" topic, I have embarked on an attempt to make the process by which societies militarize much more transparent. This is not the first word on this subject, nor hopefully will it be the last. Now more than ever we need to focus our energies on developing an understanding of the interaction of forces and actors that might lead us astray, as well as increasing our ability to articulate policy options that might contribute to our capacity to take advantage of this opportunity offered by recent events in the international environment.

Along the road to completing this research I have incurred numerous debts; most can never be repaid, and only some can receive mention. J. David Singer was an inspiration right from the start. He read countless drafts and spent endless hours forcing me to clarify my thinking. Ernest Wilson, Ted Hopf, and Carl Simon have also helped shape the final manuscript through their insightful critiques. Allan Stam, Iain Johnston, Scott Tarry, and Detlef Sprinz have also commented on various chapters and Ricardo Rodriguiz was a great help when it came to managing the data and making the computer work. And finally, the participants at the weekly Correlates of War seminar alternatingly endured my musing or harassed me during my many presentations. All were a big help; without them I would never have reached these final paragraphs. Any errors, of course, are unfortunately mine.

1

The Militarization of Societies

It is, indeed, not war or "militarization" that organizes society, but society that organizes itself in and for war. In mobilizing people and resources for war, societies remake themselves and their social-political orders for the purpose of organizing destruction.

--Michael Geyer, 1989: 79

If judged by the old criteria of militarism, we live in a very unmilitaristic time. But if we use the measure of militarization, a very different reality emerges . . . [I]t is precisely because militarization now runs so deep and so silently that we have such trouble perceiving and articulating the exact nature of this dilemma.

--John Gillis, 1989: 10

The Cold War is over. Most of the Eastern European countries have held moderately free elections. The Soviet Union, as it has been known for the past seventy years, has dissolved, and most of the newly created states that made up that union appear more as allies of the Western Bloc than adversaries. Nuclear weapons and large numbers of troops are being removed from the European theater. And rumors of military budget cuts abound, with savings presumably targeted at redressing the economic malaise that is sweeping the world. One conclusion might be that the "Rise of the Trading State" (Rosecrance, 1986) is truly at hand.

But this putative demise of the military as the central actor in world politics may be too sanguine an interpretation. The roots of the military structures on which the past one hundred years of international politics have been feeding run extremely deep. Because of the depth to which the military has penetrated many of the most industrialized societies of the world, reversing this trend may prove to be exceedingly difficult. Not only will it require a concerted effort to refocus energies that have been heretofore devoted to military production and preparations, but as John Gillis points out, it may prove equally challenging to identify the ways and articulate the extent to which the military has penetrated societies. The idea that the military could come to dominate the political and economic fabric of a society is not new, nor are the potential consequences (Galbraith, 1969; Melman, 1985; Kennedy, 1987; Ball, 1988; Dumas, 1988; Kaldor, Sharp, and Walker, 1986).

Over a half century ago, Harold Lasswell warned the world of the potential for what he termed the "garrison state." This garrison state construct revolved around the dominance of specialists in violence, the most powerful group in society, over those whose specialty is commerce. The central concept that held this security-conscious society together was that of the perpetual expectation of violence. The ruling elite, he argued, would continually point to the threat from external foes in order to extract internal compliance. The manipulation of symbols that convey a heightened degree of threat--symbols of nationalism-- would serve as a useful tool for maintaining popular support behind the increasing influence of the military over the civil affairs of state. If patriotic fervor could not be sustained through mass socialization, occasional outbreaks of military hostilities would serve to ensure continued support. The original construct (1941) argued that the garrison state would coincide with a breakdown in political democracy. A revised model (1962), however, suggested that the outward appearance of democracy could be maintained while internal decision-making would be increasingly usurped by the security sector.

While Lasswell's assertion of military dominance over society may be a bit strong, the organization of the civil sector of a society around the mission of the military has implications that go far beyond the success or failure of an economic system, though the economic dimension is clearly important. But the role of war--and violent foreign policy in general--as both a consequence of and a determining factor in the militarization of society is also of critical importance (Gurr, 1988; Van Evera, 1984). Unfortunately, far too little is understood about how these factors interact and what results from such interaction. It is here that this research will make its biggest contribution, by asking several questions. Does violent foreign policy feed the process that leads to a society organized around the goals and missions of the military? Is a highly militarized society more likely to resort to violent diplomacy as a form of internation influence? In short, is there a feedback relationship between violent state behavior and the militarization of a society? But this work will also address issues of whether a political culture, or myth, will develop that reifies the military to the extent that the perception of a threat will be maintained as a means to ensure support for policies of mobilization and, if so, how. I will also examine some of the mechanisms through which citizens become socialized to both accept and participate in the mobilization process. In effect, I will more closely explore Lasswell's thesis that the "symbols of nationalism" are manipulated in order to gain the acquiescence of the general public.

Just how militarization affects a society is of critical importance in an era when tens of millions of people are repressed, unemployed, and hungry. My analysis will work from the premise that military capability is inherently destructive and that the ultimate end-use of military hardware or organization is war. The findings of many studies suggest that military spending is an inefficient mechanism for the stimulation of an economy (for example, see Nincic, 1982), though some scholars do find that allocating resources to the military sector can have positive economic effects (Kennedy, 1974; Benoit, 1973). If states are using their military sectors as the engine for either political or economic growth, in the long run this is a poor allocation of resources. The political and economic costs, combined with the potential impact on international conflict, should encourage research into alternative methods to develop and sustain a society. This seems particularly relevant in the developing world, where the increased emphasis on security, defined in terms of military capabilities, has particularly pernicious consequences.

Societal militarization may very well be associated with the political and economic growth or decline of nation-states, which is central to a number of queries in the study of world politics. Much of the theoretical work pertaining to the onset of war is related to changes in the systemic structure within which states operate (Singer, Bremer, and Stuckey, 1972). Power transition (Organski and Kugler, 1980) and power cycle (Doran and Parsons, 1980) models tend to account for war by the rise and fall of state power vis-à-vis potential rivals. But what is less clearly understood is just what fuels the rise and decline of a country on these capability dimensions.

The power transition model argues that when powerful nations are satisfied with the systemic order and when that order is dominated by a preponderance of power in the hands of one actor, stability will result. Conversely, if there is dissatisfaction between the two leading powers, and they are approaching parity, the probability for major power war is high (Organski and Kugler, 1980). The model further argues that the growth in capabilities of a nation is the result of internal processes and is non-manipulable by other actors. Presumably, then, there are mechanisms that drive this internal development and, through this, put states on the road to war. I will argue below that organizing the general public around the preparation for war may be one vital link in this process of the rise and decline of nations.

The power cycle model (Doran and Parsons, 1980) also relates the onset of the most violent wars to the rates of change in relative capabilities of nation-states. Likewise, some of the earlier work of J. David Singer, Stuart Bremer, and John Stuckey (1972) suggests that the ordering of the systemic structure, as measured on capability dimensions, plays a role in determining the amount of war in the system. There is a virtual plethora of literature arguing one side or the other of this issue (Bueno de Mesquita and Lalman, 1988; Wayman, 1984; Geller, 1990); what is common to most is that the internal changes in individual state capabilities have some effect on violence within the global system.

In the following pages I will present a theoretical model of the underlying process by which societies militarize. I will derive some testable hypotheses from that model and then subject those hypotheses to empirical testing. As in the case of any good research, when the tests fail to offer strong support for the theoretical argument (or disconfirmation), I will often engage in well-reasoned exploratory analysis. These latter exercises should not be construed as tests of the hypotheses per se, but rather as supplying useful information with which the theoretical argument can be refined and subsequently subjected to further testing. In the end I may draw tentative conclusions based, in part, on some of the exploratory analysis. Because these conclusions are based on empirically observed patterns over time--some the result of formally tested hypotheses, others ad hoc explorations of the data--the conclusions rest on a somewhat firm foundation.

One other point should be raised before moving on. The empirical portion of this analysis pertains only to the United States and Great Britain, from the turn of the twentieth century to 1985. And although I suspect that both the model and the findings are more broadly generalizable--across both space and time--the argument, as it stands, applies mainly to industrialized nations. I attempt to broaden this focus by including a historical chapter on the evolution of the military in Brazil, though the effort, to date, lacks the empirical rigor applied to the cases of the United States and Britain.

All that having been said, let me move back a few steps in this analytical process; a number of terms need to be clarified, and I need to make explicit the underlying connections between the militarization of a society, political and economic growth, and violent foreign policy. An understanding of how these factors interact and the consequences of this interaction requires the articulation of a model from which hypotheses can be developed and tested.

LAYING THE GROUNDWORK:
DEFINITIONS AND PARAMETERS

Throughout this work I will use *militarized* and *militarization,* quite consistently. By *militarized* I mean a *condition* reflecting the extent to which civil society is organized around the preparation for war (Geyer, 1989:79). In a highly militarized society, a large segment of the general public is organized by the elite around the production and preparations necessary to maintain (a) continued elite dominance and (b) the preeminence of the "security sector" over the elite apparatus.[1] This of course does not mean that most sectors of society are either knowing or willing participants in this organizational structure. They are, however, socialized to accept and participate in its continuance. With an operational definition of *militarized being the extent to which civil society is organized around the preparation for war,*[2] I will develop indicators that are intended to reflect the degree to which this condition exists in a society. *Militarization,* on the other hand, is the *process* by which states move from a less-militarized condition toward a more-militarized one. I will propose a model of this militarization process that suggests a feedback among domestic politics, economics, and external threats.

There is an important distinction here between the term *militarization*--as I have defined it--and the more traditional conceptual relationship, *militarism*. As the quotations that began this discussion suggest, this distinction is important. *Militarism* generally refers to military-based values and ideals, whereas *militarization* refers to the preparation for war. Drawing on a wide array of literature, Neta Crawford sets out eight core beliefs of militarism, which she summarizes by arguing: "Militarism is a coherent set of beliefs about the nature of the international system and the best ways to get along in it. Militarists assume that the use of force in international relations is natural, expected, and effective in most instances and they recognize few limits to the effective use of force" (1990:44). In comparing militarism to militarization, John Gillis gives the term militarism a similar definition: "Militarism is the older concept, usually defined as either the dominance of the military over civilian authority, or, more generally, as the prevalence of warlike values in a society" (1989:1).

Militarization, on the other hand, is used to describe the organization of the political, economic, and social aspects of society around the production and preparations necessary to wage war. *Webster's New Universal Dictionary* (1983) defines *militarize* as "to make military; to equip and prepare for war." Vernon Dibble (1966-67)--while adopting the terminology of Harold Lasswell--articulates a view of the United States as a "garrison society"; in doing so, he makes explicit the elements of what Michael Geyer (1989) refers to as a militarized society.

A garrison society is one in which it makes no sense to ask whether or not civilians control the military. It is a society in which the institutions and the men who hold military, economic, and political power have become so dependent upon one another; in which their goals and interests are so complementary; and in which the traditional boundaries between military and civilian spheres have broken down to such an extent, that the very conception of civilian versus military control has no meaning. (Dibble, 1966-67:106)

As a comparison, Dibble then offers three types of alternative societies in which the boundaries between the civil and military sectors are relatively clear: (1) a militia society--such as pre-civil war England--one with few or no full-time military personnel "and no independent military establishment for civilians to control"; (2) a civilian society--pre-World War II United States--where a full-time military is completely subordinate to civilians and where military values "are at odds with, or at least different from, the values of the rest of the society"; and (3) an old-fashioned militarist society--Bismarck's Germany--where the military establishment is not subordinate to civil authority but rather dominates it (106).

These distinctions, then, turn not only on values regarding the use of force to achieve policy objectives but also on the relationship between the civil and military sectors of society. The latter is an issue that has received considerable scholarly attention (see Berghahn, 1981; Huntington, 1957; Janowitz, 1977; Finer, 1988). In a militaristic society, not only are the values regarding the use of force to achieve policy objectives quite clear, but so also is the boundary that divides the military from the civilian sphere. But it is when the boundaries between the two sectors are murky that the discussion needs to adopt the terminology of *militarized*. And it is precisely by organizing the civil sector of society around the production and preparation required to wage war that this boundary begins to dissolve. An example, again taken from Dibble, might help make this distinction clear. In arguing that it is not the size of a military establishment alone that constitutes a garrison society, Dibble states:

The garrison society consists, rather, of 1) a large and powerful military that penetrates deeply into civilian life; of 2) the great importance of civilians in military affairs, the increasing resemblance between military officers and civilian executives in politics and business, and the greater contact and cooperation between officers and civilians in politics, in science, and in business; such that 3) the traditional boundaries between civilian and military society break down; and 4) the military are blended into an alliance with government and with large corporations. (108)

The greater the involvement of the general public in preparations for war, the less clear becomes this distinction between military and civilian. The civil sector of society becomes an active participant in the mobilization efforts, and through the socialization mechanisms that feed this participation, the general public becomes not only participants but advocates, often unwitting, of continued war mobilization.

Who belongs to the "general public" and who to the "elite," who is a "civilian" and who is part of the military apparatus, are also issues that must be addressed. In the formulation of my argument, I will use the term *elite* in the manner proposed by C. Wright Mills (1956), who argued that the "power elite" consisted of a triumvirate of the heads of the largest corporations, the political leadership, and the military bureaucracy. The general public, then, are those who generally do not hold sway at the pinnacle of the state apparatus. Clearly there is a counterelite in most societies: those influential critics of state policy who do not fall into the category of the general public yet do not march with the power elite. Although admittedly they are relevant actors in the pull and haul of domestic politics, they are generally a minor part of the total society. Because of this they do not figure prominently in my analysis. The term *civil*, on the other hand, pertains in large part to that group I have labeled the general public. Some of these people are active-duty or reserve military personnel, but they are simply those who have chosen, or have been drafted into, military service. In fact, they are arguably the most highly socialized of the entire population to the ways of the power elite. When I use the term *civil*, I do so to identify the organizational structure and goals of a collective group.

There is a body of literature, spawned in part by Mills, which identifies the culprit in the increasing influence of the military within society as the Military-Industrial Complex (MIC). The theoretical and empirical work that has addressed this issue generally conceived of the "complex" as an identifiable entity that manipulated perceptions and maintained high levels of military spending by virtue of the political and economic linkages among industry, the Congress, and the military bureaucracy (Slater and Nardin, 1973). In pursuit of evidence, researchers looked not only for the relevant actors but also for the behavioral ties that bound this self-interested group to the expansion of the military sector (Rosen, 1973; Melman, 1970; Fulbright, 1970, Koistinen, 1980). The work unfolding here takes this concept a step further. If the problem revolved solely around an elite whose political and economic fortunes were intimately tied to the maintenance of a large military establishment, this would be serious but not crippling. In its more advanced stage, however, the boundary between the "entity," alluded to by the MIC literature, and the general public is no longer clearly demarcated. Society itself now becomes an integral component of the MIC. Societal acquiescence to the ways of the power elite gives way to societal encouragement to the belligerent policies that emanate from the state. The existence of an MIC is not restricted only to the most militarized societies. Many countries will have the industrial and bureaucratic infrastructures characteristic of an MIC, but not all of these countries end up with highly militarized societies. In fact, it may be that the MIC sows the seeds for the violent external behavior of the state, which, if sufficiently prolonged, begins to generate the active support of the civil sector of society.

By way of leading into a discussion of my model, let me set up two contrasting societies--in a sense the extremes on a militarization continuum--as a way of describing the organization of a militarized and a nonmilitarized society. One point that should be clear from this review is that in my formulation of the argument, we are more likely to find the highly militarized societies to also be highly industrialized; conversely, the less militarized will more likely be less industrialized. This relationship will, of course, not always hold, and at first one might even be skeptical of such a postulate. For example, Iraq, Iran, and Israel in the latter part of this century might seem to counter this assertion, and well they might. But in general the relationship between industrialization and militarization appears to be strong. Keeping my earlier definitions in mind as you follow the discussion might help make this point clearer. Furthermore, this is not to suggest a direct causal relationship between industrialization and militarization (though others have) but rather to suggest that the more traditional the society, the more difficult it will be to organize the civil sector around the objectives of the elite. It requires more than just a massive military force to organize a significant proportion of a population around the preparations for war. In highly industrial societies this organization can be carried out through the industrial, the entertainment, and the service sectors, all of which can complement the effect of a large active and reserve military force. The obvious exception to this proposition is the organization of the population in response to the initiation of a war. Regardless of the level of industrialization, the waging of war requires the mobilization of a large proportion of a society. Industrialization, therefore, is not a necessary and sufficient condition for militarization, though the theoretical arguments are suggestive and somewhat supported through prior research.

The idea that the industrialization of society is intimately tied to the amount of influence accorded the military, and to the amount of violence evident within a system, is a debate with deep roots in the social sciences (see Gilbert, 1975; Bramson and Goethals, 1964; Rosecrance, 1986). Herbert Spencer (1964), among others, has argued that an "industrial" society and a "military" society are two distinct types of social organizations, with industrial societies being not only higher on the social chain but also more predisposed to peaceful coexistence. The other side of the debate postulated that the technological sophistication of modern warfare has broken down the barrier between these two forms of societal organization. Otto Hintze prophesied that with the progression of technology, "the military and industrial types of society will probably experience not a sharpening of their differences, but a gradual blending and increasing similarity of institutions" (quoted in Gilbert, 1975:215). A more contemporary scholar, Morris Janowitz, argued that "The vast proliferation of the military establishments of the major industrialized nations is a direct consequence of the continuous development of the technology of warfare" (1964:341). This debate continues today.

Gautam Sen posits that there is a direct link between the industrialization of a society and the development of strategic industries. There are, he observes, a small number of "industrializing industries" that are necessary for achieving the goal of economic independence; these industries also happen to have strategic implications. His analysis further suggests that the fundamental characteristics of an industrialization strategy and the shape of the civilian manufacturing sector are determined by governmental attempts to achieve national security. He notes that "self-sufficiency in intermediate manufactured products which the process of industrialization evidently implies . . . is ultimately underpined by a group of industries which originated under the catalytic stimulus of defence needs" (1984:71).

Approaching the relationship between industrialization and militarization from an organization theory perspective, Stephen Van Evera[3] posits that the two are intricately linked. Although he later cautions that militarization has many causes (1984:247), he develops the argument that it is the industrialization process that fuels militarization. According to Van Evera, "The sources of militarism [sic] are deeply rooted in the nature of the modern industrial state" (398). When addressed from an organization-theory perspective, it becomes apparent to him that war springs from militarism [*sic*], which reflects the pathology of large organizations, which are created by the division of labor, which springs from industrialism. In this view, the risk of militarism [*sic*] is inherent in industrial societies. . . . An organizational approach suggests that . . . capitalism fueled militarism [*sic*] by fueling industrialization, but the cause of militarism [*sic*] lies in industrialism itself, not in capitalism per se (213).

THE IDEAL TYPES

In a more traditional, nonmilitarized society, to posit one ideal type, there are two distinct sectors. One is the civilian sector; the other is the military. (Obviously, any complex society can be disaggregated along a number of lines--mass/elite, rural/urban, ethnic, etc.--but for my purposes, the military/civilian distinction is the most salient.) The military is an arm of the state apparatus; the civilian population is a resource at the disposal of the state. In this traditional society, the two sectors operate in very different spheres. The military is organized into hierarchical units with a clear command structure; the civilians are highly decentralized, operating mostly as individual units. The military extracts from the civilian sector, both people and money, but the civilians are not organized around the mission of the military. Recruits are inducted into military service, often against their will, and taxes are paid so that the state might equip its soldiers. But there is no strong symbiotic relationship between the two sectors in such a society. The civilians do not work for the military; the military extracts from the civilians. When snared by the long arm of conscription, young civilians serve their time. But when their tour of duty is complete, most go back to civilian life; most do not join military associations or reserve forces; and most do not go to work in defense plants. Many who served will have changed their attitudes and beliefs regarding the state (Langton, 1984), but few remain in the organizational structure of the military. Only in very rare instances is there a unified sense of nationalistic fervor, and much of the time there may be more than one group contending for power. Although giving examples of an ideal type is inherently problematic, for heuristic purposes feudal Europe serves as a reasonable approximation (see McNeil, 1982; Tilly, 1975), as might pre-Imperial Japan or, more currently, some of the lesser-developed African states.

In a highly militarized society, to take the other extreme, there is a high degree of interaction between the civil and the military sectors of a society. The state not only extracts both people and money for the military but also organizes a large number of civilians under the military command structure. In a highly militarized society it may even be possible to maintain full staffing of the armed forces without resorting to a draft. Whether this is a result of economic motivations--such as employment, educational opportunities, or attitudes regarding military service--is relatively unimportant. What is critical is that enlistment in the armed forces, or working for the military bureaucracy, is a normal means of societal advancement and becomes part of the status quo. Here one might look to Nazi Germany or the post-World War II period in the Soviet Union or the United States for relevant examples.

Moreover, the societal mechanisms that help to socialize the general public to the worldview of the political and economic elite will be ubiquitous. We cannot infer from this that there develops a generally accepted "false consciousness" in the Marxian sense but rather that the information that is available to the public helps to shape one's understanding of world events. This information, to a large degree, is not only rooted in official sources, but its dissemination is often facilitated by institutions and organizations that have an interest in maintaining the status quo. For example, institutions of secondary and higher education will have programs available to the mass public that integrate into the curriculum military values, organization, and planning. A large fraction of the population will be directly or indirectly tied to the military establishment for their means of subsistence. A large percentage of the money available for research will be devoted to either military hardware or military strategy. Constraints on freedom of speech and association will be evident to the attentive public, as will be access to official information. For a number of reasons related to the foreign policy behavior of a highly militarized society, as well as mass beliefs about the acceptability of military service as a form of employment and skills training, there will be a large number of military veterans in the society. Because the ability of a state to maintain this structure of military influence is dependent on the perception of an external threat, symbols of nationalism and patriotism designed to convey this sense of threat will be highly visible within society. This will in turn lead to media and entertainment outlets that glorify military service to the country and denounce the enemy of the moment. Popular myths will evolve that not only promote the politico-centrism of the society (Sampson and Kideckel, 1989) but also extoll the virtues of the military. Military confrontations and wars will be used to mobilize the general public when the manipulation of symbols fails to do so. Not only will military service be the tool to shape attitudes toward the military and the state, but positive attitudes toward both will be formed long before the opportunity to serve is available (Bachman, Sigelman, and Diamond, 1987).

The key difference, then, in the extent to which a society is militarized is the degree of participation by the general public in the preparations for war. This participation is secured, in part, by use of symbols of nationalism and patriotism that inculcate in the public the conception that military service, military production, and "national security" are noble values to be held by upstanding citizens. The distinction between participation in the military sector of society and its civilian counterpart becomes blurred. A normal avenue for employment, research, and education becomes participation in the process of military mobilization. This status quo so pervades a more militarized society that media and entertainment outlets perpetuate this system of continued mobilization by recapitulating and glorifying the myths espoused by the security elite. Examples drawn from the United States abound, such as Rambo-type movies, the Barbie doll as an air force officer, evening news programs that uncritically reiterate the elite position, and the war toy and television industries that identify what is currently in vogue. In a society relatively free from military penetration, this blurring of boundaries is much less pronounced. Civilians produce for civilian consumption, and the military produces for military consumption. The two sectors of society have contact with each other, but they are not organized around the same hierarchical structure or principles. Clearly, this organizational structure does not revolve around direct military rule, nor is it necessary. In fact it may be argued that in a highly militarized society, it is not only unnecessary but undesirable, because civilian rule can help legitimize the military and make easier the task of maintaining public support for the diversion of resources from civil to military applications.

THREATS, POLITICS, AND ECONOMICS

A clear understanding of the process by which societies militarize has so far eluded researchers. The appropriate mix of threats, politics, and economics has been insufficiently articulated, as well as insufficiently tested. The mechanisms that help to socialize the masses to accept, and participate in, the militarization process have also been neglected. Harold Lasswell suggested that the genesis of the garrison state is in the continued expectation of violence, though its perpetuation is fed through the elite use of symbols and, if need be, the initiation of conflict (1941, 1962). Some scholars (Rosh, 1988; Lebovic and Ishaq, 1987; Mintz and Ward, 1989) test models that appear to confirm the role of external threats in spurring military spending. Alex Mintz and Michael Ward (1989), Miroslav Nincic (1982), and A. F. Mullins (1987) also argue the role of internal domestic and economic factors as a contributor to increases in military allocations. Intuitively, it seems plausible that each of these sets of factors plays a role in propelling the militarization process forward, including military spending itself, the outcome variable in each of these analyses. The model proposed here will build on Lasswell's threat-induced stimulus, which in the beginning may be an actual threat to the security of a society. But from these often legitimate beginnings, economic factors generate domestic political constituencies, which in turn require a credible threat to sustain. If a society continues on a path toward being highly militarized, the process begins to be driven by the social, political, and economic factors, even though the actual threat may dissipate. With time, the threat becomes largely concocted, the "symbols" necessary to sustain the mobilization are manipulated, and if need be, limited military action is initiated to help maintain mass support. In the early stages, a threat drives military expansion; in the latter stages, military expansion plays a role in driving the threat.

Earlier I made the distinction between a militaristic and a militarized society, with the distinguishing characteristics revolving around warlike values and military control versus the preparations for war. These two different societal attributes, however, are clearly not so dichotomous. In fact we may find that in the early stages of the militarization process, militarism is a necessary catalyst, though the strength of these values subsides with time, or the direct control of the military gives way to civil society. Though in a more highly militarized society, militaristic tendencies may once again come to the fore, leading to a society that is not only highly organized for war but also quite accepting of violence as a tool of diplomacy. In a country such as Brazil, a period of direct military control paved the way for an increase in the extent to which the industrial infrastructure became tied to weapons production; similar factors may be present in a number of other developing countries around the world. World War II, and to a lesser extent World War I, may have played this part in the militarization of the United States, when the decision-making apparatus became tightly controlled by the military, the economic sector was mobilized to produce the machinery of war, and restrictions were placed on the press in the interest of "national security." Unfortunately, exploring the contribution of societal *militarism* to the *militarization* of society will have to remain beyond the scope of this analysis, though a fuller understanding of this relationship would greatly contribute to our knowledge of the role of the military in society. But all is not lost.

If there are degrees to which a society can be said to be militarized, then traces of this evolving organization of civil society should be evident on a number of dimensions that I will outline below. If scholars such as Charles Tilly (1975, 1985), Harold Lasswell (1941, 1962) and S. E. Finer (1988) are correct, and the propensity to organize around the military is rooted in threats to the sovereignty of a nation (either real or imagined), then traces of this perceived threat should be evident either in the media targeted at the general public or in the behavior of an adversary. It should be emphasized that this does not imply a deterministic progression from a traditional society to a militarized industrial society. But it does suggest a relationship among threats, economic forces, and domestic political concerns--a relationship that has potential ramifications for the organizational structure of a society, for the behavior of the state, and ultimately, for political and economic development.

Measuring the extent to which a society is organized around the preparation for war becomes a necessary step in this analysis. And although I will discuss my indicators more fully in the next chapter, I present them now to allow the reader to more fully follow my argument. With my operational definition of *militarized* revolving around the degree of participation of the civil sector in the security elites' preparations for war, any measure of the extent to which a society is militarized should include indicators such as (1) the number of active and reserve forces, (2) the number of civilians working directly for the military, (3) the number of military veterans participating in veteran organizations, (4) the number of civilians involved in the production of military hardware, and (5) the number of military training programs in the secondary and university school systems. These indicators are summed and represented as a percentage of the labor force. The first two of these indicators tap into the size of the military as an institution, in terms of human resources. The next three attempt to identify the extent to which the military permeates the civil sector of society through employment, prior affiliation with the military and/or support of organized groups, and education.

TOWARD A THEORETICAL MODEL: MILITARIZATION AS A PROCESS

In light of the theoretical arguments positing industrialization as a driving force behind the militarization of societies, I will adopt this conceptual framework as I outline my model. The use of the term *industrialization*, however, is somewhat misleading. The shift from an agricultural economy to one dominated by manufacturing and services is the generally accepted concept behind the push of industrialization, though this does not capture the root of its relationship to militarization. More precisely, it is technological development that is one of the catalytic agents of militarization, as I will make clear later on. While the two terms may describe quite similar processes, they are not synonymous. My indicator of technological development--which will be more fully explained in chapter two--is a composite of iron and steel production, aluminum production, and sales of computer equipment. In the interest of style, however, I will often use the terms interchangeably. With this framework in mind, I will present an outline of the processes that drive the militarization of societies; and from this, I will derive specific hypotheses that will subsequently be subjected to empirical testing.

Nonindustrial Societies

In the beginning stages of the development of a nation-state, the ruling coalition is often faced with threats to its viability from both external and internal elements. The effect of this threat on the organization of a political infrastructure is evident in medieval Europe.[4] Charles Tilly (1975) argued that the genesis of the modern-day nation-state is rooted in the struggles for territorial integrity by the nobility of that era. The need to enlist and equip military forces in response to external threats laid the foundation for the civil and military bureaucracies that are an integral element of the modern state.

In the contemporary period, the origins of the threat change somewhat. Instead of feudal lords battling over territory, we are witness to--inter alia--ethnic tribes waging war over rights to leadership. The breakdown of the colonial system in a large part of the world made possible the reinitiation of lingering tribal disputes, resulting in both internal and external security threats. In response to these threats, the ruling elites were forced to recruit and equip armies in defense of their privileged positions. While some of these societies may be governed by elites who could be considered militaristic, few if any such societies would rank high when a measure of militarization is invoked. Examples include countries such as Angola and Zimbabwe in Africa and Cambodia in Asia. The governments of both Zimbabwe and Angola faced internal threats from "liberation" movements and confronted an external adversary in South Africa. In Cambodia, a number of rival factions were fighting for the right to rule, while Vietnam posed a continued threat from outside the country. The response to this entails, as one would suspect, the diversion of resources away from the building of a social and economic infrastructure to the military sector, as well as more militaristic patterns of elite control. Increasing both military spending and the numbers of military personnel would be one visible response by the state; an increase in state bureaucracy would be another.

The recent period of the Cold War also contributed to the increased influence of the military in developing countries. The two superpowers spent considerable resources wooing these new states into their orbits or attempting to dislodge the ruling elite allied with the antagonist. In the process, the United States and the Soviet Union, along with their respective allies, embarked on programs to train and arm either the state militia or an insurgent group seeking to overthrow the ruling coalition. The development of a military infrastructure, therefore, is often a product of endogenous factors driving military expansion, coupled with the import of exogenous issues and support. Again, examples abound: Ethiopia and Sudan in Africa; Honduras and Nicaragua in Central America; Iraq, Egypt, Syria, and Israel in the Middle East; and North Korea and South Korea in Asia. This is not to suggest that the Third World elites are not willing partners in the import of weapons and the related technology, but that the importation of issues and weapons from the patron state is part of the process by which new states become organized around military production and preparations.

Both the formation of a military force and the infusion of military hardware from abroad necessitate the development of a bureaucratic organization that is capable of extracting, organizing, and integrating. With time, these bureaucracies tend to become self-amplifying, as do the industries necessary to uniform, feed, house, and equip even a meager army. If the external source of military funding is disproportionately large in comparison with domestic sources of funding, then the military bureaucracy may exert undue influence in the domestic affairs of the state. This is due, in large part, to the fact that excessive external funding removes the military from the give-and-take of coalition politics that is usually central to the distribution of limited domestic resources. In the absence of an external source of military funds or technology, the mechanisms in a developing society that push the military sector to the fore are confined predominantly to the two dimensions of threat--internal and external--at least at the outset.

But the more any one state spends on its military sector, the more threatening it begins to appear to its potential rivals--both internal and external. The security dilemma, as this situation is generally called, suggests that two rivals may become locked in a cycle of an escalating arms race. And while this action-reaction response to military spending might not account for all of the military expansion, there is ample evidence to suggest that the military resources of the neighboring states of a country do drive that country's response (Rosh 1988; Lebovic and Ishaq 1987; Mintz and Ward 1989).

According to some scholars, as the resources devoted to the military sector of a state increase, they do so at a cost to the social and economic infrastructure of the society (Ball, 1988; Looney and Frederiksen, 1986), though there is some evidence to suggest that the trade-offs are not always deleterious (Benoit, 1973; Kennedy, 1983). As resources are continually diverted from the social and economic needs of a country, some of its populace may begin to view the state apparatus as illegitimate. The response by the state is repression and even greater resources devoted to the mechanisms of repression (Falk, 1977; Zwick, 1984). So as the internal threat increases in response to the continued neglect of the social and economic aspects of society, the elite becomes more embattled, spending more on the military and recruiting even greater numbers of soldiers. The need to extract from the population in order to attend to elite security concerns breeds division and discontent, adding to the cycle of continued domestic unrest (Finer, 1988; Organski et al., 1984:47). The alternative, importing the necessary equipment from a patron state, may reduce the need to extract in order to contain domestic unrest, at least in the short term, but it requires the building of an infrastructure capable of receiving and integrating this equipment.

If any particular country is at a very low level of industrialization, the militarization process may stagnate at this point. Threat begets increases in military capability, which increases the threat, which begets more military spending. The process reaches an equilibrium at some point, but society never begins to move in lockstep with the military. The values of the state might be militaristic, but the society as a whole is clearly not militarized.[5] The population acquiesces in the power of the state, and the peasants serve their time in the armed forces when they are inducted, but in general only a minor part of the society is organized around the preparation for war.

Lest we leave this portion of the discussion thinking that the military sector is simply a drain on the social, political, and economic aspects of preindustrial societies, we should be reminded that there is some evidence to suggest that the military can contribute positively to economic development (Benoit, 1973; Looney, 1989). Furthermore, there is a rather coherent line of reasoning that argues that the development of a military infrastructure also helps to develop the political and bureaucratic foundations of the modern nation-state including, but not limited to the political institutions necessary for coalition politics (Tilly, 1975, 1985; Organski, 1965). And while this debate must linger, I stand by my original assertion that although these beneficial aspects of the military may be evident, they are an inefficient mechanism for political or economic development and therefore are ultimately a drain on society.

Newly Industrializing Societies

If the country under examination is moderately industrialized, the process may not stop at a point where the military capabilities of the state are sufficient to meet an existential threat. In the newly industrializing nations, the access to technology and resources increases the prestige of military officers. The appetite for more and better weapon systems becomes the hallmark of the military bureaucracy. Few countries outside of the oil-exporting nations of the Middle East can afford to continually import high-tech weapons. If the elite wants to maintain current levels of military preparedness, they must begin domestic production of some of the previously imported hardware. Some scholars argue that the domestic production of weapons in Third World countries does not result in financial savings to the producing country but rather has an overall net cost, in comparison with importing the desired weapons (see Ball, 1988). This argument, however, focuses solely on the relative financial costs of importing versus domestic production and does not take into account issues such as domestic political pressures, national prestige, and the desire to use military production as a platform for industrialization strategies.

Industrialization strategies are often developed around the creation of certain strategic arms industries (Sen, 1984; McNeil, 1982). Basic infrastructural needs, such as roads, electricity, steel production, textile and chemical industries, and education, can be most easily justified in the name of national security--security generally being viewed as a collective good and therefore engendering a minimum of resistance. The start-up costs associated with these rudimentary components of industrialization generally must be borne by the state. In many of the developing countries of the world, this state apparatus is either composed of military officers or subjected to a heavy dose of military participation in decision-making. The military is often seen as the most nationalistic of the various ruling coalition members (Finer, 1988), and in this role it has the ability to shape industrialization strategies that serve two gods: economic development and military security. According to Gautam Sen's analysis: "It is at the initial stage of industrialization that defence-related purposes greatly influence the character of the incipient manufacturing economy. The creation of industries for military purposes lays the basis on which the civilian manufacturing economy subsequently grows" (1988:74).

As a result, military industries that are capable of manufacturing some of the basic, though rudimentary, equipment of a modern army begin to sprout. Some of this production might fall into the category of nonlethal military equipment, such as food, clothing, and furniture, or the minimal equipment of a soldier, such as small arms and ammunition (Brzoska and Ohlson 1986:20; Sen, 1988; Hilton, 1982). This not only reduces the need to import such weapons but also creates employment within the industrial sector of the economy. This, of course, requires a larger bureaucracy to oversee, regulate, and specify the production process. Likewise, the military bureaucracy requires more money to operate. But now the military can hold out the prospect of jobs in return for the diversion of resources, as well as a picture of future economic prosperity. Few people, of course, work for the military at this stage, so it is still necessary to justify increased military expansion by identifying threats to the "national security."

Brazil stands out as a good example of a country with an industrialization strategy that is heavily reliant on the production of military hardware, as we will see later on. There are, however, a number of other countries, such as Taiwan, South Korea, and the former Czechoslovakia, that are also heuristically useful for this purpose. Brazil, for example, went from a country torn by internal strife and lacking a centralized government in the early part of the twentieth century through an extended period of military dictatorship and "economic miracles," to a society quite capable of competing in many areas with the more advanced industrialized societies by the 1980s. One thread in Brazilian unification and development appears to have been the role of the military. In the early stages the military helped to unify the country and facilitate the centralization of government, and by the later part of the century the production of military hardware was central to the creation of a national steel industry, to the expanding networks of roads, rail, and electrification, to the motor vehicle and aviation industries, and to the creation of institutes for research and development. The fact that Brazil can compete in the international market place of high-tech products can be tied in part to its military-industrial complex (Franko-Jones, 1986; Hilton, 1982).

Not all countries at this stage of industrial development opt for a military-based industrialization strategy. Nor do they all rely on a large military infrastructure as the means for national security. Few of the oil-rich Middle Eastern countries, for example, expend much of their resource base in an effort to develop weapons-production capabilities, instead choosing to import most of their material equipment. If, however, a country does develop a domestic arms-manufacturing sector, a constituency will begin to develop around the continued production and organization for war and, with it, the manipulation of the perception of a threat.

As countries develop a military-industrial capability, and a trained and capable work force, they will eventually begin to import the production technology of the more sophisticated weapon systems from their former suppliers (Baek, McLaurin, and Moon, 1989; Brzoska and Ohlson 1986). This might start off as the ability to produce simple land vehicles or small naval craft, but it eventually progresses to the point of designing and producing semi-sophisticated aircraft and missile systems. Production at this level requires not only substantial numbers of trained employees but also a fairly broad spectrum of support and a vast array of supplier industries. The jobs directly tied to the production of war material ensure a degree of domestic support for the continued diversion of resources from civilian production to the military. This array of jobs, however, is not confined to the industrial sector of society. As the level of technology increases, the need to develop new production techniques and more-capable weapon systems requires the funding of research-and-development programs as well as the training of the next generation of engineers. Seemingly scarce resources now get diverted into the universities and research institutes in an effort to maintain technological capabilities applicable to the military. The society is now faced with a fairly substantial portion of its highly trained and well-educated work force participating in the production of war technology (Ball, 1988). While this might not be the most efficient use of a country's human and technical resources, this segment of the society, because of its socioeconomic status, would also tend to be one of the more influential constituency groups. The well-being of this portion of society is now tied to the continued production for war (see Stepan, 1988:84).

None of this can stand alone, however, and the domestic production of military hardware does not always originate from an economic motivation. To justify this organization around the preparations for war, the state needs to continue organizing its society in response to a specific threat. This threat may entail the perpetuation of a long-standing external dispute or the reliance on the threat to internal security that results from an insurgency. In either case the threat may be real, but it is clearly not necessary. Argentina, for example, greatly exaggerated the extent of its internal threat during the late 1970s and early 1980s (Pion-Berlin 1988) and eventually acted on a long-standing external threat in 1983. Involvement in an all-out war, moreover, may serve as the catalyst that helps institutionalize the military-industrial infrastructure. This can most readily be seen in the transformation of the United States during and after World War II. If the size of this military-based infrastructure is large enough, full-scale mobilization may later pose problems of demobilization, resulting, as Harold Lasswell has suggested, in the manipulation of a threat.

This would be the stage at which most of the arms-producing newly industrializing countries have stagnated. The weapons and military supplies that they do produce are primarily for domestic consumption, though exports may constitute a small portion of total production. Small arms and ammunition, clothing, and basic naval craft will have limited value on the export market. But those states that are able to develop the more technologically sophisticated design and production techniques are able to enter this large export market, and economies of scale begin to play a role in the weapons produced and the size of the production runs. Two main factors come into play in determining the extent of the export orientation of the country's weapons program: (1) the capacity of the producing state to absorb the weapon components into its own force structure, which can be a function of the size of the armed forces, the economic situation faced by the country, or domestic opposition to military expansion; and

(2) the costs of the design and manufacture of the particular weapon and hence the need to recoup sunk investments. The greater the industrial infrastructure needed to maintain a viable arms industry, the deeper is the level of permeation into the society. Again, in a country like Brazil, where a substantial investment has been made in the arms industry by both public and private sources, an industrialization strategy has developed around the production of certain types of weapons built mainly for the export market. The desire to maintain a viable industry in weapons technology has led to advancements in the Brazilian steel, electronics, aviation and vehicle sectors of the economy, and they have embarked on a major effort to use arms sales as a tool for economic development (Franko-Jones, 1986, 1987-88; Lock, 1986; McCann, 1981; Stepan, 1988). This economic component has ramifications that potentially go far beyond the specific industry involved. The impact of the production of military hardware on the whole of an economy can be quite substantial, and in fact, in the short-term the strength of a country's economic performance may hinge on the viability of an arms industry.

But it is not the size of the military industry alone that determines the extent to which the society is organized for war. The size of the armed forces, the number of civilians employed by the military, and the size of the bureaucracy that organizes all of these branches play a vital role in determining the extent to which the civil society is dependent on military organization. The socialization that is necessary to get the masses to produce for the event that they abhor requires the compliance of an education system, often developed by the military (Ralston, 1990), and a medium of communication that relies on the uncritical dissemination of "information." The longer is the reach of the military, the higher the level at which the civil and military sectors of a society operate as one--or at least become dependent on each other. The more people that are involved in the organization process, the more difficult it will be to halt its continued growth. So what one would expect to see is that at some point in the level of penetration, the process of militarization becomes an engine that feeds on itself. The perception of threat is still a necessary justification--because the society does not view the production for war as an intrinsic good--but the threat is no longer what drives the process: the process now drives the threat. At this stage members of the society begin to be socialized toward a military-based organizational structure; most may still abhor the thought of war, but nearly the whole of society is unconsciously becoming part of the process of preparing for it. To examine this facet of the militarization schema, we must look to that handful of industrialized countries that could be considered highly militarized.

Industrialized Societies

To maintain the high level of military preparation that exists in more highly militarized countries, such as the United States or the former Soviet Union, the state must find a way to include--either actively or passively--a substantial portion of the society into its preparations for war. This requires, inter alia, (1) the socialization of the general public around patriotic themes, which helps to ensure support during times of conflict or throughout policy debates that parcel out resources to the military, (2) a significant segment of the population actively involved in the preparations for war, and (3) the acquiescence of many of the most powerful countervailing forces within society. Employment, education, the media, and entertainment outlets are the most visible mechanisms that help enlist compliance and cooperation, as well as ensure ignorance to alternative ways of organizing societal resources. The perception of an external threat, which is still a necessary justification, is maintained through the manipulation of the symbols of "political community" (Elder and Cobb, 1983). The concept of civic duty is inspired in the minds of the young through youth-participation groups, such as the girl and boy scouts, the civil air patrol, the air explorers, and through organized church and religious affiliations. The entertainment industry begins to take part in shaping attitudes toward the military by both glorifying the role of the soldier and reinforcing a fear of the enemy. The mass media, likewise, more frequently neglects its role as a countervailing force in society and begins to uncritically disseminate the information it receives from the security elite. And the members of the ruling legislative assemblies fight for continued spending on military projects that bring resources and jobs directly to their districts. The combined effect of these forces within society is a development akin to what Richard Slotkin termed the "frontier myth" (1986) or Stephen Whitfield called the "culture of the cold war" (1991). Funding for research and development of new technologies is strongly influenced by the needs of the state's war fighting machine, and even civilian-funded research will keep a sharp eye toward the military application of any pending technological discovery. Much of the funding for research in the social sciences, moreover, is geared not toward the elimination of, or a reduction in, the capacity to engage in war but rather to the strategies of how best to use military might to prevent encroachment on national sovereignty. Numerous institutes of higher education will train young people to be good soldiers, but few will teach how to eliminate the prospects of and capability for war. It might not be necessary to have a peacetime draft because near-wartime staffing can be maintained voluntarily.

The size of the constituency behind continued funding of the military at this level of militarization is quite large. Not only are the armed forces fully staffed, but the civilian component of the mobilization effort incorporates a fairly large segment of the working population. Attempts to demilitarize, which still arise out of many quarters, both within and outside official government channels, meet with stiff resistance. To counteract these movements toward demilitarization, the elite will aggressively promote the virtues of a strong and active military sector, as well as their actual use in foreign conflicts if the efforts to redirect resources becomes too strong. To some extent this type of behavior can be seen in the United States, where advertisements, news stories, and editorials that emphasize the need to remain strong in defense of freedom can regularly be found in the print and television media.

In the beginning of this process, the expansion of the military sector is driven by actual threats to national sovereignty. In a less-militarized society, as the threat diminishes, so too will the size and scope of the military institutions. In a more militarized society, however, the military institutions are part of the mechanism that drives the threat. There are three components to the threat at this stage: the first is the domestic manipulation of a perceived threat; the second is the elite use of military force in an effort to rally public support; and the third is an existential threat resulting from an increase in the use of violent foreign policy. To maintain mass support for elite policies of mobilization, the elite may need to "concoct" or manipulate the perception of an external threat. The types of symbols used by the elite to manipulate public attitudes toward an enemy would be what Charles Elder and Roger Cobb have called "higher-order symbols." "In a stable polity, affective orientations toward higher-order symbols will normally be acquired earlier and be held longer than those directed toward lower-order ones. . . . The higher a symbol falls in the hierarchy, the more uniform the affective orientations toward it are likely to be across persons and groups" (Elder and Cobb, 1983:39). Notions of the "imperialist menace," "preserving our way of life," "the flag," "freedom" and "democracy," or the "expansion of communism" and the "evil empire" are relevant examples in the United States, though others abound. A highly militarized society will also be more prone to initiate military disputes, as suggested by Ted Gurr (1988) and Harold Lasswell (1941, 1962), or become involved in foreign conflicts, as the findings of Erich Weede (1970) and Charles Kegley, Neil Richardson, and Gunter Richter (1978) indicate. This increased dispute behavior could be a result of a number of factors, such as a sense of national efficacy, a de facto justification for the high levels of military preparedness, or an increase in the threat perceived by a potential adversary, which ultimately results in an international conflict. In any event, there will be a clear feedback relationship between the militarization of a society and its violent foreign policy.

As a result of this process, the society becomes organized around the military's preparation for war. Military organization, structures, and attitudes permeate civil society. A unique feature of a highly militarized society is that the civilian sector works to ensure the continued socialization of its members to the structure of dominance by the military. So as the existential threat abates, society remains unable to free itself from the influence of the military.

But is the only avenue out of the militarization process the political and economic decline of the highly militarized nation-state? Up to this point, I have expounded on a process that appears to have no exit, though that is clearly misleading. As with all political events, these relationships are not deterministic, the process is not carved in stone, and there are many points of entry and exit along the way. This would be evident by a cursory look at the extent to which the spectrum of industrialized countries could be considered militarized. There must be mechanisms that could either prevent the militarization of a society or reverse its trend once this uneasy state has been achieved. Rather than dwell on specifics at this point, I will merely suggest two factors that might facilitate the demilitarization of society, and later in the thesis a more complete discussion will unfold. One factor that could presage the demilitarization of society might be total defeat in war. Pre-World War II Nazi Germany and Japan, for instance, were arguably highly militarized societies, but after their defeat in war their military sectors were eviscerated, leaving them little in the way of a military infrastructure. More important, their civil societies were also purged of the vestiges of military mobilization. Another factor that might prevent or reverse a trend toward militarizing a society might be a combination of a vastly reduced existential threat coupled with severe economic constraints placed on both the state and the society, something akin to what is being experienced in the United States today and may have contributed to the demise of the former Soviet Union. Ironically, the same economic forces that propel the militarization process forward may also compel a retraction. If those scholars who have chronicled the economic costs of military expansion are correct (Melman, 1970, 1985; Smith and Smith, 1983; Ball, 1988), we might expect the financial deficit to catch up someday. If so, we might also expect that those same forces that help to embellish the threat would now begin to depreciate its magnitude. Melvin Small (1974) finds that, indeed, sources of news and information can work both ways.

A FRAMEWORK FOR AN EMPIRICAL TEST:
THE HYPOTHESES

To summarize the preceding discussion, I present the core of the argument as a series of hypotheses. In subsequent chapters I will return to a discussion and test of these hypotheses.

H1: Increased militarization leads to an increase in violent foreign policy by the state. The more tightly society becomes organized around the preparations for war, the more likely it is that it will have to put its preparations to use. This can be a result of either domestic pressures or international tensions, or some combination of the two.

H2: Increased violent foreign policy leads to greater societal militarization. The more the state relies on violent international behavior to achieve policy objectives, the more likely that the military will take on a greater role in society. We would expect to see this, inter alia, as an increase in the level of participation by the general public in the mobilization of resources for war. Hypotheses H1 and H2 together reflect the self-amplifying feedback relationship that exists between the organization of society and the behavior of the state.

H3: Highly militarized societies tend to be more highly industrialized. In the age of part-time or mercenary armies, there was relatively little interaction between the military and the civil sectors of society. But in a modern high-technology era, the role played by civilians is instrumental in determining the military capabilities of the elite. With the exception of periods of total war, when nearly all societies coalesce around the war effort, it is generally only the more industrialized societies that have the industrial infrastructure capable of efficiently producing the modern weapons of war and thereby incorporating a broader segment of society in the preparations for war.

H4: The more militarized the society, the greater is the extent to which the perception of a threat will be maintained in the mass media. In a more highly militarized society, rather than the elite demobilizing its military resources in response to a decreasing threat, we would expect to see an increase in the manipulation of the perception of a threat. The level of mobilization might decrease from the heights reached during the peak of the war, but the demobilization will not reach precrisis levels. This ratchet effect will require the manipulation of the perception of a threat in order to maintain mass support (Lasswell, 1941; Rosen, 1973; Russett, 1970).

H5: The symbols that help to create and maintain a culture generally predisposed to war or armaments are more evident during periods of high mobilization. Without positing a direct causal relationship, I argue that patriotic and war-related themes will be more evident in highly militarized societies. Whichever way the causal arrows point, a heightened level of patriotic entertainment will assist in organizing public support for elite policies. It is this heightened patriotic fervor that will be manipulated when support for continued military preparations begins to wane.

In the following chapters the theoretical arguments and any empirical evidence supporting each of these hypothesis will be discussed in greater detail. Each hypotheses will then be tested through the use of a number of statistical techniques, both parametric and otherwise. The spatial and temporal domains for the entire study will be discussed below, while the specific statistical models to be used in each stage of the analysis will be presented in the appropriate chapters.

THE CASES TO BE ANALYZED

The bulk of the analytical component of this study will be broken into two separate longitudinal, within-country analyses of both the United States and Great Britain from the turn of the twentieth century until 1985. Britain and the United States were chosen for a statistical analysis for a number of reasons, both theoretical and methodological. Both countries have covered much of the developmental spectrum outlined in my theoretical model, though each was the industrial "leader" at different points in time; each country was also considered to be the "leader" of the international system, though again during different historical periods. And both countries have a history of relying on their respective militaries as tools in the game of internation influence (Gochman and Maoz, 1985). There are also the obvious similarities of being two Anglo-Saxon countries with very similar backgrounds and a common language. The closely linked heritage of these two countries makes their selection particularly interesting by allowing me to hold potentially confounding factors constant while observing the crucial variation--such as stage of industrial development and systemic characteristics--evident over eighty five years of time. "It is often the relative similarity of situations that enables the marginal difference and its causes to be appreciated. By focusing on a relatively homogeneous field, [we increase our] capacity to do in-depth analyses" (Dogan and Pelassy, 1984:118). Methodologically, the United States and Great Britain are attractive cases because of their respective histories of in-depth reporting on a great number of societal variables. Being relatively "open" societies, much of the required data could be either gleaned from official sources or derived through estimating techniques that make use of available data on closely related indicators.

A historical case study of the evolution of the Brazilian military is also used as a descriptive tool of analysis for many of the opposite reasons used to justify my choice of the United States and Britain. Although Brazil is a large country and has a considerable amount of regional influence, it has never even approximated systemic leadership, is generally not an innovator of technology but an emulator, and has reached nowhere near the level of political and economic development found in the other two cases. Furthermore, Brazil does not have a large armed force, nor is it particularly violent in pursuit of foreign diplomacy. Brazil does, however, have a substantial Military-Industrial Complex. Because of these vast dissimilarities with the two cases used for statistical analysis, Brazil serves as a good point of departure for expanding this theoretical argument beyond the general category of advanced industrialized countries.

THE ORGANIZATION OF THE FOLLOWING CHAPTERS

The outline for the remaining chapters of this book will follow a somewhat compartmentalized format. In chapter 2 I will test the hypothesis that the extent to which a society is militarized is determined, *caeteris paribus*, by the violent foreign policy of the state and the size of the political and economic constituencies; in effect, I will be trying to identify the militarization process. Chapter 3, then, will reverse the hypothesized causal path and examine the extent to which the militarization of society leads to increased belligerence on the part of the state elite. This chapter will address the theoretical questions of the effect of the internal organization of society on the external behavior of the state. The fourth chapter will be a synthesis of the second and third chapters. Having argued that the role of violent foreign policy and the militarization of society are part of a self-amplifying feedback process, in chapter 4 I will test the extent to which these two factors do indeed feed off one another. Chapter 5 will then examine some of the mechanisms in society that help to socialize and organize the general public to accept and participate in the mobilization of resources for the military. The specific issue to be addressed is the role of movies and toys in popularizing the symbols that will later be manipulated in order to facilitate the mobilization process. Chapter 6 will present a historical narrative outlining the evolution of the influence of the Brazilian military in their society. Although this chapter is less rigorous than the preceding chapters, the insights offered by this analysis should give us an opportunity to evaluate the prospects for generalizing this theoretical argument to a broader category of cases. In the final chapter I will summarize and discuss my findings, paying particular attention not only to the process that leads toward a more militarized society but also to mechanisms that might help reverse the course.

2

Identifying the Militarization Process: The First Half of the Puzzle

> We must worry not about a sudden take-over of power by our soldiers but about how to prevent slow accretions in the scope of military influence in the "normal" political system.
>
> --Bruce Russett, 1970:181

> For years the military hardliners in the Soviet Union have needed to describe a threat--from NATO, from the United States--in order to justify the tremendous expenditure of their gross national product on the military as well their own privileged position.
>
> --Ronald Lehman, 1991

In chapter 1, outlined an unfolding process by which a society might move from a less to a more militarized level of organization. As the model was presented, I argued that the militarization of a society is a process that unfolds through time and is related to changes in the political, economic, and institutional makeup of society, as well as the external environment in which the state interacts. Others have chronicled the costs associated with diverting resources from civilian to military sectors of society (Melman, 1970, 1985; Dumas, 1988; Smith and Smith, 1983; Kennedy, 1987), though few have demonstrated the empirical linkages between the various domestic and international factors that contribute to the militarization process over a sufficiently long historical period (see Nincic, 1982; Russett, 1990).

In this chapter I will examine some of the factors that contribute to the militarization of both the United States and Great Britain, including the role of the violent external behavior of the state. I will argue that political and economic inertia, the level of technological development, the existence of an existential threat, the maintenance of the perception of an external threat, and the violent foreign policy of the state all contribute to an increase in the extent to which the society is militarized. Each of these factors forms a part of the broad category of literature that examines the motivations and forces behind military allocations (see Allison, 1983; Sen, 1984; Rosh, 1988; Rosen, 1973; Gurr, 1988, respectively). This study covers the years 1900 to 1985, measured four times per decade at alternating two- and three-year intervals.[1] In the following chapter I will then turn the equation around and examine the extent to which militarization effects the amount of international conflict engaged in by the state. In each case I am fully aware that the statistical models used at this stage might very well produce biased estimates of the hypothesized relationships. This twofold approach, however, is used because (1) it will help to develop the models in a coherent manner, (2) it will permit me to engage in some exploratory analysis with which to reevaluate the theoretical arguments, and (3) it addresses these arguments as they are generally found in the literature. I will correct for these conceptual and methodological shortcomings in the forth chapter.

At this juncture it is important to keep in mind my operational definition of the term *militarized*. As I use the term, I mean the extent to which the civil sector of society is organized around the production and preparations for war; my indicator is the percentage of the labor force that is directly or indirectly organized around or producing for that event that they allegedly abhor, war. One result of using such an indicator is that it isolates the political and economic constituencies and moves us away from focusing on a military-industrial complex as the driving force. Instead we end up with an indication of the size of the labor pool working as active proponents for continued mobilization. Conceptualizing this issue as a societal-level phenomena rather than simply a function of the state's allocation of resources does two things: (1) it moves us away from a reliance on realpolitik explanations for levels of military preparedness; and (2) it challenges the notion advanced by Samuel Huntington (1957, 1968), that a professionalized military and a highly militarized society are incompatible.

ASSEMBLING THE BORDER:
THE THEORETICAL LINKAGES

International Disputes

To date, there is little empirical evidence demonstrating a relationship between international belligerency on the part of the state and the increased penetration of civil society by the military. Charles Gochman (1990:151) even goes as far as to suggest that "the extent of mobilization of resources as a consequence of a dispute is likely to be quite small," though he argues that we should expect an increase in mobilization as a result of a war. While he may be technically correct if he sets out to examine the role of disputes on short-term changes in military spending or the number of active-duty personnel, his statement negates the role of military crises as a tool for both developing a "national security" ideology and rallying support for an already high level of military mobilization. Much of the extant literature examining the relationship between the mobilization of resources and international conflict posits that the causal arrows flow from changes in capabilities to changes in the amount of conflict in the system (Diehl, 1985; Morrow, 1989; Singer, Bremer, and Stuckey, 1972). There is, however, a body of theoretical work positing the relevant connections between violent foreign policy and increased militarization.

In his seminal article on the garrison state, Harold Lasswell argues that for the elite to expand their instruments of control, they must ensure that civilian consumption is voluntarily restricted. This can be achieved, he posits, by manipulating the perception of a threat, by socializing the public to the ideology of the elite, or failing both of these, through the use of international "bloodletting." According to Lasswell:

The elite of the garrison state will have a professional interest in multiplying gadgets specialized to acts of violence. The rulers of the garrison state will depend upon war scares as a means of maintaining popular willingness to forego immediate consumption. War scares that fail to culminate in violence eventually lose their value; this is the point at which ruling classes will feel that bloodletting is needed in order to preserve those virtues of sturdy acquiescence in the regime which they so much admire and from which they so greatly benefit. (1941:465)

Ted Gurr makes the theoretical linkages between international violence and the militarization of the state more explicit, positing a number of propositions that purportedly account for a feedback between the development of a garrison state and international belligerency. One of the consequences of repeated conflict involvement, according to Gurr, is that the state will develop "specialized organizations ready to fight future wars" (1988:48). He further argues that the greater the military capability of a state, the more likely it is to engage in international conflict, which leads him to the proposition that "states with limited power capabilities tend not to become militarized" (52). If he is empirically correct, then we can deduce from his propositions that international conflict is one of the mechanisms that lead to militarization. Gurr's model posits, then, that the greater the involvement in foreign conflicts, and the more successful the forays, the more entrenched become the military institutions within the society.

Witt Raczka argues that in order for the state to generate the support necessary for the extraction of resources for military purposes, three factors must be present in society: the availability of the required human and material resources; political legitimacy; and the perception of external hostility. If any one of these is missing, he argues, then resource extraction will be minimal. "Military mobilization is an economic, political, and strategic problem at the same time. There need be an external stimulus, a threat or an opportunity--real or imaginary--for political authority to resort to resource extraction" (1989:14). One implication of his analysis is that if the security elite has a strong-enough interest in maintaining the level of resource extraction, then it may resort to the manipulation of the perception of an external foe. Initiating a military confrontation with an easily suppressible adversary may be a sufficient catalyst for the mobilization of mass support.

These arguments make intuitive sense and suggest that Gochman's assertion should be examined more closely. In a society where elite authority is maintained by virtue of the political legitimacy accorded the state, the mobilization of resources by the military is to a large degree a domestic political issue, in many ways like most others addressed by the legislative or administrative components of the government. A constituency develops around a particular political agenda, which in the process of competing for funding and access must be able to demonstrate its strength vis-à-vis other constituency groups. The military sector, it would seem, has a mechanism with which to mobilize this support unlike any other constituency. The deployment of troops into a hostile situation abroad can have the effect of "rallying the public around the flag." Even if this display of public support is rather short-lived, the size of the constituency can be made large enough, quickly enough, to ensure that funding is not diverted from the cause. This is in part a reflection of the size of the pool of human resources having strong ties to the military, but is also related to the depth of the affective emotions attached to the defense of the motherland. International crises, therefore, might not affect short-term fluctuations in the level of mobilization within a society, as Gochman points out. But in the pull and haul of domestic politics, we should expect an organization to use the resources at its disposal to mobilize its constituency in response to proposed changes in allocations; military disputes are one of the tools in this organizational grab bag, albeit a tool of last resort. International violence, therefore, should help to prevent the encroachment into military budgets and contribute to the tendency for already high levels of mobilization to persist. And although foreign conflicts may result from factors other than elite attempts to shape domestic attitudes, the outcomes with respect to levels of mobilization can be similar.

A counter hypothesis would, of course, argue just the opposite: that the use of violence as a tool of foreign diplomacy would wear thin on the electorate and that the more frequent the use of force in situations that do not pose direct threats to national sovereignty, the more likely that public opinion would demand a retrenchment in the size and scope of the military. While empirical evidence is needed to discriminate between these lines of reasoning, this latter type of action and reaction is not implausible.

Directly related to the state's ability to generate support through the use of force in the international environment is the previous track record of foreign interventions. As Gurr points out, those states that have been successful in international conflict tend to develop an ideology that highlights the efficacy of military force. One outgrowth of this history of dispute behavior is the maintenance of a sizable pool of military veterans in society. When it comes to organizing constituencies in response to threatened reductions in the size of an organization, there are few more active lobbyists than veteran groups. The shared values and comradery associated with prior military service make the veteran pool a critical component in elite attempts to mobilize support. It is no accident that major foreign policy speeches by a U.S. president are often delivered to veteran organizations.

There is evidence to suggest that veterans of the armed forces are more conservative and nationalistic than those who did not serve. A heightened sense of nationalism increases the propensity of individuals to support the state and makes them more susceptible to the manipulation of the symbols of nationalism by the security elite. Jerald Bachman, Lee Sigelman, and Greg Diamond argue this point rather persuasively, concluding that: "Based on much literature, there is widespread agreement that military personnel tend to be above average in nationalism, conservatism, and traditionalism. They have also been characterized . . . as professional, patriotic, . . . altruistic . . . authoritarian, militaristic, and aggressive" (1987:169). They sum up their position on the role of military service in the indoctrination process by stating, "The overall connection between service and promilitary values has been firmly enough documented so that interest now centers on *why* rather than *whether* such a connection exists" (170, emphasis in original). Presumably the more frequent the involvement in war or international disputes, the greater are the numbers of young men and women who will have filtered through the military. In short, then, prior military service tends to inculcate a belief in and acceptance of the state's use of force in international settings. The more members of a society that are subjected to this type of indoctrination, the easier will be the elite's task of manipulating support for continued mobilization. But this will increase not only the constituency of the military bureaucracy; a large veteran pool will also increase the demands on the political leadership for additional funding for traditional veteran causes, such as health, education, and retirement benefits.

From the theoretical arguments presented above, we would expect violent foreign policy to be one of the factors that help to organize the society around the preparations for war. From one vantage point, this mechanism is a product of success in previous disputes that helps to generate an "elite political culture, or myth" extolling the virtues of political violence. From the other perspective, "bloodletting" is a tool to mobilize the general public behind the violent policies of the security elite. Whichever the mechanism that drives the relationship between military disputes and the militarization of a society, and it is probably both, violent foreign policy contributes part of the explanation for the extent to which society is militarized.

Technological   Development

While the theoretical linkages between the progression of technology on the
one hand and militarization on the other may not be readily evident, a closer
analysis reveals some very interesting connections. If we use industrialization as
an indicator of technological advancement, then Gautam Sen (1984) develops the
argument that strategic industries are the focal point for industrialization
strategies, while Stephan Van Evera (1984) argues that industrialization breeds
militarization through the division of labor and organizational inertia. If one
were to categorize countries on these two dimensions, using a scale of high,
medium, and low, and then pigeonhole each country into the appropriate sector
of a contingency table, the result might tend to confirm a positive relationship
between militarization and industrialization (see figure 2.1). A number of factors
work toward this conclusion.

When armies relied predominantly on foot soldiers, and the weapons
employed consisted mainly of a piece of metal hammered into the shape of a
lance or a sword, there was little penetration of the civil sector of society by
military preparations. Artisans or craftsmen produced the weapons, generally at a
very low rate of production, and mercenaries often performed the fighting (see
McNeil, 1982; Ralston, 1990). Civil society, of course, was regularly subjected
to the brutality of the army, but rarely was society organized around the
preparations for the coming carnage. In fact it was not until the reign of
Napoleon that the concept of a standing conscripted army came to the fore. The
production necessary to equip and feed an army at this time was still rather
minimal when compared with modern-day armed forces. Even the food required
by these advancing armies was often acquired through plunder and pillage rather
than organized production.

Even in the early part of the twentieth century, the weapons of war were quite
rudimentary by today's standards, though this period marked the beginning of
what has been called the "American system of manufacturing" (Smith, 1987).
The ability to mass-produce weapons or the components for interchangeable
weapons systems had a significant impact on the ability of the state to field and
equip an army. According to Merit Smith, technological developments in
interchangeable manufacturing, machine tools, and railroads were all intimately
tied to the military enterprise. From an institutional perspective, Bruce Brunton
(1988) argues that changing patterns in military production in the United States
can be understood by looking to the intersection of the industrial and "security"
needs of a growing country. Like Gautam Sen, he sees the needs of industry and
the military as mutually dependent. James Cypher (1987), on the other hand,
suggests that military spending can be seen as a disguised form of industrial
policy.

With the continued advancement of technology, both capital and consumer,
the role of the foot soldier has taken on diminished importance, though the
human element of militarization is still quite substantial. Missiles, jet fighter

aircraft, long-range bombers, nuclear arsenals, and communication technology have changed not only the face of warfare itself but also the preparations necessary to wage war. A large standing army is still a prerequisite for military capability. In fact, the need to absorb, retaliate, maneuver, penetrate, and communicate, it is said, requires an ever vigilant military force. But now the preparations for war require the involvement of a much broader spectrum of the population. Scientists are needed to keep military technology on the cutting edge, engineers are required for design and development, production workers are needed to assemble, schools are needed to train this modern army in the use of these high-tech weapons, and bases are needed to house the soldiers and store the equipment. A bureaucracy, of course, is instrumental in overseeing and organizing this entire mobilization process. The size of this endeavor ensures that there will be retirement and education benefits to be dispersed, as well as medical facilities to be constructed and staffed. All of this, of course, is quite evident when looking at the progression of the military sector in an advanced industrial society, though the theoretical argument should hold for newly industrializing societies, if not those on the lower end of the technological ladder.

The irony in this evolving state of affairs is that the military component of the modern armed force no longer claims vast numerical superiority over its civilian counterpart, as can be seen in figures 2.2 and 2.3. These graphs depict the ratio of the combined active and reserve military personnel to the number of civilians working in the military bureaucracy or in weapons plants, where, for example, in the United States the ratio of soldier to civilian was three to one at the beginning of the century, yet slightly less than one to one by 1985. And along with the expansion of those sectors directly tied to military preparations comes the need for increased indirect participation. Bankers are needed to cash payroll checks, realtors to facilitate the distribution of property, and store clerks to sell the consumer goods to this expanding cadre of producers. In the day of the foot soldier armed simply with a sword or a rifle, the extent of this production was minimal. The technological advancements associated with the process of industrialization appear to have contributed to the dispersal of the roots of the military as an institution. Along with this penetration into the civil sector of society comes the popularization of the military in general, and violence as a tool of foreign policy in particular.

Political and Economic Inertia

Like any large organization, the military has its own parochial interests at the forefront of its planning and budgetary processes. As the amount of resources--both human and capital--intimately tied to the military expands, these organizational interests engender greater domestic political influence. Although interservice rivalries may at times seem more salient than the interests of the

Figure 2.1
A Hypothetical Distribution along
Industrialization and Militarization Axes

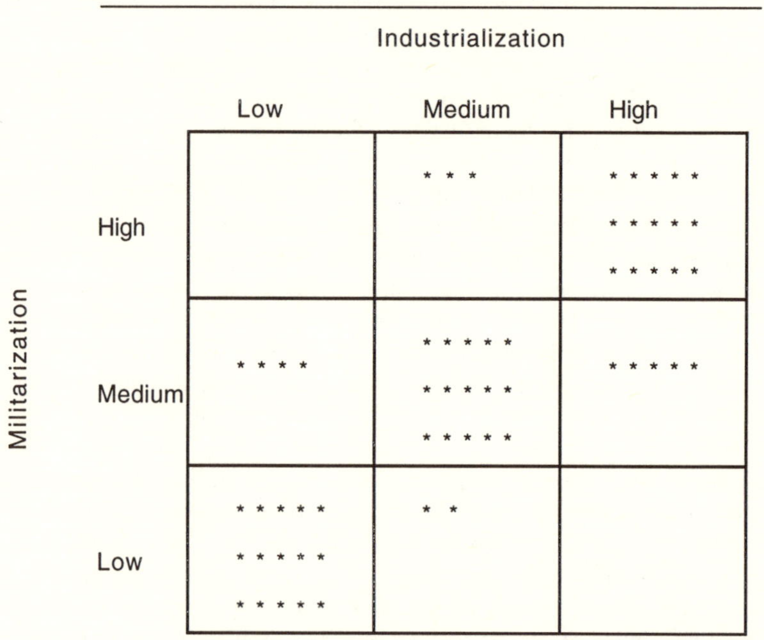

Industrialization

	Low	Medium	High
High		* * *	* * * * * * * * * * * * * * *
Medium	* * * *	* * * * * * * * * * * * * * *	* * * * *
Low	* * * * * * * * * * * * * * *	* *	

(left axis label: Militarization)

Note: the asterisks are not meant to convey observed numerical relationships but rather serve as an example of how the distribution of cases might be expected to align.

military per se, in the final analysis it will be the institutional role of the military as a whole that will defend its organizational interests most enthusiastically. Both the individual branches of the armed forces in the United States and the Department of Defense have offices specialized in promoting the virtues of their organization (Fulbright, 1970; Yarmolinsky, 1971). These public relation arms of the military are directed toward both legislative and public consumption, though their mission is quite explicitly the promotion of organizational interests.

If organizational interests are indeed part of the explanation for the extent to which a society is militarized, then we would expect to find evidence of this organizational staying power across time. Furthermore, this bureaucratic inertia may have several components, with each playing a more central role at various points along a temporal dimension, though all have direct ties to the political and economic constituencies that develop around the individual themes. These factors include: the push of technology, which captures the support of the scientific and industrial communities; the size of both the civilian and the non-civilian forces organized under the heading of "defense," which may be a function of and help determine the health of the labor force; the amount of current-year funding for the military and related programs; and the size of the congressional constituency that actively supports promilitary legislation. None of these constituencies are completely independent of one another, and, in fact, one may argue that they are quite interdependent. But in any event, there is some evidence that these factors do influence the size of military budgets and the type of weapon systems produced (Nincic, 1982; Russett, 1970).

If the political-economic-bureaucratic argument is correct, we should expect that the extent to which a society is militarized at time "T-1" will help predict the level of military mobilization at time "T". Communities that support a military base--and are to some extent supported by the base--workers who build munitions, soldiers on active and reserve duty, civilians who run the military bureaucracy, and veterans who have either a nostalgic view of the military or an ideological predisposition to support the military as a tool of foreign policy will exert strong influence on those charged with allocating national resources. The size of this constituency group will help ensure stability during budgetary processes.

Threats: Both Existential and Manipulated

Absent a hostile environment, even the most militarized society would begin to demobilize. Regardless of the amount of political legitimacy accorded the state and the inertial forces behind continued mobilization, the extraction of resources for military purposes will be increasingly difficult to maintain due to domestic political and economic pressures attributable to concerns such as budget shortfalls and infrastructural decay. Those who argue that the diversion of resources from civilian to military consumption will have pronounced economic costs may be empirically correct, though they have tended to neglect the domestic political benefits that may accrue through military mobilization (Melman, 1970; Dumas, 1988; Ball, 1988). The costs that are incurred by society tend to be rationalized in the name of "national security" and defense of the motherland. In the absence of a threat to the security of the state, the economic costs associated with continued mobilization would become not only increasingly evident to the general public but also more difficult to rationalize. Political legitimacy and the perception of a hostile international environment, along with the material capability required to organize and equip an armed force, are necessary and sufficient conditions for the extraction of resources for military purposes (Raczka, 1989). Take away the threat, and there will be little or no extraction. This threat, however, need not be existential in nature.

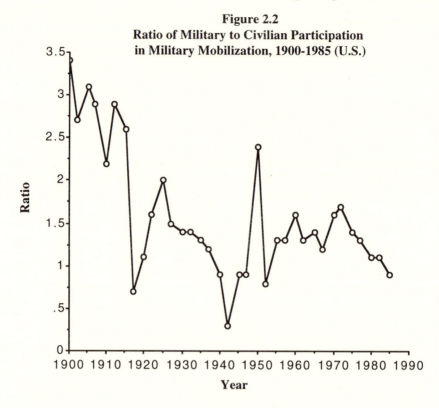

Figure 2.2
Ratio of Military to Civilian Participation
in Military Mobilization, 1900-1985 (U.S.)

A number of scholars have demonstrated that a threatening external environment may lead to increased allocations to the military sector (Rosh, 1988; Lebovic and Ishaq, 1987; Mintz and Ward, 1989). Miroslav Nincic (1982) argues that a hostile appearing adversary may account for some of the variation in weapons procurement and military spending. Charles Tilly (1975) suggests that a threat to the territorial integrity of the state will lead to an expansion of the military bureaucracy and form the rudimentary foundations of the modern nation-state. This argument coincides with that proposed by Otto Hintze, who goes as far as to argue that the state and the military were nearly synonymous at the "dawn of history." Moreover, he claims that throughout the ages, "pressure from without has been a determining influence on internal structure" (1975:183). The literature on arms races and the theoretical concept of the security dilemma also point to the role of the external environment as a factor in shaping internal military allocations. At the extreme, during mobilization for a war, we would expect that the external environment would shape internal decision-making regarding the extraction of resources for military purposes. We might also expect that a persistently hostile external environment would prevent large-scale

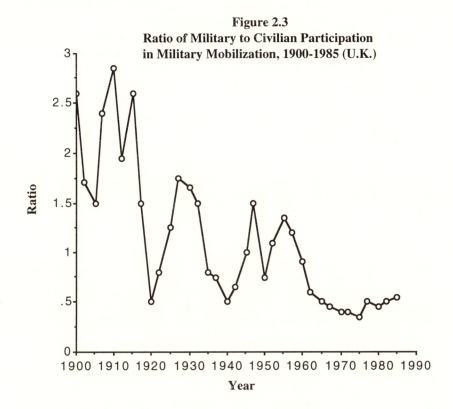

Figure 2.3
Ratio of Military to Civilian Participation
in Military Mobilization, 1900-1985 (U.K.)

reductions in the level of mobilization, if indeed this did not lead to a solidification of the influence of the military sector within society.

But an existential threat is not a prerequisite for maintaining high levels of military preparedness. What is required is not that the threat be real, but that the perception of a threat be maintained in the public eye. John Kenneth Galbraith (1983) argues that military leaders will maintain at least the perception of an external threat in order to prevent them from taking on a strictly ceremonial role within society. As mentioned earlier, Harold Lasswell suggests that the managers of the garrison state will manipulate perceptions of an external threat, even to the extent of engaging in international "bloodletting," in order to maintain access to their privileged positions. Likewise, the literature on the Military-Industrial Complex generally assumes that there is a self-interested elite that will manipulate the perception of a threat in order to maintain high levels of military preparedness (see Slater and Nardin, 1973).

Maintaining the perception of an external threat could be carried out through a number of mechanisms. There is, of course, the resort to international violence--in a sense, picking a fight with an adversary with whom you have a high probability of rapidly defeating--though this might generally be the tool of last resort. Before taking such extreme action, the state would attempt to use the mass media to identify an antagonist, chronicle the need for continued military preparedness, or point to the "evil" that threatens the global environment. Along this line, G. Ray Funkhouser (1973) demonstrates that the amount of media attention given to a topic in the United States is related to the public's perception of "the most important problem facing America."

That the media are sometimes an effective tool both for filtering out information deemed by the elite to be counterproductive and for feeding in information deemed critical to an elite worldview has been amply demonstrated (Gamson and Modigliani, 1989; Herman and Chomsky, 1988; Lee and Solomon, 1990). The motivating forces behind this "manipulation" are said to include a mixture of corporate profits, ideological preconceptions, and organizational self-interests. In the United States the military, in particular, has had a substantial impact on the content of news that reaches the public. To carry out this task of maintaining the desired images at the forefront of news reporters and news consumers, the individual departments of the armed forces have developed large, efficient, and well-funded public relation bureaus. News clips, media briefings, community forums, congressional and reporter "junkets," and even audio and visual production facilities ensure that the military is able to get its message to the public. This public relations machine has had notable successes in controlling media access to "news," as was evident in the Cuban Missile Crisis, the recent invasions of Grenada and Panama, and the conflict in the Persian Gulf, though it was less "successful" during the Vietnam War. Much the same story can be told about the military bureaucracy in Great Britain, as was clearly evident during the Falkland/Malvina War (Harris, 1983).

SOME TESTABLE HYPOTHESES

Having outlined the theoretical argument behind the militarization of societies, I can now make explicit a few hypotheses that emerge from my discussion. These hypotheses will subsequently be tested against data from the United States and Great Britain during the first eighty-five years of the twentieth century.

H1: The increased use of violence in foreign diplomacy leads to an increase in the extent to which society is militarized. The more the state relies on violent international behavior to achieve policy objectives, the more likely that the military will take on a greater role in society (Gurr, 1988). The development of organizations ready to fight future wars would be one outgrowth of continued involvement in international conflicts. We would expect to see this, inter alia, as the maintenance of or increase in the level of participation by the general public in the mobilization of resources for war.

H2: Militarization is positively related to the level of technological development. In the age of part-time or mercenary armies, little in the way of industrialization or civil participation could foretell the extent to which a society was organized around military preparations. But in a modern, high-technology era, the level of technological advancement plays a central role in determining the military capabilities of the state. It is in part the level of technology involved in the production of weapons that involves so much of the civil sector of society in the preparations for war. A large standing army alone-- as found in many developing countries--is not enough to organize a substantial proportion of society around military preparations. Only the more technologically advanced societies can efficiently produce modern weapons. Therefore, militarization should be positively associated with industrial-technological capabilities.

The question of whether technological developments "cause" militarization, or vice versa, is an interesting issue, though not quite the chicken-and-the-egg dilemma. While it is true that the military might promote the development of certain strategic technologies, that in itself does not lead to the direct involvement of civilians in the weapons-production process. But as that technology gets refined and transformed from a basic technology to one with military applications, the involvement of the civilian labor force takes on a new dimension.

H3: The more militarized the society, the greater the "manipulation" of the perception of a threat in order to maintain public support for the transfer of resources to the military sector. In response to an external threat, we would expect that an elite would mobilize its resources to address any impending challenge. In a more highly militarized society, as the existential threat diminishes, we would expect to see an increase in the manipulation of the perception of a threat rather than the demobilization of the military and its infrastructure. The level of mobilization might decrease from the heights reached during the peak of the crisis, but in the aftermath, the demobilization will not reach precrisis levels. This ratchet effect (Russett, 1970) will require the maintenance of the perception of a threat in order to maintain mass support. In short, if the threat is not "objective," then it will have to be "created" in the minds of the general public.

STEPS TOWARD EMPIRICAL TESTING: THE RESEARCH DESIGN

A multiple regression model using a least squares estimator was used as the primary means of testing the hypotheses, though various forms of non-parametric analyses--such as contingency tables and graphs--were used to tease out additional information when the statistical models were less revealing.

To empirically test these hypotheses, I needed to generate data for a number of variables. And while this makes for rigorous and reproducible findings, it adds a burden to the reader. Before moving on to the tests and the results, I need to operationally define these variables and discuss index construction. Although this may seem unwieldy and tedious at this juncture, the process is central not only to solid research but also to the interpretation of the findings.

THE OUTCOME VARIABLE: MEASURING MILITARIZATION

In measuring the extent to which a society is militarized, we must take account of all those people who are directly or indirectly organized by the military around the mobilization or preparation for war. This requires the development of a militarization index that will incorporate the various participants in this organizational process. The composite index that I have constructed is composed of six indicators; each attempts to tap into a specific component of the society: (1) active and reserve military forces; (2) civilians employees of the military establishment; (3) direct and indirect employees in weapons industries; (4) membership in organized veteran groups, or in Great Britain, the number of people receiving war pensions; (5) enrollment in military-based education programs; and (6) induced employment from weapons industries. The rationale and the data sources for each indicator will be spelled out below. In restricting my index to these six indicators, I left out much that could legitimately be claimed as pertinent to any measure of the degree of militarization. What is missing may be as important as those indicators included, but for theoretical reasons, omissions were made. Some of the more glaring indicators omitted from my measure include (1) military spending, as either an absolute figure or as a percentage of gross national product or government budget, (2) amounts and direction of research and development funding, and (3) distributional relationships such as government funding of education or health as a percentage of military spending. Whether or not this research suffers from the lack of inclusion of such indicators is an empirical question, but the intent of my militarization index is to capture the extent to which military preparations permeate society. Because funding-based indicators are subject to the fungibility of accounting procedures, as well as changes in the health of the economy as a whole, they may not be the best mechanism to tap into this construct.

All of my indicators are based on numbers of people; therefore, the index will be an expression of the percent of a population that is organized around the mobilization and preparations necessary for war. There would appear to be two bases from which I could derive this ratio: the total population or the labor force, or "effective population" (Organski, Bueno de Mesquita, and Lamborn, 1972). Because most of those who are involved in the preparations for war are part of the working-age population, my militarization index will be calculated as a percent of the labor force. Using this indicator will also give a sense of the economic burden associated with high levels of military mobilization. A less-inclusive indicator of militarization that is commonly used is military personnel per capita or as a percent of the labor force. Gary Goertz and Paul Diehl (1986), however, argue that the number of military personnel per capita is not an entirely valid measure of the resources devoted to the military, in large part, because the more modern the military force the more reliant it is on technological sophistication over sheer numbers. Technological developments, as I have argued above, shift the burden of preparing for war from the soldier to the civilian; therefore, any indicator based solely on military personnel will miss a critical element of the mobilization process. My militarization index accounts for this changing makeup of the "military participation ratio" by including not only those who will be called on to fight but also those who will organize and produce for the next battle.

Active and Reserve Military Forces

The need to account for the size of the active-duty forces seems rather straightforward. Clearly these forces are one of the most involved sectors of the population in the preparations for war. They not only are the potential combatants but also are mobilized on a full-time basis and in general are a foreign policy tool used by the state. The income of active-duty forces is derived from their involvement in the mobilization process, and any dependents are equally reliant on continued employment.

Reserve forces, however, are a somewhat different issue. For the most part, these soldiers do not derive the bulk of their income from military service; they are activated only on rare occasions and are in training for only a short period each year, yet they need to be included for a number of reasons. As individuals, reservists are committed to respond to the call-up of their units and, in doing so, incur the costs of active-duty service; they also receive some of the benefits. These are people who either have been through an extensive period of active military service or, at a minimum, have undergone extensive military training. As can be seen in the recent Persian Gulf war, reserve forces have been mobilized in large numbers and have taken forward positions in the combat zone. It is clear from this recent example that the operational planning of the military bureaucracy relies quite extensively on this pool of reserve forces whose normal direct involvement with military service is somewhat limited. However, this is not solely a modern-day phenomenon. The reorganization of the American army--and the political fight that it entailed--turned to a large degree on the organization of a ready reserve mobilizable in time of "national emergency" (Skowronek, 1982).

Data for these two indicators in the United States were derived from the *Statistical Abstract of the United States* and the *Annual Report of the Department of Defense*; for Great Britain, the relevant sources are the *Annual Abstract of Statistics* and the *Statement on Defence Estimates*.

Civilian Employees of the Military Establishment

Although civilians under the employ of the military establishment do not contribute directly to the projection of force by the state, they are a vital component of the bureaucratic and economic impetus behind continued mobilization. Without a large civilian support staff, the projection of force would be much more difficult for a modern-day army. The ties that bind are economic, political, and bureaucratic. It was argued earlier that the interests generated by the development of a large military-bureaucratic structure engender strong political and economic constituencies. These constituencies, in turn, use their influence to maintain continued military mobilization. People who work for the Department/Ministry of Defense will generally become part of the family of supporters for continued mobilization. Not only are job security and income factors that motivate this constituency, but so too are health care, retirement, and education.

Data on the numbers of civilians working for the Department of Defense were generally taken from the *Statistical Abstract of the United States*, though for some years the data were estimated. British data were derived from both the *Statement on Defence Estimates* and the *Annual Abstract of Statistics*; some data had to be estimated (see appendix 4 for the estimation procedure).

Direct and Indirect Employees in Weapons Industries

Like both active-duty military personnel and civilians working for the defense bureaucracy, those employed in weapons industries have strong economic ties to the continued preparation for war and, in some instances, to war itself. One need not be the staunchest supporter of elite policies to be engaged in war production, but working in a defense plant does entail at least a modicum of loyalty to the power elite--or, at a minimum, the quiet acquiescence to their foreign policies. Security checks and oaths of loyalty ensure that those who are active critics of the elite will rarely find employment in military industries, and the hierarchically based authority structure common to the defense plant ensures that those who do join rarely become critics.[2] It is in large part the economic tie that binds those who produce the weapons of war to support for continued mobilization. In fact, it not only binds them to the process but makes them active lobbyists on behalf of continued funding, expansionist foreign policies, and the promotion of the elite worldview.[3]

During the post-World War II period in the United States, these data were supplied by the Defense Department; this also holds true during the World War I period. Reporting for the earlier years is much more sketchy, and in most instances I had to either estimate the data or adopt the estimations of other researchers. For Great Britain, these data required much more estimation, though there were periods during which official government data were available in the

Statement on Defence Estimates or the *Annual Abstract of Statistics* (see appendix 4 for estimating procedures).

Organized Veteran Groups

Veterans of military service are generally considered to be highly supportive of the worldview of the security elite. Research suggests that on average, they tend to be more patriotic, nationalistic, and militaristic. Not all veterans, however, are active supporters of either the state or the military as an institution. Not only do some veterans actively support causes that are distinctly antimilitary, but as can be seen from the number of veterans participating in antiwar movements in the United States during the Vietnam conflict, a fair number of veterans do not fit the statistical mold described above. But large groups of veterans do tend to be active supporters of the promilitary policies of the state. These are veterans who belong to organized veteran organizations. Most of these groups are well organized, with local meeting halls, national headquarters, and active lobbyists working on behalf of both veteran interests and foreign policy issues. A perusal of the mission statements of some of the largest veteran organizations makes it clear that these groups actively work to promote the continued expansion of the military bureaucracy and, in some instances, the use of military force (see VanBuskirk, 1991:14; VFW, 1991:10; DAV, 1989; Lister, 1982). But whether or not each individual member supports the policies advocated by the organization is less important than the amount of political influence claimed by these groups by virtue of the size of their respective constituencies. Larger membership rolls tends to result in greater political access and influence.

Data on the number of people participating in veteran organizations were obtained from the membership rolls of the Veterans of Foreign Wars, Disabled American Veterans, and the American Legion.[4]

Military-Based Education Programs

Both the United States and Great Britain have extensive programs with which to bring military values, structure, and discipline to young people. These programs can be most readily observed through the organization of students in school, both at the secondary and the university levels. One might suggest that the impact on students is of marginal importance or that many, if not most, of the students who participate in such programs never go on to become active or reserve soldiers, let alone work in the arms industry. But during a time of "national emergency" these organized students can become part of a ready-made civil defense team, as they did in Britain during World War II or in Nazi Germany, as the carriers of the banner of the Third Reich. But most important, young "soldiers" who are part of military drill teams in high school go on to become adult members of society. Not only are these students mobilizable while they are young, but their youthful training helps ensure that they will be mobilizable when they are older and their influence is greater. Some, of course, derive income and a university education from their participation in the ROTC program, most of whom then go on to become reserve soldiers. Private "military academies" would appear to have a similar effect on the attitudes and perceptions of their graduates, though no account was taken of them in my indicator.

Data on military-based education will be restricted to the ROTC and JROTC programs for the United States, with data for the most part obtained from the military services, and to the Cadet Associations for Great Britain. Some estimation was necessary; see appendix 4 for details.

Induced Employment from Weapons Industries

Numerous jobs are attached to those industries and services that cater to those who derive their income directly from military employment or weapons contracts. The income of those who work directly for the military is generally spent within a given economic region. For example, the presence of a military base has quite a large effect on the local economy in which it is located, and the political uproar that is generated at the hint of a base closing can attest to the economic spin-off attributable to the military payroll. The technical term for this is *induced employment* and can be estimated by an employment multiplier. The U.S. Department of Defense estimates that for every direct or indirect job associated with the preparations for war, between two-tenths and eight-tenths of a job is created in the service industries providing for those directly under the military employ (Department of Defense, 1983).[5]

Figures on military-related induced employment are rarely, if ever, reported and in fact, for the most part, are simply crude estimates. Kyohei Sasaki (1963) estimated the employment multiplier from defense spending in Hawaii during the period 1949 to 1959 to be 28 induced jobs per 100 direct or indirect jobs created by military spending (1.28). Through a similar econometric procedure, M.E.F. Jones estimated the employment multiplier for a number of industries during the interwar period in Britain. Many of the industries for which estimates were derived figure prominently in that category of professions that make up the "munitions industries." Some examples may be helpful. The iron and steel industry created approximately 68 induced jobs for every 100 people directly employed; the shipbuilding industry, 44 induced jobs per 100 direct; the coal industry only 6 jobs per 100; chemical industries, 49 jobs per 100; aircraft industries, 27 jobs per 100; and building materials, 150 induced jobs per 100 directly employed (1985:434). For purposes of this analysis, I will use the mean (.5) of the range of jobs that the Department of Defense attributes to the induced effect of direct military employment. Though admittedly the value of this multiplier is a somewhat arbitrary choice, it is certainly not a capricious one. I also acknowledge that the induced employment that results from military spending is probably not stable over time. In an effort to reduce the probability of overestimation, the induced employment figures that I derive are a result of applying the estimated employment multiplier to only the number of those employed directly or indirectly in the manufacture of weapons. It is not applied to active duty forces or civilians working for the Defense Department, even though the earnings of each of these groups do support a broader community. Indicators of this abound, and one need only look to the political upheavals in the United States during the round of base closings in 1991 to witness the impact of military spending on local communities. In these instances, it was not only the military itself that resisted such widespread base shutdowns; the local residents also lent a strong voice to the case against closing bases.

These six indicators form the core of my militarization index and, as such, are summed and represented as a percent of the labor force (see figures 2.4 and 2.5). The result of this index is a fairly comprehensive measure of the extent to which the civil sector of society participates in the mobilization of resources for war. But it is not a totally complete view of societal involvement. Some factors have been omitted, which might be legitimately included. The number of people receiving military pensions--in the United States--and the number of dependents on those actively working for the military are the two most glaring examples. Employment in the space and nuclear-energy sectors has also been left out of the analysis.

PREDICTOR VARIABLES

Technological Development

A valid and reliable measure of the level of the technological capacity of a country is somewhat problematic for cross-sectional analyses, though it is easier to achieve when adopting a longitudinal design. For this analysis, an index was created using three separate indicators: iron and steel production; aluminum production; and sales of computers and peripheral equipment. These three indicators were chosen to reflect the increased technological sophistication in the production of military hardware over time. In the early part of the century, for example, basic metals were the critical component in the manufacture of weapons, though by the latter part of the century electronic circuitry nearly defined the technological capabilities of any particular military force. Because each of these indicators employs different units of measure, and each is introduced into the economy at various times throughout the century, I normalized each indicator to the year at which data for that indicator was first available. For example, iron and steel production equals 100 in 1900; aluminum production equals 100 in 1925; and computer sales is normalized to 100 in 1962.

These normalized scores were then summed across the three indicators to create an index of technological development. At the turn of the century, the index is composed of only iron and steel production, though by the 1960s the index includes all three components.

For the United States, data for iron and steel production were taken from the Correlates of War Capabilities dataset, aluminum production from the *United Nations Statistical Yearbook*, and computer sales from the *Statistical Abstract of the United States*. The same sources were used for British data, with the exception that the *Annual Abstract of Statistics* was the source for data on British computer sales.

The Perception of Threat

The extent to which the perception of an external threat was maintained in the public eye was measured through the content analysis of the Sunday *New York Times* and the *Sunday Times of London*; the unit of analysis was the article. Three randomly picked months were chosen--March, May, and October-- for which an "article count" was carried out on each Sunday paper during those months.[6] The result of this procedure is a net count of the frequency of articles per week that maintain a positive image of the military; the number of articles in each year was normalized for the number of weeks in the months sampled. Articles were counted that (1) identified an external foe or reported on an international crisis that threatened the interests of the United States or Great Britain, respectively, (2) chronicled the need for military expansion, increased military spending, and the need to reorganize the armed forces or deploy them outside the territory, (3) referred to patriotic themes or, conversely, used unpatriotic language to identify an organized group or foreign government, and (4) reported on issues of emerging military technology or the introduction of new technology into the armed forces of either the United States or Great Britain, respectively. Since antimilitary or antiwar articles might serve as a countervailing force within the mass media, the number of articles reporting on antimilitary or antiwar themes or discussing issues of arms control and disarmament or peace negotiations between antagonists were also counted. The latter two categories were subtracted from the former group, giving a net count of the number of articles portraying positive images of military mobilization (see appendix 1 for coding rules).

Compromises were made in choosing the *New York Times* and the *Sunday Times* as the sole source for coding this data, though the trade-offs appear to be justifiable and supported by precedent (e.g., Peterson, 1981). Admittedly, neither of these papers is directed at the mass public but rather could be considered part of the elite press. My intent, however, was to measure the extent to which the mass media was "manipulated," though this posed nearly insurmountable problems. Although throughout the entire time period under study, the *New*

York Times, for instance, did not claim the national stature that it now does, the front page of the Sunday edition, it could be argued, serves as a fairly reliable indicator of those articles picked up and printed in the mass-circulation papers. A similar argument would apply to the *Sunday Times of London*. Moreover, since many of the less cosmopolitan mass-circulation papers tend to be more conservative than their internationally oriented brethren, any errors associated with this measure will most likely work against a test of the theoretical argument presented here. However, as a check on the reliability of the *New York Times* as an indicator of the stories that reach the general public, I carried out a similar article count of the front page of the *Detroit News*, in each year, for the month of October. The *Detroit News* is clearly a paper targeted at a local audience and does not carry the elite-press stature of the *New York Times*. The outcome that I expected to find was that the number of stories portraying a positive image of the military would be smaller in the *News* than in the *Times*, though the correlation between the number of stories in each would be quite high. Indeed, in most years there were more promilitary stories in the *Times*, though this was not universal, and the correlation between article counts was .86. This latter statistic suggests that the *New York Times* is a fairly reliable indicator of the extent to which a promilitary image is maintained in the eyes of the general public, at least in the United States.

A second charge might be levied at my use of mass-circulation newspapers as a measure of the extent to which a perception of a threat is maintained in the public eye. A somewhat intuitive conclusion is that press reporting is simply capturing those times when force is being used in the international environment and, therefore, the society is facing an external threat. In effect, my indicator of the use of violence in pursuit of foreign policy objectives and my measure of manipulated threats are collinear. In fact, this is a far-from-complete picture. News reporting reflecting promilitary themes in the *New York Times* and the number of international disputes engaged in by the United States are correlated at a .40 level. Clearly there is a fair amount of reporting on military issues that is not directly related to U.S. involvement in disputes. A cursory glance at the coding sheets confirms this observation. Although this pattern generally holds true for British press reporting, the correlation between press articles and dispute behavior is significantly higher, .61.

Disputes and the Existential Threat

My indicator of elite use of violence to achieve foreign policy objectives was the number of ongoing militarized interstate disputes in each specific year. Data on the number of disputes in which the United States and Great Britain were involved as either the initiator or the target was taken from the Correlates of War Dispute dataset. A dispute was counted if it had begun or was ongoing in the specific year under analysis or the immediately preceding year ("t" and "t-1"). The

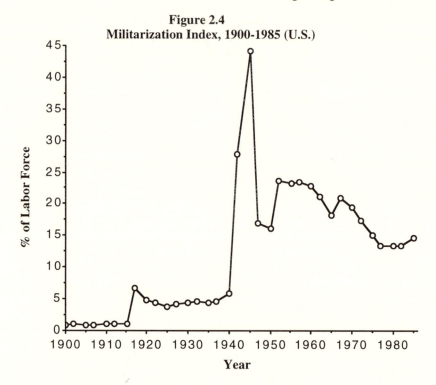

Figure 2.4
Militarization Index, 1900-1985 (U.S.)

inclusion of the lagged year was based on the notion that not only current violent behavior would contribute to societal militarization but that there would be a residual "holdover" from the previous year.

The model was also controlled for the existence of a war, as classified by Melvin Small and J. David Singer (1982), or the presence of a serious dispute with another major power. While this variable might not capture the total breadth of factors that could potentially compose an existential threat faced by the state, it appears to be a reasonable proxy. Realpolitik proponents, as well as some empirical evidence (Rosh, 1988; Lebovic and Ishaq, 1987), suggest that the military spending of a rival or neighboring state contributes to the perception of an external threat. Such a measure, however, would not only have to *a priori* account for a wide array of dyadic relationships, but in light of the known difficulties in accurately measuring both absolute levels of military allocations and yearly changes, it is not entirely clear whether the perception drives the calculation or vice versa. In short, in order to employ a military-spending indicator of an existential threat, I would need to *a priori* identify the external threat and only then measure changes in military allocations. In J. David Singer's (1958) formulation, threat is composed of the interaction between the perceived capability and intentions of an adversarial state. Inferring intention from behavior would appear to be a justifiable position (for example, see Huth,

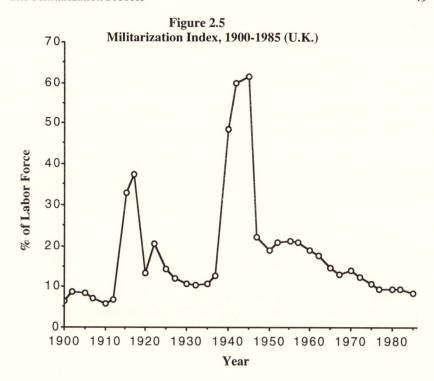

Figure 2.5
Militarization Index, 1900-1985 (U.K.)

1989), as would inferring capability by virtue of major power status. It is very likely, moreover, that any threat that would be identified *a priori* would be a member of the major power system and would also have been involved in disputes or a war with the United States during the time period under study.

The extent of mobilization during the previous period is included in the statistical model as an indicator of the bureaucratic and economic inertia working to maintain the level of mobilization.

The functional form of the equation is as follows:

$$Y = \alpha + \beta_1 X_1 + \beta_2 X_2 + \beta_3 X_3 + \beta_4 X_4 + \beta_5 X_5 + \varepsilon,$$

where

Y = militarization (MILI),
X_1 = # of ongoing international disputes (DISPUTES),
X_2 = militarization at time t-1 (MILI t-1),
X_3 = natural log of index of technological development (TECHNOLOGY),
X_4 = maintenance of the perception of a threat (MANIP), and
X_5 = dummy variable for existential threat (EXISTENTIAL).

THE PICTURE BEGINS TO TAKE SHAPE:
WHAT THE EVIDENCE TELLS US

The results of the regression analysis lend tentative support for the hypothesized relationships as they apply to the United States, with one glaring exception (see table 2.1). The role of international disputes as a factor contributing to the militarization of society appears to be in question. The negative coefficient associated with the dispute variable implies that dispute involvement is associated with demilitarization, though the level of statistical significance affords little confidence in this conclusion. Of the remaining variables, though some are statistically weak, the direction of the findings, as well as the strength of the coefficients, suggest that the model is essentially pointed in the right direction. The role of maintaining the perception of an external threat in the militarization of society appears to be quite strong, as does the effect of previous levels of militarization. Both coefficients are strongly positive and statistically significant. The effect of technology, on the other hand, is substantively in the hypothesized direction, though it suffers from weak statistical significance. A threatening international environment, furthermore, has a strong substantive impact, though it also lacks statistical significance at conventional levels of confidence. A first-cut analysis, therefore, lends some support for the theoretical argument, though it clearly calls for further refinements in the theoretical model.

The same analysis carried out for Great Britain identifies a somewhat similar pattern; however, the use of force as a tool of foreign policy appears to have a positive impact on changing levels of militarization (see table 2.2). This finding lends some credence to the argument that the use of violence in the international environment will serve to increase levels of military preparedness within society, though weak statistical confidence should breed caution. But it also leads to the question of why this relationship does not appear to hold in the United States.

Table 2.1
Regression Results (U.S.): Outcome Variable, Militarization

Variables	Coefficient	Standard Error	T-Ratio
DISPUTES	-.15	.41	-.36
MILI (t-1)	.57	.13	4.42**
TECHNOLOGY	.69	1.56	.44
MANIP	1.27	.55	2.30*
EXISTENTIAL	4.98	4.01	1.24
Constant	-4.83	9.18	-.52

Adjusted R2=.72 Standard Error=5.35 Mean (Y)=12.32 Durbin h=1.03

* p<.05
**p<.01

Now that the hypotheses have been formally tested, with results that are encouraging though not overwhelming, it is time to engage in some exploratory analysis. First, the question just posed deserves serious treatment, and second, well-reasoned arguments can help make sense of the findings and suggest modifications to the theoretical model. These might not be completely distinct issues. One explanation for the differing role played by violent foreign policy in the United States and the United Kingdom is that there is a threshold in the extent to which a society is militarized above and below which the relationship to the use of violence is fundamentally different. During less-militarized periods, the public will be more hesitant to support foreign excursions; during highly militarized periods, the public may become overly accustomed to such violent state behavior. In the former instance, this may result in a retrenchment in the latitude accorded the military, while under the latter circumstances, the public may even limit the peaceful options available to the elite. If indeed this relationship is nonlinear, then it may be captured by explicitly modeling this threshold effect. Furthermore, if the relationship does differ above and below some cutoff, then the weak findings resulting from the misspecified model are quite understandable. To make this more tangible, we need only to look at the violent foreign policy of and public attitudes in the United States. Before World War II, the United States was basically a militia society with strong public tendencies toward isolationism. World War II ushered in a change in the attitudes of the American public toward the military, an increased influence of the military in political decision-making, and a marked increase in the use of force as a foreign policy tool.

When categorizing the data for the United States into "high," "medium," and "low" levels of militarization and dispute involvement, we clearly see that periods of high militarization coincide with times when the use of force is quite common; periods of low militarization are also times when force is used more selectively (see figure 2.6). This is confirmed by a test for the difference of

Table 2.2
Regression Results (U.K.): Outcome Variable, Militarization

Variables	Coefficient	Standard Error	T-Ratio
DISPUTES	.57	.37	1.54
MILI (t-1)	.20	.10	2.00*
TECHNOLOGY	.80	.84	.94
MANIP	15.46	3.44	4.48**
EXISTENTIAL	3.14	2.56	1.22
Constant	-.36	5.54	-.06

Adjusted R^2=.80 Standard Error=6.27 Mean (Y)=18.35 Durbin h=-.21

* $p<.05$
** $p<.01$

means in the number of ongoing disputes in the pre- and post-World War II eras, where the post World War II period had on average about three more ongoing disputes per year than in the period before the war. Categorical data from Great Britain, however, does not show this clear pattern between the extent to which British society was militarized and the use of violence by the British elite, nor does a difference of means test. We will come back to examine this more closely later.

One inference that can be drawn from this preliminary empirical evidence is that, *ceteris paribus*, internal factors account for a large part of the military-based mobilization of society. This conclusion seems much more applicable to the United States than to Great Britain, though in either case the argument appears to be supported by the data. The external environment, however, cannot be neglected when looking for potential causes of societal militarization. Whether the use of force by the state covaries with changing levels of militarization--as seems more evident in Britain--or whether there is a threshold in the extent to which a society is militarized, above which the use of force becomes more commonplace, the data indeed demonstrate that there is an empirical relationship between the external behavior of the state and the organization of society. However, the findings appear tentative enough that further model specification and analysis are called for.

The two weakest findings in the analysis of U.S. data pertain to the roles of technology and violent foreign policy in the militarization of society; these coefficients are also statistically weak for British data. The previous discussion and exploratory analysis suggest that accounting for the potential changing role of disputes above and below some threshold, particularly in the United States, might significantly increase the strength of the statistical findings among predictor and outcome variables. To formalize a test of this argument, I included an interactive variable in the analysis that attempts to model this threshold effect. A dummy variable was created that was coded zero if the level of militarization was below 12 percent (the mean of U.S. militarization levels) and coded one otherwise.[1] This dummy variable was then multiplied by the DISPUTE variable, in effect creating an interactive variable that has values greater than zero only during periods when the society was above this threshold of militarization. The interpretation of this new coefficient would be to identify the added effect of high levels of violent foreign policy on militarization during periods when society was more highly militarized, whereas adding the two coefficients will identify the substantive impact of dispute behavior on militarization during periods of high mobilization.

The new findings demonstrate that the use of force by the United States does have a statistically significant and substantively meaningful effect on levels of militarization (see table 2.3). The different signs associated with the coefficients for dispute involvement over the entire time period (DISPUTES) and those years during which the level of mobilization was above the threshold (HIGH-DISPUTE) confirm that the weak relationship identified in the earlier analysis was an artifact of poor model specification. At lower levels of militarization, the use of force in the current or the previous year results in a demobilization of forces. But at higher levels of militarization, increased dispute involvement tends to increase the level of military mobilization. Data from

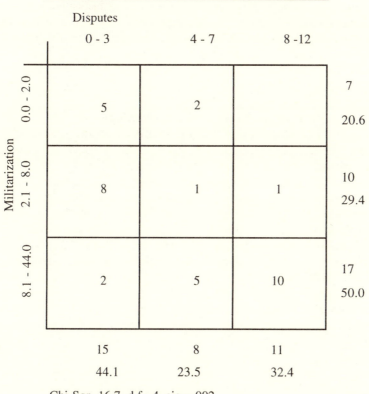

Figure 2.6
Categorical Analysis of Disputes and
Militarization in the United States

Militarization	Disputes 0 - 3	4 - 7	8 -12	
0.0 - 2.0	5	2		7 20.6
2.1 - 8.0	8	1	1	10 29.4
8.1 - 44.0	2	5	10	17 50.0
	15 44.1	8 23.5	11 32.4	

Chi-Sqr 16.7, d.f.=4, sig.=.002
Kendal's Tau b=.56, sig.=.000

Great Britain identify a similar pattern (see table 2.4). This finding is consistent with the theoretical arguments of both Harold Lasswell and Ted Gurr, who posit that international violence will help to solidify the role of the military within society, though the evidence supports the argument only for a much narrower category of cases, namely those in which society is already quite militarized.

Under the restrictions of this new model, the role of technology appears to have a differing effect on militarization, depending on the society. In the United States the relationship is clearly negative, though in Britain the coefficient is positive but statistically weak. This runs counter to some of the strong theoretical arguments outlined earlier. The confounding problem, it appears, can be attributed mainly to trends in technological development over the post-1940 era, where growth is clearly exponential. Trends in militarization over that same period, however, are generally declining, though still well above pre-1940 levels. A visual examination of the data on the ratio of civilian to military personnel does suggest that with the increase in technological sophistication came a more participatory role of civilians in the preparations for war, which is highly consistent with the theoretical argument outlined earlier, but the multivariate analysis does not play a confirming role.

Table 2.3
Regression Results, Revised Model (U.S.):
Outcome Variable, Militarization

Variables	Coefficient	Standard Error	T-Ratio
DISPUTES	-1.86	.54	-3.41**
HIGH DISPUTES	2.41	.53	3.99**
MILI (t-1)	.48	.10	4.52**
TECHNOLOGY	-3.23	1.61	-2.01*
MANIP	1.29	.44	2.87**
EXISTENTIAL	8.79	3.35	2.61*
Constant	22.19	10.03	2.21
Adjusted R2=.82 Standard Error=4.32 Mean (Y)=12.32 Durbin h=-.55			

*p<.05
**p <.01

POINTING THE WAY AHEAD: INFERENCES
ABOUT THE REAL WORLD

The implications of these findings for our understanding of the militarization process, as preliminary as they are, are impressive. Over a temporal dimension covering eighty five years and comparing two countries, a few relationships appear evident: (1) the political-economic inertia behind militarization can be quite strong, though as is evidenced by British data, previous militarization does not necessarily prevent gradual demilitarization; (2) the use of military force to achieve foreign policy objectives is not only more prevalent during periods of high militarization, but during these periods the use of force contributes to increases in levels of militarization; and (3) the use of force during periods of low militarization is associated with the demilitarization of society, somewhat consistent with a democratic politics argument. If this could be borne out by more in-depth analysis, it may suggest that the democratic process can be subverted by societal militarization. Unfortunately, that query will have to await its own systematic investigation. A further finding is that the existence of an existential threat can lead to an increase in the level of militarization, as one should expect, but this too is not a necessary condition, as the data from Great Britain suggest. The role of technology in the militarization of society, however, is unclear at this stage. Although in a multiple regression analysis, technology levels are either associated with demilitarization or, as in the case of Britain, support the hypothesis, and although our confidence level is a bit suspect, this appears to be more an artifact of the rapidity of the growth in technological sophistication in the post-World War II period.

Table 2.4
Regression Results, Revised Model (U.K.):
Outcome Variable, Militarization

Variables	Coefficient	Standard Error	T-Ratio
DISPUTES	-1.17	.78	-1.50
HIGH DISPUTES	1.76	.71	2.46*
MILI (t-1)	.09	.10	.89
TECHNOLOGY	1.27	.80	1.58
MANIP	16.55	3.18	5.20**
EXISTENTIAL	1.04	2.41	.43
Constant	.78	5.20	.15

Adjusted R2=.83 Standard Error=5.77 Mean (Y)=18.35 Durbin h=-.41

*p<.05
**p<.01

In general, these findings lend qualified support to the ratchet argument put forth by Bruce Russett, and they confirm much of what Miroslav Nincic demonstrated: that domestic pressure and the international environment both contribute to the explanation for military allocations. These findings also suggest that at a minimum, the realpolitik paradigm offers only a partial accounting for the militarization of societies. For the most part, these findings hold across both Britain and the United States, though there are differences that need to be examined more closely.

Possibly more interesting is the role played by the media specifically and the maintenance of the perception of a threat in general. The theme of news reporting on issues relating to the military has a strong and positive effect on levels of mobilization. Those who argue that a Military-Industrial Complex has been the driving force behind the high levels of military preparedness in the United States have assumed that the perception of a threat would, if necessary, be artificially maintained. The evidence presented here lends credence to that charge. In light of the findings from chapter 5--examining the relationship between militarization on the one hand and societal symbols of war and patriotism, on the other--it seems that positive images of the military are maintained in the public eye and are subsequently manipulated during periods of high mobilization. William Gamson and Andre Modigliani (1989) find a similar dynamic taking place with regard to nuclear energy.

These findings challenge the notion that technological development has a direct impact on increasing levels of militarization. In fact, taken literally, this would suggest that technological development retards the militarization process, at least in the United States. This result, however, appears to be an artifact of the phenomenal growth in the level of technical sophistication in the postwar period. Nevertheless, in both countries the ratio of civilian to military participants in the preparations for war more closely follows the trends in technological development. This latter point constituted a large part of the theoretical foundation for arguing that there would be a positive relationship between technology and militarization. The likes of Alexis de Tocqueville, Otto Hintze, Morris Janowitz, Harold Lasswell, and Stephen Van Evera could take some solace in these findings, though they are far from conclusive.

Perhaps of critical importance to this research effort is the impact of the use of force by the state on societal militarization. The results of this analysis demonstrate that the relationship between the resort to violent foreign policy and the militarization of society is not as straightforward as some might suggest. In a more highly militarized society, there is a positive relationship, suggesting that an increase in the use of force will lead to an increase in the level of militarization; yet on the lower end of the militarization scale, the opposite appears true. This finding is also consistent between the United States and Great Britain. One inference that can be drawn from this finding is that violent foreign policy is used by the state in an effort to mobilize public support for the diversion of resources to the military sector, though only when there is already a burgeoning Military-Industrial Complex.

A few words should be said about the apparent differences between the results of U.S. and British data. With the exception of the finding regarding the role of technological development in the militarization of society, discrepancies are a matter of statistical confidence rather than substantive impact. Although weak statistical support calls into question the direction of the impact, the coefficients across cases are generally consistent. One difference could of course be cultural, though I will leave that discussion for another day. Two explanations stand out most prominently, and it is to these that I will turn. The first comes from examining the trends in militarization during the twentieth century (see figures

2.4 and 2.5). Britain, faced with greater threats to its survival during the two world wars, clearly mobilized to a much higher level than the United States, though at the conclusion of each war it demobilized more drastically. In fact Bruce Russett's ratchet argument does not adequately describe the British experience. The post-World War II trend in Britain is much less volatile than that of the United States and for the most part demonstrates a slow but steady reduction in the level of militarization. The second factor that might partially account for some of the differences in the findings can be attributed to the role played by each actor in the international system. Until World War I, Britain was considered the dominant actor in the global system. And although this period was at the end of the Pax Britannia, there was no other actor yet capable of claiming the mantle. By the end of World War II, the United States was one of two superpowers, and Britain had taken on a much diminished role in the international system. And while system leadership itself might not have a strong direct impact on levels of militarization, it might indeed effect the extent to which violence is used in pursuit of foreign policy objectives and through this levels of militarization. This will be examined in the following chapters.

A final word of caution about the findings just presented is necessary. If the data used in this analysis were generated through a feedback process between societal militarization and the violent behavior of the state, the assumptions that underlie the least squares estimation technique would be violated. We would expect, therefore, that the findings are highly inconsistent. In short, we need to explicitly model the feedback relationship in order to generate reasonably reliable estimates of the impact of the various components of the militarization process. Although we should not expect wild swings in the direction of the findings, we cannot consider this misspecified model to be the final word.

3

Accounting for Violent Foreign Policy: The Second Half of the Puzzle

In Chapter 1 I laid out the overall theoretical argument, while chapter 2 subjected one side of the hypothesized feedback to empirical testing. Although not the complete picture, the results demonstrated that both internal and external factors contribute to the militarization of the U.S. and British societies. While the findings differ marginally between the United States and Great Britain, the basic arguments outlined in the earlier chapter tend to be supported by the data, at least with some modifications. However, if there is a feedback between the external behavior of the state and the internal organization of society, then we must also look for factors that contribute to the violent foreign policy of the state. The central aim of this chapter is to model those factors that contribute to elite use of violence in the international environment--in effect, the other side of this hypothesized feedback. I will focus primarily on three variables that should account for much of this violent foreign policy: (1) the extent to which the society is militarized; (2) the clarity of the systemic order; and (3) the role of system/bloc leadership. Once we understand the independent factors that drive both the militarization of society and the use of force by the state, I will explicitly test for a feedback among them, in chapter 4.

Much of the literature examining the causes of international violence tends to focus on accounting for international war, but international war does not capture the range of violent foreign policy engaged in by the state. For example, military disputes short of war are much more common than war itself, though that broader category has received much less systematic attention (an exception is Huth, Gelpi and Bennett, 1992). Much of what does exist, moreover, focuses primarily on dyadic level explanations.[1] And while dyadic level analyses--such as the role of contiguity or enduring rivalries--contribute greatly to our understanding of the violent behavior of a state, we seem to know little about the effect of either the internal organization of society or the constitution of the systemic order on the violent foreign policy of the state. In this chapter I will examine the theoretical grounding for our understanding of the use of force, as well as any empirical findings uncovered to date. My discussion, however, will sidestep issues such as geographic proximity or other dyadic explanatory variables. With that background, I will then go on to test hypotheses incorporating the structural and behavioral factors that might account for the violent foreign policy of the state.

ASSEMBLING THE PIECES: THE THEORETICAL OUTLINE

Internal Militarization and External Behavior

While enough has been said about Harold Lasswell's thesis regarding the relationship between external belligerency and internal militarization, it should be clear from his model that increased militarization will result in an increase in state-led coercion. Lasswell, however, is not alone in positing this relationship. As suggested in the previous chapter, Ted Gurr sees the militarization of the state and the use of violence to achieve policy objectives as part of a self-amplifying feedback. This feedback is driven in part by the evolution of a political culture that reifies the role of a successful military. J. David Singer (1970) also points out that internal militarization can increase the level of international belligerency. All of these arguments make intuitive sense and suggest that further analysis is warranted. Two main factors point to internal militarization as a cause of external violence: (1) domestic political and economic concerns; and (2) heightened tensions in the international environment associated with highly mobilized adversaries.

To justify continued or increasing levels of funding, staffing, and production for the military, the security elite must generate public support; one mechanism available to the elite is the use of force in a foreign conflict. By rallying the public "around the flag," they may be able to justify continued mobilization. For reasons of political expediency it might make sense, then, for an elite to embroil the society in an armed conflict if maintaining, or increasing, levels of militarization is in their immediate interest (Snyder, 1991). In short, the domestic militarization of society could inexorably lead to the militarization of elite foreign policy.

The motivations behind such behavior by the state need not be devious or duplicitous, as much of the Military-Industrial Complex (MIC) literature might suggest, but simply a matter of political and economic pressures. Jack Snyder demonstrates that logrolling politics can play a central role in expanding the military commitments of the elite and can retard the ability of a political system to utilize self-correcting mechanisms in the pursuit of rational foreign policy. Moreover, in a highly militarized society the public may, almost subconsciously, encourage the use of force by the elite. If the level of military preparedness is sufficiently high, this foreign policy implement will tend to look like the most attractive option available to the state leadership. And if a great deal of prestige--both internal and external--is accorded the military, the propensity to demonstrate its political capital might result in an increased incidence of coercive diplomacy. As John Kenneth Galbraith (1983) has argued, if a military sits idle for too long, it will begin to lose credibility among its domestic constituents.

Bruce Russett argues that one result of a state's attempt to use the diversion of resources to the military sector as a tool to maintain domestic political and economic stability is the unintentional side effect of increasing international hostility. It can "reinforce the domestic arguments for similar policies in other countries . . . [and] generate higher levels of threat-perception among the political elites" (1990:23). The net effect could be to increase the level of international tension resulting in more militarized foreign policies. If Russett is empirically correct, then the "security dilemma" or the "arms spiral" can be driven by domestic political considerations, and these domestic concerns can then lead to an increased incidence of international conflict. However, attempts to manipulate domestic policies are not the only factors contributing to international tensions.

It is argued by some scholars (Kennedy, 1987; Singer, 1989; Gilpin, 1981) that the decline of a major power, or the "global hegemon," will be both a cause and an effect of the increased allocation of societal resources to the military sector. And although I will discuss this issue more fully below, the increased reliance on the military for either political or economic stability not only can exacerbate the decline but also can lead to the increased use of force by the state.

Theoretically, then, societal militarization can affect the amount of violence evident in elite foreign policy in three ways: (1) by domestic pressures associated with high levels of military mobilization, which lead to either public acquiescence or active support for elite use of international violence; (2) by increasing international tensions vis-à-vis a neighboring state or perennial adversary; and (3) by exacerbating the decline of a global or regional power and encouraging attempts to maintain its status in the system through the use of force. It should be evident that each of these mechanisms or behaviors is fully consistent with the others, resulting in the internal process of militarization feeding on itself and fueling the effect on the external militarized behavior of the state.

In the first instance, if a sizable proportion of society has links that tie them directly to the continued production and preparations by and for the military sector, then they might be more likely not only to acquiesce in the violent foreign policy of the elite but also to unwittingly encourage such behavior. A similar argument can be made about self-interested coalitions (Snyder, 1991). The second mechanism can be conceived of in terms of the security dilemma or an arms spiral (Jervis, 1976) and is often operationalized as an arms race in which two adversarial states respond to the arms buildup of the other. There is some empirical evidence that the existence of an arms race is associated with the outbreak of war, though the findings across studies are not sufficiently consistent to permit reliable generalizations (Wallace, 1979, 1981; Diehl, 1983, 1985; Morrow, 1989). And finally, the breakdown of the systemic order, or the perception of changing relative positions in that order, has been linked to the onset of major-power war (Singer, Bremer, and Stuckey, 1972; Doran and Parsons, 1980; Organski and Kugler, 1980), though again, little systematic evidence has demonstrated that international violence short of war follows from fluctuations in systemic clarity.

If the theoretical arguments are correct, it should be clear that these factors interact quite readily. For example, the perception of declining relative power might generate an increased level of military mobilization, which in turn both looks threatening to a neighbor or adversary and engenders greater domestic political and economic momentum. The spiral tightens as the diversion of resources to the military increases; the increased use of violence in elite foreign policy should be one result. The sequence could also begin from a different starting point, where, say, an already high level of militarization leads to political pressure to make use of the military as nonviolent diplomatic initiatives become less successful. This increased belligerency appears threatening to an adversary, which ultimately results in more resources being devoted to the military sector, which then helps precipitate the relative decline of the state. The declining systemic order makes easier the challenge to the status quo by dissatisfied states and makes more likely the attempt by the declining power to use force to maintain the system hierarchy.

All of this is not simply a scholarly hunch. There is some empirical evidence that internal militarization leads to the increased use of violence by the state. Robin Luckham (1980) shows that on the African continent, the more highly militarized the state, the more prone are its elite to employ violence in pursuit of policy objectives, against both internal and external opponents. This line of reasoning has been demonstrated somewhat more systematically by those who search for the causes of political repression. Whether military allocations or regime type was used as the predictor, the increased influence of the military was positively associated with the level of domestic political abuse by the state (Zwick, 1984; Henderson, 1982; Regan, 1990).

Using a distinction between verbal and violent foreign conflict behavior, Erich Weede (1970) finds that internal militarization--measured in terms of expenditure and military personnel data--is positively, though weakly, associated with both forms of conflictual foreign policy. And Charles Kegley, Neil Richardson, and Gunter Richter (1978) find a positive correlation between militarization (military spending/GNP) and both domestic and foreign conflict. Each of these studies, though somewhat problematic, offers a modicum of support for the hypothesis that internal militarization increases the propensity of the state to resort to violence in an effort to achieve its foreign policy objectives. Paul Diehl and Jean Kingston (1987), however, find no evidence to support the hypothesis that arms increases significantly affect the probability that a major power will become involved in disputes. This is in direct contradiction to the previously mentioned studies and poses a serious challenge to the theoretical argument presented here. But before abandoning the notion that the militarization of society plays a contributing role in the propensity of the elite to employ violence, it should be noted that the Diehl and Kingston study relied on a simple dichotomous coding of dispute involvement. In doing so, the authors failed to examine whether militarization is related to the frequency of ongoing violence in any one year. For example, their findings would be consistent with a condition in which a country was involved in one dispute for every year that it fell at a low end of a militarization continuum, with twenty disputes per year for each year at the high end of the continuum. In all instances, the dichotomous variable would indicate the existence of a dispute, and the variation in the level of militarization would be quite extreme. This research strategy would not capture the variation in dispute behavior over a range of militarization values.

The literature on arms races takes us a bit closer to empirical support for the thesis that militarization leads to an increased likelihood of the use of violence in elite foreign policy, though the outcome that is examined is generally confined to war. Michael Wallace (1981) finds that an arms race tends to precede the outbreak of war under certain circumstances, whereas Paul Diehl (1983) demonstrates that an arms race and the outbreak of war between disputants are only weakly correlated. By including a control for the risk propensity of the state, James Morrow (1989) shows that an arms race alone is not sufficient to cause war but that certain types of states are more prone to gravitate from an arms race to a war. But whether or not the existence of an arms race increases the probability of dispute involvement is still indeterminate from these analyses.

We must use caution, however, when trying to draw inferences from the class of events labeled "arms races" to the more general proposition evident in my theoretical argument. Most of the findings just discussed apply only to the specific instance of an arms race or a unilateral arms buildup, though the question remains as to whether a high level of militarization will increase the propensity to employ violence in foreign interactions, regardless of whether or not the level of militarization is the result of an arms race. However, if the arms spiral and the security dilemma concepts have any empirical validity in the international environment, then one outgrowth from the increased international tensions that accompany national armament programs should be a greater propensity to employ violence in pursuit of policy objectives.

In sum, both our theoretical understanding and the scant empirical evidence point to the internal militarization of society as a contributing factor in the extent to which a state will resort to the use of violence, be it domestic or international. But clearly, other factors present the opportunity and possibly the incentives.

System Clarity

The role of the international system structure on the outbreak of war has a long tradition of attention from social scientists, though with more theoretical than empirical support for the importance of a systemic level of analysis (for example, see Waltz, 1979; Singer, Bremer, and Stuckey, 1972; Gilpin, 1981; Deutsch and Singer, 1969; Organski and Kugler, 1980). It has also been asserted that most wars are preceded by at least one militarized dispute, if not a series of disputes. By linking these two theoretical propositions, we can draw the inference that changes in the system structure--or the clarity in the distribution of capabilities therein--should result in an increase in the incidence of disputes. While this proposition has not been empirically tested, it does seem to be a plausible argument and approachable from a number of theoretical directions.

The declining role of a system-leader might account for the breakdown of order within the global community of nation-states and, through this breakdown, an increase in the use of violence to achieve political objectives. If, indeed, the system leader--or system leaders--work to maintain the status quo within that system, and if the rewards associated with the status quo are unequally distributed to the benefit of the guarantor of the status quo, then an inability to clearly define an international hierarchy should increase the number of challenges to the faltering leadership. Furthermore, the declining major powers may resort to more inflexible responses, such as using force to quell the aspirations of the dissatisfied lesser power and diverting increasing amounts of resources to their military sectors. This reasoning is supported by the arguments of Robert Gilpin (1981) and Paul Kennedy (1987), who posit that an increased diversion of societal resources to the military sector, by a country sitting near the pinnacle of systemic power, will inevitably lead to a decline in that state's ability to determine the rules of interaction within that system. Not only do the number of challenges to the status quo increase, but so too does the propensity to employ violence on the part of the system leader in an effort to maintain the status quo. J. David Singer et al. (1989) would draw the noose even tighter around the neck of the over-allocating state, arguing that it is not only the hegemon that is susceptible to the effects of declining relative influence but that all of the dominant powers in the system will respond to their own relative decline. This decline, according to Singer, will result in the increasing resort to the use of force by all actors in the system.

The role of uncertainty plays a crucial part in the theoretical arguments relating system structure to international violence. According to Kenneth Waltz (1969, 1979) a bipolar system is inherently more stable--and, presumably, less conflict prone--than any form of multipolar environment, whereas Karl Deutsch and J. David Singer (1969) see a multipolar world as more stable than one with two dominant blocs or poles. A further refinement of this debate posits that a unipolar, or hegemonic, order is the most stable. The underlying concept that drives this debate is the effect of uncertainty on the behavior of actors in the system. Those who argue that the smaller the number of dominant actors, the less conflict-prone will be the system, view uncertainty as a destablizing factor. As the hierarchy of the international system becomes less clear, so too does the certainty with which retribution will be meted out for attempts to disrupt or challenge the status quo. From this theoretical perspective, the less clear the roles in the international system, the more prone to violence will be the members of that system.

On the other hand, uncertainty is viewed by Deutsch and Singer as an inhibitor to the use of violence to alter the status quo. The uncertainty in this case is rooted less in the question of whether a challenge to the status quo will result in a punitive response and more in which actors--if any--will come to the aid of the aggrieved party. Aggression may engender no collective response by the other major actors in the system, or it may result in a unanimous decision to work against the aggressor. It is this uncertainty--of who will respond and how--that counsels caution in the policies of potential challengers to the status quo.

Zeev Maoz (1982) argues that if the systemic hierarchy is not sufficiently clear and stable, then those actors who feel that they do not command their rightful place at the table of elders will become frustrated with their lack of a role in defining the rules of interaction. This frustration may provide the motivation required to challenge the status quo; a violent foreign policy on the part of the frustrated actor may be one result. Although the initiator in Maoz's model is clearly the frustrated state, this need not be so. Robert Gilpin's (1981) hegemonic model suggests that one of the responses available to the declining state is to increase its sphere of influence and expand its capability base. If the international environment is truly anarchic, as realpolitik proponents would argue, then expanding one's sphere of influence and capabilities might entail a fair amount of coercion. Therefore, an unstable and fluid system would have at least two potential sources of increased violence: the frustrated initiator trying to force a change in the status quo; and a threatened declining power trying to maintain its dominant position through the use of force.

The common thread in each of these theoretical arguments is that the clarity of the international system will be a causal factor in the level of violence evident in the foreign policies of the individual states within the system. And although the empirical evidence to support this assertion is inconclusive, there is a fair amount that we do know about the relationship between system structure and the propensity to fight wars.

The most logical place to start this survey is with the study by J. David Singer, Stuart Bremer, and John Stuckey (1972). The results of their analysis of the role played by the concentration of capabilities on the outbreak of major power wars demonstrate that the makeup of the system does have an impact on the war-proneness of states within the system. Even though the authors outline a number of caveats that suggest the tentative nature of their findings, they do come to a fairly strong conclusion regarding the postdictive ability of the systemic hierarchy for the magnitude of major-power war.

Bruce Bueno de Mesquita has also tested for the effect of systemic level variables on the occurrence of war in the major-power system (1978; 1981; and with Lalman, 1988). In the earlier studies he finds very tentative support for the thesis that systemic factors influence the amount or level of international war, at least those wars involving at least one major power. In the latter study, which compares the predictive ability of an expected utility model with one focusing on systemic-level variables, Bueno de Mesquita and Lalman conclude that systemic factors account for very little of the variation in the propensity for war among European states; the expected utility model, however, accounts for significantly more of the variation in the outcome variable.

More recently Paul Huth, Christopher Gelpi, and D. Scott Bennett react to the weakness of many of the earlier findings regarding the role of system structure on international violence by testing a more sophisticated model incorporating controls for state-level attributes, including risk propensity, along with system-level variables. Their findings support the argument that the concentration of capabilities in the system affects the dispute-proneness of at least a certain class of international actors: enduring rivals. They conclude their analysis by arguing that system uncertainty has an effect independent of the state's risk propensity and that "increases in system uncertainty have a negative effect on conflict initiation . . . supporting the Deutsch and Singer argument that multipolar systems are more stable than bipolar ones, at least as far as dispute initiation is concerned" (1992:21).

Others who have contributed to our empirical understanding of the role of system structure on likelihood or magnitude of war include Frank Wayman (1984), William Thompson (1986), and Charles Doran and Wes Parsons (1980), among others. Each of these authors presents evidence to suggest that the structure of the international system plays at least some part in the propensity of states to engage in international violence. Furthermore, Terry Boswell and Mike Sweat (1991) examine competing models of hegemony, for the period from 1496 to 1967, in order to test the theoretical argument that the existence--or relative decline--of a global hegemon will affect the amount of war in the system. Their findings indicate that during the period encompassing the post-Industrial Revolution, the existence of a global hegemon reduced the intensity of major wars; in the pre-industrial period, the findings were inconclusive.

Each of the above-mentioned analyses presents some evidence to bolster the argument that the makeup of the international system, inter alia, determines the amount of violence within the major power system. In fact, an inference that can be drawn from this collection of studies is that more than simply the constitution of the systemic order affects the likelihood of war; also, the clarity of that constitution contributes to the level of violence between states. All of this leaves us short of a direct generalization from systemic clarity to the violent foreign policies that fall short of war, though the evidence presented by Huth, Gelpi, and Bennett takes us a step closer. All is not lost, however.

It is a commonly accepted notion that the outbreak of war is generally preceded by a series of militarized international disputes. It would be the very rare instance in which a war commences without any prior violent or threatening interaction between the disputants--the "bolt from the blue attack." On the other hand, not all disputes or series of disputes culminate in war. In fact, according to Correlates of War data, war is a fairly rare event in international politics. Violence short of war, however, is a much more common occurrence and, on the whole, an apparently legitimate tool in the pursuit of policy objectives.

Based on the theoretical arguments just presented, and the somewhat weak empirical evidence of a relationship between system structure and war, it should be fairly clear that systemic-level variables--in particular, the clarity of the hierarchical order of the members of the system--can contribute to our understanding of the use of violence in pursuit of foreign policy objectives. An unclear systemic order not only might increase the motivation and the opportunity for states to employ violence in their international interactions but it also might offer violence as one of the few alternatives to achieve desired outcomes. In a highly disorganized system, the ability to reach cooperative agreements may be threatened by the lack of expected continuity (Axelrod, 1984), while the ability of any one or more actors to prevent the use of violence is severely diminished. This combination would lead to an increasing number of challenges to the current order, as well as increased attempts to reimpose order on the system. Violence would be the likely result.

System Leadership

While this is not an issue that needs excessive attention, the role of system or bloc leadership should increase the propensity of a state to become embroiled in international disputes; the likelihood that those disputes will turn violent should also increase with a leadership role. Why?

Three points will suffice to make this relationship clear: (1) the system/bloc leader is expected to enforce the rules of interaction that directly affect those under its tutelage; (2) a nonsystem/bloc leader is more likely to let the leader address challenges to the status quo, in essence creating the free-rider problem; and (3) the system leader must carry the banner of ideology--or the unifying construct that holds the bloc together. In the first instance, the benefits that accrue to the leader of the system, or the central actor in a bloc, make it incumbent on the leader to stand firm against challenges to either bloc cohesiveness or system "lordship." Because the leader will generally have a disproportionate share of military and economic capabilities, it is the most likely candidate to defend the existing order as well as to have the most to gain from it. Second, the minor members of any bloc or alliance will tend to contribute less to the maintenance of the existing order than will the senior member (Olson and Zeckhauser, 1966). This should hold true for the use of force, as it apparently does when members interact over economic issues. And finally, the leadership role in large part revolves around the maintenance of an ideological banner or a central defining issue. Members of blocs or alliances coalesce around some general theme, whether it be a trade issue, a religious fervor, or a political orientation. But it becomes the job of the leader of that bloc to maintain the cohesiveness around that organizing concept and to ward off challenges from outside the collective. For Britain, this leadership role entailed keeping the shipping lanes open to the free trade of goods and resources; for the United States, leadership involved not only the defense of the free market system but also the prevention of the spread of an antithetical ideology, communism.

SOME TESTABLE HYPOTHESES

Following the format of the previous chapters, I will present the most salient hypotheses as a form of theoretical summary. A research design will then be outlined by which these hypotheses can be tested against data from the United States and Great Britain.

H1: Increasing militarization of society leads to the increased use of force by the state in pursuit of foreign policy objectives. The mechanisms that drive this relationship are both internal and external, with theoretical reasoning and empirical evidence lending credible support for the hypothesis. The literature on arms races and the theoretical construct of the security dilemma, as well as the work by Paul Kennedy and others on the fate of "over-allocators" to the military, all point to militarization as a major factor in state-led coercion.

H2: The greater the concentration of capabilities in the systemic order, the lower is the propensity of the state to employ violence in pursuit of foreign policy objectives. There are two distinct sides to this argument, though the strongest logic rests with those who suggest that a bipolar or hegemonic system will be more stable than a multipolar one. Although the evidence is not unanimous, there appears to be considerable empirical support for the stability hypothesis (two exceptions are Huth, Gelpi, and Bennett, 1992, and Hopf, 1991).

H3: The leadership role in the international system is positively associated with the propensity of the state to embroil itself in international conflicts. Leadership almost by definition entails being at the forefront of unfolding events or crises. As such, the system or bloc leader will be the target of challenges to the existing order and will be obligated to defend encroachments on the organizing ideology. We should expect, therefore, that a system leader will be more prone to use violence in "defense" of the status quo.

THE RESEARCH DESIGN

Indicators and Their Measurement

The discussion in the previous chapter regarding the operationalization and measurement of my indicator of militarization precludes my having to reiterate that procedure here. However, I have changed the measurement of the outcome variable, DISPUTES. Rather than measuring violent foreign policy by the number of disputes ongoing in years "t-1" and "t," as I did in the earlier chapter, I counted disputes ongoing at times "t" and "t+1." The reason is that the militarization of a society at time "t" cannot lead to the increased use of force at time "t-1," though we would expect that levels of militarization would have some impact on violent foreign policy during the current year, as well as some residual effect in the following year. System leadership was coded dichotomously, with a "1" indicating that the country exercised its role as system leader. For the United States this included the years 1945 through 1985 and for Great Britain, the years 1900 through 1915 (Boswell and Sweat, 1991).[2] The clarity of the international system structure was measured on a ratio scale following the well-accepted pattern set by J. David Singer, Stuart Bremer, and John Stuckey (1972). Their measure of capability concentration is derived from six indicators: demographic (total and urban population), industrial (iron and steel production and energy consumption), and military capabilities (military expenditures and military personnel). It is constructed in a manner such that a system in which one country held all of the possible shares of these six indicators would have a concentration score of one; if the capabilities were distributed evenly across the system, the concentration score would be zero. In actuality, the concentration measure varies from .21 to .63.

Methodology

The hypotheses were tested with a linear regression model using a least squares estimator and correcting for the effects of autocorrelation with a Corchrane-Orcutt procedure. The functional form of the original equation is as follows:

$$Y = \alpha + \beta_1 X_1 + \beta_2 X_2 + \beta_3 X_3 + \varepsilon,$$

where
Y = # of ongoing disputes @ t and t +1 (DISPUTES),
X_1 = level of militarization (MILI),
X_2 = system concentration (SYSCON), and
X_3 = system/bloc leader (SYSLEAD).

BEGINNINGS OF A COMPLETE PUZZLE: THE FINDINGS

The results of the analyses do little to clarify much of the ambiguity evident in earlier research findings. Not only does the strength of the relationships differ between Britain and the United States, but for two of the three variables in my model, the coefficients have opposing signs (see tables 3.1 and 3.2). Using British data, there is fairly strong support for the first hypothesis, that increased societal militarization is associated with more frequent resorts to force. System concentration, on the other hand, is associated with a decrease in the dispute propensity of the state. This finding differs from that of Huth, Gelpi, and Bennett and lends some confirmation to the argument that the more hierarchical the system, the more peaceful are the system members.

Table 3.1
Regression Results (U.S.): Outcome Variable, Disputes

Variables	Coefficient	Standard Error	T-Ratio
MILI	.05	.11	.44
SYSCON	3.41	10.58	.32
SYSLEAD	4.11	2.25	1.83*
Constant	1.60	3.09	.51
Adjusted R2=.48 Standard Error=3.26 Mean (Y)=5.51 D.W.=1.86			

* p<.10

The findings for the United States, however, give quite a different picture of the effect of militarization and systemic constraints on the violent foreign policy of the state. System concentration has no discernible statistical impact on the use of violence in the international environment; nor do levels of militarization in the United States. In essence we have no confidence that there is any relationship between these variables. System leadership, however, has a strong substantive impact on the amount of violence engaged in by the United States, and we have a fairly high degree of confidence in this finding. This lends credence to the argument that it is the system or bloc leader that serves as the lightning rod for attempts to penetrate the cohesiveness of the existing order. One inference that might be drawn from the divergent findings between the United States and Britain is that the free-rider problem is alive and well. The United States finds itself embroiled in more international conflicts as a result of rising to the position of the leader of the Western alliance, whereas there is no impact of system leadership during Great Britain's brief tenure. Any inferences at this point, however, must be quite tentative.

Table 3.2
Regression Results (U.K.): Outcome Variable, Disputes

Variables	Coefficient	Standard Error	T-Ratio
MILI	.21	.04	4.92***
SYSCON	-12.5	6.53	-1.90*
SYSLEAD	-.74	1.83	-.40
Constant	5.42	2.65	2.03
Adjusted R2=.54	Standard Error=2.80	Mean (Y)=4.51	D.W.=1.78

* p<.10
*** p<.01

To complete this analysis, I must contend with or account for not only the divergence in findings between U.S. and British data but also the rather weak support for my theoretical argument. But before moving on to try to explain these discrepancies, I should first engage in a bit of exploratory analysis. For the moment I will stand behind the notion that the underlying theoretical arguments are essentially correct but that the operationalization of these concepts must be reconsidered. For example, *absolute* levels of militarization may contribute to the political and economic momentum behind continued funding of the military and therefore increase domestic pressures to justify existing levels of mobilization; this might show up as an increase in the use of force as a tool of diplomacy or in a more pervasive use of some of the mechanisms that help maintain the perception of a threat. But the increased international tensions generally attributed to the security dilemma may be more a function of *changes* in the level of militarization. The effect of changes in militarization may be more salient than absolute levels for a number of reasons. A substantial alteration in the extent to which a society is militarized may not only be more perceptible to an adversary, but if that change is toward higher levels of militarization, it may appear more threatening. If a neighboring, or adversarial, state reacts in kind, an arms spiral may ensure, leading to an increase in international tensions. Changes in militarization, however, may also be more readily evident to a domestic audience, leading to pressures to justify increased expenditures and ultimately to the more frequent use of force by the elite.

Furthermore, the perceptual component of the security dilemma may be exacerbated by a state's place in the system hierarchy, with changes in militarization producing an external behavior in a "system leader" different from the external behavior in a country not at the top of the hierarchy. The basic theoretical model remains essentially intact, but clearly more attention needs to be paid to just how "increases" in militarization are perceived by and influence the political leadership. In an attempt to partially examine this refinement to the original model, I created a new variable, DELTAMIL, which reflects the changes in the level of militarization across time periods. The findings from this reanalysis are presented in tables 3.3 and 3.4.

The most striking finding of this revised model can be seen in the case of the United States. Not only does the impact of system leadership increase in both substantive and statistical significance, but the role of changes in the level of militarization on the violent foreign policy of the state is quite strong, and in this instance we have a high degree of confidence in the finding. The effect of system concentration, furthermore, changes to the hypothesized direction, though our level of statistical confidence is extremely low. What this demonstrates is that it

Table 3.3
Regression Results, Revised Model (U.S.):
Outcome Variable, Disputes

Variables	Coefficient	Standard Error	T-Ratio
DELTAMIL	.19	.09	2.08**
SYSCON	-7.71	10.79	-.71
SYSLEAD	7.33	2.23	3.27***
Constant	4.79	3.33	1.43
Adjusted R2=.53 Standard Error=3.12 Mean (Y)=5.61 D.W.=1.92			

** p<.05
***p<.01

is the change in the level of militarization in the United States that affects the likelihood that its elite will resort to the use of force in the international environment. Furthermore, for the United States, taking on the leadership role in the Western alliance at the culmination of World War II meant a substantial increase in the number of disputes that are ongoing at any one time. These findings suggest that the cost of being the dominant actor in the alliance is an average of about three more militarized disputes per year than could be accounted for by other variables.

The revisions to the model, however, do little to change the substantive impact of the findings for Great Britain. Any real change can be seen in the effect of system leadership on violent foreign policy. Although the sign of the coefficient is the same as in the previous model, the substantive impact is about five times greater, and we have a bit more statistical confidence in the result. This, however, comes at a cost of substantive and statistical significance of the effect of system concentration on the violent diplomacy of the state. There seems to be little apparent difference between absolute and changing levels of militarization on the propensity for the British elite to use force as a tool of foreign policy. And even though the level of confidence is low, the substantive effect of system concentration is quite large. The data from both the United

States and Britain suggest that as the distribution of capabilities in the global system becomes less concentrated, the amount of international violence increases. This finding not only appears to differ from conclusions of Huth, Gelpi, and Bennett, but also seems to support those who have found that a bipolar world is more peaceful than a multipolar one, at least from the British and American perspective.

Table 3.4
Regression Results, Revised Model (U.K.):
Outcome Variable, Disputes

Variables	Coefficient	Standard Error	T-Ratio
DELTAMIL	.18	.04	4.45***
SYSCON	-8.69	6.38	-1.36
SYSLEAD	-3.81	2.54	-1.50
Constant	8.55	2.90	2.94
Adjusted R2=.51 Standard Error=2.89 Mean (Y)=4.51 D.W.=1.76			

*** p<.01

One remaining concern should persist. Because of the extreme levels of military mobilization, and demobilization, that took place around the world wars--World War II for the United States--there is some question about the sensitivity of these findings to those extreme perturbations. The results of dropping the war years from the analysis demonstrate that for the United States,

Table 3.5
Regression Results, Excluding War Years (1942 and 1945)
(U.S.): Outcome Variable, Disputes

Variables	Coefficient	Standard Error	T-Ratio
DELTAMIL	.28	.11	2.43**
SYSCON	.56	11.20	.05
SYSLEAD	7.01	2.11	3.32***
Constant	2.04	3.50	.58
Adjusted R2=.59 Standard Error=2.97 Mean (Y)=5.45 D.W.=1.92			

*** p<.01
** p<.05

the findings are not dramatically altered; in fact, the fit of the data is appreciably better. Societal militarization is a stronger predictor of dispute behavior, as is system leadership (tables 3.5 and 3.6); the effect of system concentration, however, becomes moot. For Britain, dropping the world-war years eliminates any trace of an empirical relationship between the predictor and outcome variables, and the overall fit of the data to the model is dramatically reduced. Obviously, the world wars played a much more determining role in Great Britain than they did in the United States.

INTERPRETING THE RESULTS

The central objective of this chapter was to empirically examine the extent to which the militarization of society affects the external behavior of these two major powers. The results of my analysis suggest that there is a strong empirical relationship, and the finding is similar for both the United States and

Table 3.6
Regression Results, Excluding War Years
(1915, 1917, 1940-45) (U.K.): Outcome Variable, Disputes

Variables	Coefficient	Standard Error	T-Ratio
DELTAMIL	.02	.05	.52
SYSCON	-3.67	7.93	-.46
SYSLEAD	-2.81	2.04	-1.37
Constant	5.31	3.30	1.64
Adjusted R2=.06 Standard Error=2.52 Mean (Y)=3.30 D.W.=1.81			

Great Britain. Three factors should have emerged as I presented the results: (1) that societal militarization does have a positive impact on the amount of state-led violence; but (2) that the strength of the findings in each individual case was in part a function of how the relationship between militarization and the resort to arms is conceptualized; and (3) that the world wars played a much more central role for Great Britain than the United States.

The role of the world wars appears to almost determine the strength and direction of the findings for Great Britain, while having little impact on the results of U.S. data. An answer to the sensible question of "why" can only be touched on here, and even then it is more speculation than empirical demonstration. An examination of the data on militarization (figures 2.5 and 2.6) suggests that the mobilization patterns in Britain were driven to a much greater extent by the wars than was the pattern in the United States. Britain mobilized more fully, and demobilized in a more continual pattern, for and after the two world wars. The United States, on the other hand, maintained a fairly high level of mobilization throughout the post-World War II period. This period also coincided with the U.S. role as one of two superpowers. It is apparent from the data on militarized disputes that Britain was more prone to use force in the global arena in the early part of the century than in the latter part. This suggests--or at least leads one to suppose--that if we were to go back another century in the analysis of British data, the relationship between militarization and the use of violence would be much more systematic and less tied to the extremes of global war. Britain in the nineteenth century played a role more similar to that of the United States in the latter part of the twentieth century. In short, the evidence suggests that this could be tied quite explicitly to the role of a dominant actor in global politics.

The different interpretation of the effect of militarization on the violent behavior of the state at first poses a more difficult problem. For the United States, it is the magnitude of the *change* in militarization between periods that is strongly associated with the resort to force by the state, whereas in Great Britain both the absolute level and the changes in militarization are equally good predictors. Much of the theoretical argument that I have outlined earlier turned on the issue of mobilizing the support of the general public for elite policies of military mobilization, essentially a domestic politics argument. This would suggest that levels of militarization would be most relevant. And while this may still be essentially correct, it may operate more subtly under certain circumstances.

Although domestic politics may still be operative in the relationship between militarization and the use of force in the global arena, the strength of the effect of changes in militarization suggests looking elsewhere. International tensions associated with increases in the level of militarization would appear to account for much of this relationship. This is consistent with Bruce Russett's (1990) argument. Rapid, or large, fluctuations in the extent of militarization by one of the dominant actors in the international system could be sufficient to cause increases in the use of force in the international environment. As a dominant actor in the system substantially increases its level of military preparedness, it may not only limit the range of options available for conflict resolution but also increase international hostility toward it. Domestic politics might still have a marginal impact on the state's ability to sustain involvement in foreign conflicts, though political concerns will not be the main engine behind its propensity to use force. International or systemic factors play a more central role, at least at first.

The effect of systemic level variables, however, is somewhat inconclusive. The hierarchical makeup of the systemic order is at best a very weak predictor of the amount of conflict engaged in by either of these two major powers. On the other hand, system/bloc leadership is a strong predictor of the dispute behavior of the state, though this finding too needs to be tempered by the short time-frame (1900-1915) during which Britain was coded as a system leader during the twentieth century. While the spatial and temporal dimensions of this analysis limit the general inferences that can be drawn, the findings at the systemic level add support to those who argue that a more concentrated systemic order will tend to be less conflictual.

With the unidirectional components of this analysis complete, I can now move on to a more rigorous test for a feedback between internal militarization and the use of force as a foreign policy tool by the state. This next segment will use a system of equations to demonstrate the effect of a hypothesized self-amplifying feedback. Again, a note of caution is in order. If the correct specification of this model is as a system of equations, then it could call into question the results in this and the previous chapter. The assumptions of econometrics will have been violated, if indeed there is a feedback, resulting in biased and inconsistent estimates on all of the variables examined in the previous two chapters. However, it was necessary to go through this exercise for two reasons: (1) most of the literature--both empirical and theoretical--discusses these relationships as unidirectional phenomenon, at least implicitly; and (2) an inductive approach was necessary to more correctly specify some of the most critical components of the more rigorous system of equations.

4

The Feedback between Societal Militarization and Violent Foreign Policy: Merging the Two Halves

In the previous two chapters I tested a number of hypotheses pertaining to both the increased militarization of U.S. and British societies and their respective propensities to employ violence in the twentieth-century international environment. In each case the models proved to be moderately successful at predicting changes in either of the outcome variables, though overall the findings are at best only suggestive of the hypothesized feedback discussed in the opening chapter. To make a compelling case for the existence of a feedback between the internal organization of society and the external behavior of the state, this must be explicitly modeled and tested.

It was argued in the introductory chapter that the underlying process that produced the data used in this study involved a feedback between the extent of societal militarization and the violent foreign policy of the state. And when the findings of each of the preceding chapters were less conclusive than the theoretical case suggested, I fell back on the crutch that if indeed there was a simultaneity problem, then the results of each individual analysis would not be terribly robust. It is now time to put the two equations in their proper order and to empirically test the proposition outlined earlier.

Such a feedback is quite intuitive in the field of world politics, though it has remained at the level of speculation, devoid of empirical grounding. If indeed there is a self-amplifying process between these attributes and behaviors, then it not only would have direct policy implications but also should leave identifiable traces. When a state finds itself frequently embroiled in international disputes that escalate to the use of force, one response that might be expected is that the elite will take the steps necessary to prevail in such disputes. And as Ted Gurr (1988) points out, frequent success in the use of force will lead to the elevation of the instruments of force to a virtuous role in society. Therefore, a high level of military readiness, coupled with a military that is held in high esteem within the ranks of society, might limit the range of options considered when an international incident arises. But the interaction between these two behaviors is, of course, not so simple.

Following a format somewhat similar to that of the previous two chapters, I will outline the theoretical argument, discuss a research strategy, and present and interpret the findings. This chapter, however, will be an abbreviated version of the earlier ones because much of the groundwork has already been laid. Operational indicators and data sources have been adequately spelled out in chapters 2 and 3, as has much of the basic theoretical argument. The statistical procedure used, in this case a system of equations using a two-staged least squares estimator, will need some explication, though the interpretation of the findings should be straightforward.

ORIENTING THE LANDSCAPE: THE THEORETICAL ARGUMENT

The idea that the militarization of a society and the propensity for the state to use that military preparation as a foreign policy tool are part of a feedback mechanism is not new. J. David Singer, Harold Lasswell, and Ted Gurr have all either explicitly spelled out the foundations of a feedback relationship or implicitly assumed that such an interaction exists. It should not require a great leap of imagination, however, to see that internal militarization and external belligerency feed off one another. There are three basic mechanisms that drive this feedback: (1) the need to rationalize or justify existing levels of military preparedness; (2) the effects of international tensions on attitudes and perceptions; and (3) the military's role or stature in society. The first is predominantly a domestic politics argument; the second functions primarily at the level of international politics; and the third may be a product of the other two.

Internal Politics

There is a plethora of literature chronicling the impact of domestic political and economic concerns on the diversion of resources from the civilian to the military sector of society, much of which falls under the rubric of literature on the Military-Industrial Complex (MIC). Jobs, education, social status, and access to technology are some of the factors that help create momentum behind continued mobilization. An already high level of militarization can put pressure on the political and economic elite to not only prevent the demobilization of society but also justify current or higher levels of mobilization based on an external threat. The "least expensive"--and possibly most efficient in terms of cost-benefit considerations--is to maintain the perception of a threat through the socialization of the general public, or as Lasswell (1941) put it, to inculcate in the public mind the continued expectation of violence. Symbolic politics and the process of emnification--or creating an enemy (Rieber and Kelly, 1991)--would be the primary means to maintain public support. But the political use of symbols will often reach a point of diminishing returns, at which time more drastic measures may become necessary. The use of force to achieve some putative foreign policy objective, then, becomes the fallback option.

In one scenario, the cycle starts with an already high level of militarization. Two ways to reach that point--which may be a sufficient though not necessary condition--are via a period of direct military rule or the mobilization of resources in response to a global war. These two conditions, or course, may go hand in hand. But this is not the only mechanism by which domestic concerns can lead to external belligerency. Bruce Russett (1990) demonstrates that under certain circumstances, domestic unrest or discontent will be externalized by the state; his evidence lends support to Gurr's (1988) theoretical model, which postulates that the externalization of internal dissention will exacerbate tendencies toward militarization. If the state externalizes its domestic problems by using force in the international environment, and is successful in such forays, it will contribute to the development of a political culture that holds the military in high esteem.

So, domestically, the feedback can be understood in terms of either the effect of political and economic momentum that results from already high levels of military mobilization or the externalization of discontent that appears to the domestic audience to be successful. In the first instance, high levels of militarization will require some sort of rationalization mechanism, which will serve to more fully entrench the military into society, which then will require a continued show of force to sustain public momentum. The second mechanism operates from a slightly different perspective. Domestic discontent leads the political leadership to attempt to divert attention by embroiling the country in an international "incident." The success of these efforts will be partially a function of the elite's ability to create an enemy out of the target of their military force, and once successful, the stature of the military as an institution will be elevated. This victorious military will then justify additional resources in order to stand guard over its newly created enemy. At some juncture the inertial forces behind the entrenched institution will come to the fore.

International Politics

There are a number of ways in which international interactions accelerate the feedback between militarization and the use of force by the state. The thesis that a declining-power in the global arena will respond maladaptively has received a fair amount of attention (see Gilpin, 1981; Kennedy, 1987), though the declining power syndrome does not hold the monopoly on the internal-external militarization feedback. The increased international tensions associated with the military buildup of an adversarial or neighboring state can lead to a similar response at home. And as Russett (1990:23) points out, this international hostility can be a result of actions taken in response to domestic political and economic considerations. In each instance, increased militarization can result in an increased propensity to resort to force in the international arena.

There are at least two types of maladaptive behavior by the declining power that can exacerbate the feedback: (1) in an effort to reverse the apparent hemorrhage of relative capabilities, the state can increase its flow of resources to the military sector, thereby creating the appearance of an ability to influence global affairs; or (2) the state can try to increase its resource base through armed acquisition. These two approaches to dealing with a decline in the structural clarity of the international system are obviously linked. Furthermore, the theoretical arguments underlying these responses have been adequately spelled out by Robert Gilpin (1981) and others, and there is some evidence that both types of efforts are a chimera rather than a solution (Kennedy, 1987). In the first instance, spending more on the military in an attempt to create the illusion--if not the actual fact--of maintaining the ability to determine the distribution of goods and services within the global system can have deleterious consequences for international stability by leading to domestic pressures to justify or rationalize current levels of mobilization or by leading neighboring or adversarial states to respond in kind, thereby increasing the level of international hostility. In either case the spiral tightens, and what started as an attempt to redress a perceived international imbalance results in an increase in both militarization and the use of violence as a tool of diplomacy.

Obviously the international mechanisms behind militarization and the use of violence to achieve policy objectives have many points of entry or exit. For example, it need not be the declining state that is the focus of inquiry. Any member of the international system may respond to the maladaptive behavior of one of the leading members of the system with what appears to be defensive precautions. Increasing the level of military preparedness might be one response. But this too could result in international tensions, eventually leading to direct military hostilities and then to the need to maintain or expand the level of precautions taken to ward off the newly discovered threat. In a sense, this is a grossly simplified version of a partial rationale behind U.S. military spending over the past forty five years. Increased military preparedness begets an increased level of international tensions, which then serves to rationalize current levels of spending or to justify increases. A further rise in international tensions results, as well as domestic pressures for rationalization and further increases in allocations.

The Status of the Military in Society

The strength of the feedback is partially determined by history. As Gurr pointed out, successful military excursions will generally add to the political clout accorded the institution of the military within society. Increased political influence and a popular myth detailing the invincibility of the generals will result. If the military is seen as the defender of the values held dear by the public, then the military will tend to be more successful in securing resources during the political debates over the distribution of the budget. A large and successful armed force will spin off a large and vocal pool of veterans, as well as incorporate a fairly sizable portion of the work force in the production of the tools of warfare. The more entrenched the military, the greater are the domestic and international pressures pushing in the direction of an increased use of force to achieve policy objectives. However, as I discussed earlier--and we will see in the following chapter--this public myth surrounding the military, and the values that help structure public support for the need to maintain a "strong defensive posture," can be and are subject to social manipulation (Hesse and Mack, 1991; Whitfield, 1991; Small, 1974).

History can also play another role. Previous wars or military conflicts influence the perception of the strength and tenacity of the adversary and help shape the strategy designed to confront an enemy. Technology plays a crucial part in the process, and secrecy is the mechanism of choice for maintaining the influence of the security elite. The need to stay at the cutting edge of weapons technology--to avoid another Pearl Harbor or to prevent a missile gap--not only absorbs material resources in the name of "national security" but also constrains human and intellectual resources. Security clearances are needed to ferret out foreign spies, to restrict the flow of critical information, and to secure the allegiance of some in the academic and political community; many of those who do not pledge allegiance at least acquiesce. The press, likewise, is constrained by secrecy, both formal and informal. One effect of maintaining a veil of secrecy in the name of "national security" is to severely diminish the influence of countervailing forces in society. This is justified, in part, on the historical patterns evident in the behavior of the "enemy." When it comes to rationalizing the level of military mobilization, the security elite has access to not only a marginally critical press--at the worst--but also the ability to use official "history" in a manner consistent with their policy objectives. There will be little standing in the way of the security elite's resort to force as a tool to convince the public of the need for a strong military. We should keep in mind, however, that history itself can play a countervailing role in the inertial forces behind the militarization of society, as was apparently evident with the U.S. involvement in Vietnam. But this too is not so clear cut. A decade after the "Vietnam syndrome" set in, an equally aggressive anti-Vietnam syndrome was used to justify a sharp increase in the level of military mobilization, with the war against Iraq, as well as the invasions of Panama and Grenada, helping to--inter alia--remove the stigma of Vietnam from the American psyche.

The three mechanisms that help drive the feedback among the militarization of society and the use of force by the state do not operate in isolation from the society in general. Each of the above-mentioned mechanisms is in part determined by, but also helps to determine, the relationship between societal beliefs and attitudes regarding "national security" and the role of the military in both society and the international system. The process of emnification will serve as an example. If the militarization of a society requires the perception of an enemy (Rosenberg, 1973; Rieber, 1991; Ferguson, 1989), then symbols that convey this sense of threat will permeate the social fabric. From children's cartoons (Hesse and Mack, 1991) to children's toys (chap. 5), an image of the enemy will be prominently displayed. Rewards and punishments will be meted out for either compliance with or dissension from the social norm that acknowledges a specific enemy (Lasswell, 1941, 1962; Goldschmidt, 1989). And institutions of socialization, such as religious organizations, schools, and the media, will help to acculturate the public to the ways of the security elite. The existence of an enemy will then be used to constrain dialogue and restrict access to evidence that might counter this perception of the enemy. Emnification, then, is both a result of the process of militarization and a contributing factor in its continuance.

A unique aspect of the militarization process is that when a society becomes highly militarized, it may no longer require a specific set of domestic institutions that manipulates perceptions in order to sustain public support for the policies of the security elite--a Military-Industrial Complex, though the process still requires an identifiable enemy. The larger society may itself become the engine driving the continued militarization of its political, social, and economic fabric. In effect, Richard Slotkin's "frontier myth" (1986) is replaced with the myth of "defense of freedom and the motherland." But in the process, the "freedoms" that were to be defended become victims of the creation of the enemy. There is no longer an open and free dialogue in the mass media (Herman and Chomsky, 1988; Lee and Solomon, 1990; Whitfield, 1991; Ginsberg, 1986). Academic discourse is constrained by the pledge of secrecy and the need to secure funding, and perceptions of the international environment become subject to what anthropologists call politico-centrism--"an internalized belief in the superiority of one's own political system and an automatic suspicion of our adversary's" (Sampson and Kideckel, 1989:163). A Military-Industrial Complex is possibly a necessary condition to reach the higher stages of militarization, but once there, it is clearly not sufficient to sustain the process.

A TESTABLE HYPOTHESIS

In light of the preceding discussion, only one hypothesis will be explicitly tested in this analysis. But because the models that were tested in the previous two chapters did not conform to the specification that I have argued theoretically--that there is a feedback between the extent of militarization and the number of ongoing disputes--the earlier findings should be somewhat suspect. In effect, I am retesting all of the hypotheses spelled out above, but for reasons of brevity I will only explicitly state the new hypothesis to be tested.

H1: There is a positive feedback between the militarization of society and the use of force by the state to achieve foreign policy objectives. Coefficients for both the variables MILI and DISPUTES should have a positive sign, suggesting that the more the state finds itself embroiled in international disputes, the greater the involvement of the civil society in the preparations for war. Conversely, the greater the involvement in the preparations for war, the more prone will be the state to use force to achieve desired outcomes.

THE RESEARCH DESIGN

Methodology

The statistical model involved a system of simultaneous equations, which was tested with a two-stage least squares estimator (TSLS). The reason a system of equations is most appropriate--rather than the two unidirectional linear models employed in the earlier chapters--is that if the data were generated as a result of a feedback relationship between militarization and the use of violence by the state, then the assumptions that underlie an ordinary least squares estimator (OLS) are violated. One of those assumptions is that there is no systematic covariation between the error term--or the stochastic component of the model--and the other predictor variables. But if there is a feedback between militarization and the use of force, then this assumption no longer holds. Inconsistent estimates of the coefficients on all the variables in a unidirectional model would result; any interpretation of the findings, therefore, would be somewhat problematic. To control for this covariation, a system of simultaneous equations is employed.

Since using systems of equations often implies a test of causal processes, a word about this type of "causality" is in order. Although the term *causal modeling* is often applied to simultaneous equation models, it can be somewhat misleading. As with most data analysis in the social sciences, causality is not generally tested with the procedures widely available, at least in the sense of meeting necessary and sufficient criteria. A system of simultaneous equations, however, does allow for much stronger inferences about causal relationships than do unidirectional econometric models. Procedurally the system of equations controls for the simultaneous effect of one endogenous variable on the other while controlling for all other exogenous variables. In this instance, the results will identify, say, the effect of societal militarization on the violent foreign policy of the state while controlling for the simultaneous effect of violent foreign policy on militarization. We can therefore isolate the independent effect of each endogenous variable on the other. This is not exactly "causality", but it is a bit further along than mere "associations."

Systems of equations, furthermore, are subject to the constraint that they meet necessary and sufficient conditions for identification. These conditions ensure that the equations to be estimated are not linear combinations of each other and that each equation has enough information independent of the other equations so that unique parameter estimates can be derived. These two criteria are known as the "rank" and the "order" conditions. A system of equations consists of a series of endogenous and exogenous variables, each of which is either included or excluded from the equation being estimated.[1] Meeting the "order" condition for identification requires that the total number of excluded variables in each equation be at least equal to the total number of equations minus one. This is simply a counting procedure. Testing for "rank" conditions of identification is more difficult. Many economists, however, argue that determining the rank condition of identification is unnecessarily demanding and that, in general, meeting order conditions is adequate for estimation purposes (see Kelejian and Oates, 1989). The order condition is met with the model as it is specified below, though understanding how this condition is fulfilled might be more intuitive by examining the structural equations. The system of equations is as follows: (see figure 4.1)

Equation #1 $Y_1 = \alpha + \beta_1 Y_2 + \beta_2 X_1 + \beta_3 X_2 + \beta_4 X_3 + \beta_5 X_4 + \varepsilon$, and

Equation #2 $Y_2 = \alpha + \beta_6 Y_1 + \beta_7 X_5 + \beta_8 X_6 + \varepsilon$

Where:
$Y_1 = \Delta$ militarization (DELMILI),
$Y_2 = \#$ ongoing disputes at time t (DISPUTES),
$X_1 = $ lagged militarization (MILI, t-1),
$X_2 = $ logged industrialization (TECHDEV),
$X_3 = $ maintenance of perception of threat (MANIP),
$X_4 = $ existential threat (EXIST),
$X_5 = $ system/bloc leadership (SYSLEAD), and
$X_6 = $ system concentration (SYSCON).

It can be seen from these structural equations that equation 2 has four excluded variables, and equation 1 has two variables excluded. The order condition has been met, and in fact the system is overidentified on this criterion.

Two last points about a two-stage least squares estimation procedure should be raised. First, the coefficient of determination--R2--that is commonly used as an indication of the amount of variation in the dependent variable that is accounted for by the independent variables in the model is quite suspect when using TSLS. Because the properties of the R2 statistics are not very well defined in this type of procedure, the standard error of the estimate will give a more reliable indication of the fit of the data to the model. And second, although a

Figure 4.1
Simultaneous Equation Model of the Feedback
between Militarization and Violent Foreign Policy

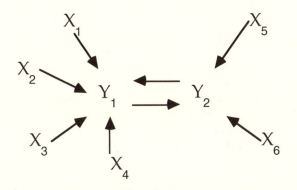

TSLS procedure does not provide unbiased estimates, the estimates are asymptotically consistent and even in small samples consistent relative to an OLS procedure. This increased consistency affords us a much greater degree of confidence in the statistical results and therefore a much clearer understanding of the underlying processes that are being modeled.

Variables and Indicators

In the previous chapters I have sufficiently outlined the variables in the model, as well as their respective indicators. With one exception, there is no need to duplicate this earlier work; that exception is my indicator of the extent to which the state resorts to the use of force. In chapter 2, I used the number of ongoing disputes at times "t" and "t-1", whereas in chapter 3, the indicator reflected the number of ongoing disputes at times "t" and "t+1". The reasoning, of course, concerned the specific model being proposed and was in effect a way to build in the appropriate hypothesized lags and leads. When modeling a feedback, however, we need to be very sensitive to the appropriateness of lags or leads, particularly if they are endogenous to the system. In this model the use of force by the state is an endogenous variable, and therefore a lag or a lead will confound the analysis. For example, if societal militarization and the use of force are in a simultaneous feedback relationship, then militarization at time "t" cannot be a cause of an increase in disputes at time "t-1", as would be the implicit assumption if I used the indicator employed in the second chapter. A similar problem would hold if I included disputes at time "t+1" in the analysis of the feedback model. For these reasons, my indicator of the use of force by the state to achieve foreign policy objectives is the number of ongoing disputes at time "t".

As an alternative, the system of equations could be expanded to include another endogenous variable for the appropriate lag or lead, for instance, by incorporating another endogenous variable that taps into the change in militarization at time "t+1". This would, in effect, allow me to test the marginal impact of disputes under way at time "t" on militarization at time "t+1", while at the same time examining the impact of militarization at time "t" on disputes at time "t". This procedure was carried out. The expanded model, however, did not affect the direction of the coefficients associated with DISPUTES and DELMIL, nor did it much alter the degree of statistical confidence. Furthermore, the larger model had only a marginal impact on the results of the entire system of equations. Rather than muddy the waters on an already overly complex procedure, I did not include the more complicated model in this discussion.

THE COMPLETED PUZZLE: THE FINDINGS

As in the earlier chapters, the results from the system of equations are less consistent than one might hope for, yet overall they tend to support much of the theoretical argument heretofore discussed. There are two ways to interpret the findings: (1) in relation to the earlier OLS results; and (2) on their own merits. I will start with the latter and then conclude by briefly comparing the results of the two different estimating techniques.

Keeping in mind the results from chapter 3, *changes* in militarization rather than *levels* of militarization was used as one of the endogenous--or outcome--variables in this analysis. You will recall that changes in militarization was a much stronger predictor of the dispute involvement of the state than was the absolute level. In the system of equations, change in the extent of societal militarization remains a strong predictor of violent foreign policy, though the feedback is not so clear-cut. For the United States, in fact, I find a rather peculiar feedback. While militarization appears to have a positive effect on the number of ongoing disputes--positive in the sense of leading to an increase in the use of violence--the state's use of violence in the international arena has a negative effect on militarization (see figure 4.2). So the hypothesized feedback does not show up as a self-amplifying mechanism but rather as two forces working against each other. All of the other variables in the model--for the United States--predict in directions consistent with the theoretical arguments, with the exception of the level of militarization in the previous period. Furthermore, all are statistically significant at or near the conventional levels of confidence. The one exception, lagged militarization (MILI, t-1) not only runs counter to the theoretical argument but also is statistically robust, an interesting finding that we will come back to later.

The data for Great Britain present a reasonably similar picture of the underlying militarization process, though there are differences that need to be pointed out.[2] The first is that the hypothesized feedback between societal militarization and the violent foreign policy of the state appears to be confirmed, at least tentatively (figure 4.3). The coefficients associated with both variables are positive, though the effect of violent foreign policy on militarization is statistically weak. Systemic-level variables have a negative relationship with the state's propensity toward violence, though neither is statistically robust. And as with the U.S. data, the level of militarization in the previous period is negatively associated with changes in militarization during the current year. Both the extent to which the media maintains the perception of a threat and the existence of an existential threat are positively associated with changes in militarization, though only the effect of the media reporting on military issues is statistically significant at conventional levels.

The findings at the systemic level are of particular interest at this juncture. The results of the analysis appear to lend support to advocates and evidence identifying a hegemonic actor as a critical component in patterns of global violence (see Boswell and Sweat, 1992). The effect of system leadership, for instance, differs wildly between the United States and Great Britain, suggesting that the decline of one hegemonic leader and the rise of the successor may be evident. Likewise, system concentration findings are consistent with arguments about the role of hegemonic actors in international politics. In the former instance, system leadership is strongly and positively associated with violent foreign policy by the United States, though negatively associated with violent foreign policy in Great Britain. Furthermore, this evidence suggests that the more concentrated the distribution of capabilities within the international system, the lower the propensity for either of these two major powers to resort to the use of force.

When judged by the criterion of whether we gain information by using a more sophisticated statistical model, the answer must be clearly, yes. Not only do we see that the bureaucratic politics is not as strong as we are often led to believe, but the coefficients on many of the variables change quite substantially from those derived with the unidirectional models. But for the most part, the changes are in magnitude, not direction, suggesting that the feedback might not be as central to the militarization process as the earlier reasoning had posited. However, we can only rest on this conclusion with caution.

INFERENCES ABOUT THE "REAL" WORLD

What do the results of this new model tell us about the militarization of society and the hypothesized feedback involving violent foreign policy? The interpretation of these findings is similar to any other regression analysis,

Figure 4.2
Results of Two-Stage Least Squares Estimation (U.S.)

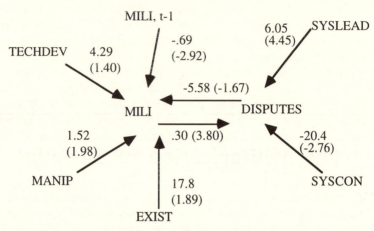

Standard Error of Estimate (Equation 1: Y1)= 3.05; Mean=.72
Standard Error of Estimate (Equation 2: Y2)= 1.52; Mean=2.82

though the coefficients associated with the outcome variables--the two endogenous variables in the system--should be interpreted as, for instance, the marginal impact of violent foreign policy on societal militarization when controlled for the simultaneous effect of militarization on violent diplomacy. I have attempted to ease the task of deciphering these results by superimposing the coefficients and their t-ratios over the graphical depiction of the model (figures 4.2 and 4.3). For example, if we focus on the United States, an additional article per week on the front page of the *New York Times*--on average--is associated with a 1.5-percent increase in the level of militarization. Furthermore, an increase of about .7-percent of the labor force involved in military preparations during the previous time period is associated with a 1-percent decrease in the extent of militarization during the current period. An average increase of one ongoing dispute, moreover, leads to a 5.5-percent reduction in militarization, a rather awkward finding, though consistent with the notion that democratic politics can work to restrain the free hand of the state elite.[3] The awkwardness of the conclusion is predicated in large part on the simultaneity of the effect, though this may be less problematic than it first seems. But what is uncovered here--and in any such econometric analysis--is not a direct "cause and effect" relationship but rather the existence of a strong statistical pattern over time. As mentioned at the outset, in a literal sense, causal modeling this is not.At this juncture it remains the role of theoretical reasoning to untangle the empirical findings, and on this criteria the finding of a simultaneous "cause and effect" is on much firmer ground.

Figure 4.3
Results of Two-Stage Least Squares Estimation (U.K.)

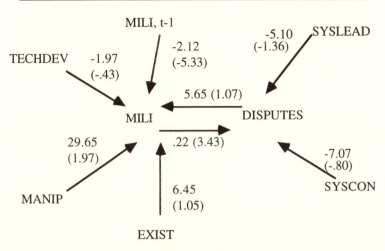

Standard Error of Estimate (Equation 1: Y1)=6.35; Mean=-.06
Standard Error of Estimate (Equation 2: Y2)=1.35; Mean=.55

System-level variables appear to have a rather strong impact on the use of violence by the state. Carrying the mantle of system or bloc leadership comes at a cost of better than six additional disputes per year, while an increase in system concentration--measured by the distribution of capabilities across the system--results in a decrease in international disputes, lending tentative support to those who argue that the smaller the number of poles, the less violent the international system (e.g., Waltz, 1979).

A particularly interesting finding is the negative relationship between previous levels of militarization and current trends; this finding also holds in the case of Great Britain. This result, it seems, runs counter not only to conventional wisdom but also to many of the theoretical arguments and much of the empirical evidence that can be found in the literature (Allison, 1983; Kurth, 1973; Nincic, 1982; Mintz and Ward, 1989). One possible inference is that the overall trend is toward the demilitarization of U.S. and British societies, though obviously that trend is neither constant nor monotonic. One might expect current levels of militarization to be highly and positively correlated with its lagged value, particularly in a bivariate test. But in a regression of previous *levels* on currents *trends*, a strong negative finding is reasonable, even if surprising. Absent a strong perception of a "clear and present danger," a democratic political process would most likely result in an inability to sustain high levels of militarization without subsequent retrenchments in this form of resource allocation (see Russett and Hartley, 1992). Furthermore, this finding is entirely plausible given the added benefits of a more fully specified model.

On the whole the findings are fairly consistent between results obtained with British and U.S. data, though the statistical confidence in the relationships tend to be weaker in Great Britain than those for the United States. Two questions regarding these results need to be addressed. First, what factors might account for the divergence in findings between the United States and Great Britain? And second, what inferences can be drawn from the disconfirmation of the feedback in the United States?

To take the latter question first, the intuitive conclusion would be that rather than violent foreign policy and the militarization of society feeding off one another, militarization leads to the increased use of force by the state, but the use of force has costs that are borne by the military establishment. It is a fatigue factor, to put it into simple terms. Public attitudes toward the military may permit--or lead--the elite to use force in pursuit of policy objectives, but once the "campaign" is over, a period of retrenchment ensues. This is reasonably consistent with a democratic politics argument in which the public will condone the use of force but will tire of the effort when the costs become excessive relative to any potential benefits. Presuming that the military excursions by the state are "successful"--and for the United States this is generally true--then this lack of a self-amplifying feedback directly challenges Gurr's theoretical model (1988). Even when I controlled for the effect of violent foreign policy in the previous period on current militarization, this counteractive effect of disputes was evident. But this cannot be the final word.

The theoretical argument outlined earlier posits that one response by the state in a highly militarized society would be to more frequently resort to the use of force abroad. However, the range of options available with which to employ force in the international environment is quite broad, including direct covert intervention to destabilize a foreign government, overt military intervention on behalf of a sitting government, or the use of military assistance to aid an antigovernment insurgency, though none of these would be captured by the indicator of choice in this analysis. Furthermore, each of these behaviors would be thoroughly consistent with the theoretical argument. In fact, in a highly militarized society these types of international interventions might be the action of choice by a security elite seeking to maintain a viable military institution. In each case the use of military force would be relatively painless, when viewed from the perspective of the domestic political constituencies, yet could be manipulated in a manner that highlights the threatening nature of the targeted adversary. To put this into Lasswell's terminology, the expectation of violence could be maintained, while the amount of bloodletting would be minimized. We would probably also expect to see during this period a heightened use of symbolic politics to facilitate the mobilization of public attitudes. If the theoretical reasoning is sound--and in this instance it seems to be--then before resting on the disconfirmation it might be best to make the model and the testing procedures compatible and then subject it to reanalysis. In this case, the indicator of the use of violence by the state needs to be broadened in an effort to capture this more diverse range of options.

Because there is some support for the hypothesized feedback in Great Britain we must address the question of why there is a difference. The most reasonable place to look is to the rather obvious impact of differing roles in the international system during the twentieth century. System leadership could, of course, have an effect on the way that militarization and violent foreign policy mutually influence one another, and to some extent this is borne out by the evidence linking system leadership to the number of ongoing disputes. The feedback may be self-amplifying in Great Britain because, as a non system-leader for most of the period under study, Great Britain used force in the international arena in a more traditional military role. Unlike a dominant member of the international system, a non system-leader has neither the interest nor the ability to intervene clandestinely, except under more limited circumstances. Furthermore, maintaining the ideological "purity," or cohesiveness, of the system or bloc *is* the role of the system leader. We would expect, therefore, that Great Britain would be a free-rider when it comes to "weeding out the Communists" or "stabilizing" friendly governments and "destabilizing" unfriendly ones. There would be little need for a second-tier country to engage in the type of international bloodletting that would help inculcate the perception of a threatening global environment in the minds of the general public. The system or bloc leader can adequately fulfill this need. Symbolic politics will generally suffice to keep the perception of a threat alive.

One further point should be clarified. The results from chapter 3 suggest that we look to the effect of the world wars when interpreting the findings in this chapter. As you will recall, most of the variation in British violent foreign policy could be accounted for by the impact of the two world wars. For the United States, however, World War II had the opposite effect on the strength of the predictions. It is also apparent from examining the data on militarization that the patterns are quite different in these two countries. In the twentieth century, Britain mobilized a substantial proportion of its labor force for World War I and World War II, yet with the termination of those wars, demobilization was rather steady, though far from complete. The United States, on the other hand, mobilized quite extensively for World War II, and has remained at a fairly high level of mobilization ever since.

Dropping the war years from the analysis does little to clarify the substantive impact of the finding regarding the feedback between societal militarization and the use of violence by the state. As in the earlier chapter, the exclusion of the war years strengthens the results of the analysis for the United States but has the opposite effect when using British data. Yet even if excluding years when the countries were involved in large-scale mobilization for global war produced significant changes in the substantive conclusions, there is no overarching theoretical reason to omit particular years based on the level of militarization. In fact, it is in part the mobilization for wars that I am trying to model. Throwing out specific war years because the conflict achieves some arbitrary threshold does not seem to advance our understanding of the militarization process. If the theoretical model is correct, a successful big war should simply be more effective at helping to create a political culture or myth extolling the virtues of the military than would a less drastic use of force.

SOME FINAL COMMENTS

Having empirically examined the hypothesized feedback between the militarization of society and the use of force by the state, and finding only tentative support for the self-amplifying thesis, I now offer three concluding remarks: (1) overall, the findings were generally supportive of the theoretical argument; (2) there is modest support for the feedback hypothesis, though further research is necessary to more fully examine this process; and (3) the role of system or bloc leadership may have a large impact not only on the propensity of the state to engage in violent diplomacy but also on the type of force used in pursuit of policy and its relationship to the militarization of society.

At a time when the prospects for substantial demilitarization are at their highest point in decades, we seem to know surprisingly little about the process by which societies militarize--and therefore about the mechanisms that might facilitate the demilitarization process. The more fully specified model proposed in this chapter demonstrates at a minimum that the militarization of societies follows a fairly similar process across countries--at least across those with common historical and cultural traditions. But it furthermore identifies some potential behaviors or attributes that propel or retard the intrusion of the military into society. The content of press reporting, for instance, is a strong predictor of changes in militarization, and therefore emphasis might be placed on the countervailing role of the mass media. The evidence also suggests that the trend is toward the demilitarization of society and that we should be leery of conscious efforts to invert that trend.

Doubt is cast on the empirical validity of a self-amplifying feedback process between societal militarization and the use of violence by the state, at least when judged by the evidence presented here. Although the theoretical arguments are convincing, the data are less than conclusive. It is in the playing out of this feedback that the greatest difference can be found between Great Britain and the United States. Even though the data do not lend strong support to the theoretical argument, they do suggest broadening the scope of the operational indicator used to measure state-led international violence before abandoning the theoretical approach altogether.

When coupling the divergent findings on the role of violent foreign policy in the militarization of society, we gain some insight into how different players in the international arena use the force at their disposal. The self-amplifying nature of the feedback in Great Britain suggests that when this country gets embroiled in a foreign conflict, it gears up for the fight. Possibly the use of force by a member of the system who is not occupying a leadership role is more traditional in nature. The security elite sends an army, a battalion, or a division to confront some international adversary. This type of behavior requires only a limited degree of mobilization. But the leader of some collective group of states has a more encompassing role to fulfill. In attempting to maintain the status quo or to propagate the dominant ideology, the system leader has a much more diverse repertoire for the use of force. When the use of force consists of employing a few dozen "advisors," training mercenary armies, or sabotaging a society's infrastructure, the short-term mobilization that is required is minimal. The size of the standing and reserve armies, moreover, is sufficient to handle all but the most violent conflicts.

With all of this in mind, we need to take one more turn to complete the story. I have argued that a highly militarized society can remain so only with the active support of the public, and as Lasswell and others have posited, the perception of a threat must be pervasive lest the security elite be faced with either of two choices: to substantially demobilize their resources; or to make use of their military might. The least expensive way of influencing public attitudes-- relative to the use of military force--is through the use of symbolic politics and the mass media.

5

Societal Symbols and Societal Militarization*

When Harold Lasswell warned of the evolution of a garrison state, much of his argument was driven by the ability of the security elite to mobilize support through mechanisms of social manipulation. The political use of symbols and the socialization of the general public to the ways of the elite, he argued, would contribute to the quiet acquiescence in the transfer of power from those who emphasized commerce to those who develop and deploy the means of violence. In this chapter I will examine some of the mechanisms that might help facilitate this public passivity. Specifically, I will explore the role of war toys, war movies, and promilitary themes in the mass media as agents in the socialization of the public to policies that emphasize military mobilization in the United States and Great Britain, from 1900 to 1985. If symbols of patriotism and the "manipulation" of perceptions and attitudes are central to a security elite's ability to penetrate civil society, then traces of this not only should be evident across time but also should give us some insight into the process by which societies militarize.

Lasswell, however, was not the only scholar to warn of the elite manipulation of the perception of an external threat in order to maintain continued support for the military. Although President Dwight Eisenhower popularized the term, C. Wright Mills (1956) and others (see Rosen, 1973; Koistinen, 1980) identified the culprit in the continual expansion and institutionalization of the military as the Military-Industrial Complex. A triumvirate of the heads of the largest corporations, the political leadership, and the military bureaucracy, it was argued, would manipulate public attitudes toward the military "in order to forestall opposition and preserve their privileged positions" (Slater and Nardin, 1973:28). Institutional spheres such as education,

---

*This chapter is based on an article that originally appeared in the *Journal of Peace Research* and is reprinted here by permission of the Editors.

religion, and the media, along with their respective agents of social control--educators, religious leaders, as well as publishing, television, and entertainment personalities--function to create and popularize symbols that convey a heightened sense of patriotism, nationalism, and the efficacy of the military. In a highly militarized society, the self-interested motivations that allegedly drove the Military-Industrial Complex contribute to a collective motivation on the part of the general public. Jobs, education, retirement, and health benefits all tied to the continual funding of the military as an institution will ensure societal support, even though factions within the power elite may become more reluctant advocates. In a highly militarized society, the symbols that help maintain this patriotic fervor should be evident in any number of media targeted at the general public. Two of the more visible will be mass print media and entertainment outlets.

While the Military-Industrial Complex literature has attempted to verify the existence of a self-interested "entity" that would manipulate the perception of a threat (see Rosen, 1973), very little work has empirically examined the relationship between the development of the symbols to be manipulated and their subsequent manipulation in an effort to ensure continued support for military mobilization. To put the argument that follows into perspective, a contemporary historical anecdote may be useful.

As recently as the late 1980s, Iraq was on the receiving end of grants, loans, and even the machine tooling required for weapons production from both the United States and Britain. Presumably the Iraqis could have been considered an ally--or at least a country with some mutual interests. Even prior knowledge of Saddam Hussein's intentions to annex part of Kuwait was apparently received with cautious acquiescence by both the British and the American governments. But after Iraq's invasion of Kuwait, and after a decision was made to attempt to turn back this fait accompli, public opinion needed to be mobilized before the respective countries would bear the potential human and financial costs. This process was particularly transparent in the United States.

In the process of shaping the attitudes of a largely uninformed electorate into one that virtually demanded the use of force to expel the "Iraqi dictator," a number of dubious assertions and comparisons were invoked; symbolic politics played a critical part. The media to a very great extent faithfully reported just what they were told. Examples abound: a witness testified before Congress that Iraqi troops were taking babies from incubators, shipping the incubators to Iraq, and leaving the babies to die; the perception that Iraq was poised to invade Saudi Arabia--the oil threat--was generated; Saddam and Hitler were equated; posters of the American flag reading "these colors don't run" popped up all over the country; local towns held fund-raisers to support the troops; and yellow ribbons adorned many a tree. Oddly enough, toy manufacturers stocked the shelves of retail outlets with "Desert Storm" war toys, which sold out with amazing speed.

Trying to ascertain whether this is all a conscious effort by a Military-Industrial Complex misses the point. Parts of it fit that mold; others do not. For instance, the testimony about incubators and babies turned out to be false, presented by a dubious witness and with the clear knowledge of the U.S. government. On the other hand, it is unlikely that toy manufacturers are very closely tied to the Military-Industrial Complex but rather opted to capitalize on a good market. In any event the results are the same, at least in terms of mobilizing support for the military effort. The perception of a threat is created and maintained in the public eye, and the symbols that help solidify that support become ubiquitous and self-generating. The key to this inquiry is to determine whether there is a systematic pattern in the relationships among symbols of patriotism, the maintenance of the perception of a threat, and the militarization of societies.

SYMBOLIC POLITICS AND SOCIETAL MILITARIZATION: THE THEORETICAL CONNECTIONS

One of the key components of the argument that I have outlined is that the general public not only will become socialized to accept the encroachment of the military within society but also will become active supporters of this increasing influence. There are several distinct points of entry into a discussion of how the public becomes socialized to accept and participate in the organization of society for war. I will dwell on two in particular: (1) the ability of the media to shape attitudes toward the military; and (2) entertainment outlets that emphasize issues of patriotism, glorify the military, and shape cognitive patterns regarding the role of force in foreign policy.

When I speak of the manipulation of symbols and perceptions, one might intuit that there is some identifiable group or individual who is "out there" doing the manipulating. And while there may be some element of this conscious attempt to manipulate the public that undergirds the militarization process, this is not the most serious component of the symbolic politics argument. Rather than a tangible person or group doing the "dastardly deed," it is society itself that creates, advocates, and perpetuates the myths that are a necessary component in the militarization of society. Since the creation of such myths quite explicitly serves the interests of the security elite, they will actively encourage the myth-making process, but by themselves this task may be unmanageable. The development of myths about a country's role in the global village, or even an individual's role in his/her country, helps to shape perceptions of an enemy. As Richard Slotkin points out, the metaphors that develop from and come to characterize these common myths "not only define a situation for us, they prescribe our response to that situation. At the very least, they tell us how we ought to value the situation--whether we are to identify with it or against it" (1986:19) .

The idea of collectively identifying with or against any particular group is a critical aspect of the process of emnification. To create an enemy that lives in the minds of a large percentage of a population requires a sustained effort that draws on the historical myths prevalent in society, makes use of the metaphors that grow out of those myths, and presents an animate object that can be the target of public disdain or the source of public fear. The symbolic politics argument takes root here. The strategic use of symbols in society can facilitate and perpetuate each aspect of this enemy-building process. To more fully understand the role of symbols, particularly their role in societal militarization, we need to examine how symbols are created, perpetuated, and manipulated.

THE DEVELOPMENT OF SYMBOLS

The first step in this symbolic politics argument is linking the individual to the nation, or more specifically, understanding how and what type of symbols facilitate this task. In their study on the development of political values in children, Robert Hess and Judith Torney found that the identification of symbols of the nation are developed very early in life, engender positive images, and are persistently held. It is the schools, they argued, that are at the vanguard of this socialization process. The authors also demonstrated that images of "good" and "bad" political objects were developed at a very young age, even though complex conceptual information was beyond comprehension. Furthermore, the children in their study "appeared to have opinions about Communism as a threat to our country" while the term *democracy* was associated "with our nation and valued highly" (1967:25). This basic attachment to the nation did not appear to diminish with age or intelligence. "It should be noted that for the items 'America is the best country in the world' and 'The American flag is the best flag in the world', the responses of all groups at all age levels were highly positive and the variance was very small" (129).

To link issues of symbolic politics to the militarization of societies, we need to demonstrate that the general public is socialized to issues of nationalism and patriotism and that symbols that convey this feeling of national allegiance are not only ubiquitous but manipulable. It is also important to understand that these symbols are highly valued and persistent through time, because it is these symbols of nationalism that will be trumpeted in an effort to mobilize the general public. In the conclusion to their study, Hess and Torney argued that "children's attachment to the country is strong, positive, and unchanging over time, and that this attachment is essentially an emotional tie . . . that is particularly important in time of national emergency" (213).

According to Charles Elder and Roger Cobb "Symbols serve as a rallying point for the mobilization of support for demands and provide a catalyst for the organization of a political movement. The solidarity of a mobilized group will depend heavily upon the extent to which unifying symbols capture the fears, anxieties, and frustrations of its adherents" (1983: 17). Symbols are one of the building blocks required in the development of political legitimacy, and as such they serve to structure popular involvement in politics and undergird authority by legitimizing the distribution of power (18). Decision makers, according to

Elder and Cobb, actively manipulate political symbols and tend to rationalize actions through them (28). Those symbols engendering the broadest and most enduring attachments are referred to as symbols of "political community" (36). The flag, America, the Constitution, and freedom are symbolic images of political community and agreement in the United States, and "evidence suggests that they are indeed the objects of widespread and intense affective sentiment" (39).

Other institutions of socialization, such as the media, peer groups, church affiliations, and the family, play a role in the development of political attitudes toward the nation (see Tolley, 1977; Silbiger, 1977; Beck, 1977). Which of these is of greatest import in the socialization to issues of nationalism is an empirical question that has yet to be answered definitively. But there is evidence to support the notion that education, particularly the early development of affect toward the nation, is a critical component in the formulation of symbols of political community. For example, in a study of sixth-graders, Howard Tolley found "One third [of respondents] believe that war is good if the U.S. beats the communists. Far more, however, regarded defense of the nation's freedom as the primary objective" (1973:399).

MAINTENANCE AND MANIPULATION OF SYMBOLS

Having outlined some of the evidence which demonstrates that symbols of nationalism are developed early and are resistant to change, we need to see how these symbols are reinforced through time and manipulated when popular support for military mobilization begins to wane. Who is actually behind the manipulation is unclear; early literature on the Military-Industrial Complex would argue that a core elite should draw the focus of scholarly inquiry. But in a highly militarized society, the manipulation may be more that the general public hears what it wants to hear, though what it hears is of course tempered by an elite view of the world.

John Kenneth Galbraith suggests that this support for a strong national defense is fairly easily maintained because the power wielded by the military as an organization ensures that most citizens will willingly submit to military ideology. In fact, he argues, "Support for a strong national defense is an expression of normal patriotism; no truly good citizen dissents" (1983:160). He illustrates the need to maintain at least the perception of an external threat, lest the military be seen to serve only a ceremonial function, by arguing that dissent or opposition is subject to "the suspicion or assertion that those involved are aiding, abetting, or motivated by the enemy. At minimum they are unpatriotic; at most their dissidence verges on treason, invoking the traditional threat of punishment. Deeply conditioned attitudes affirm the value of patriotism, and these become of absolute importance when there is external danger" (165).

One mechanism for maintaining this perception of threat is through the control of information, for which the military in particular, and the security elite in general, has unparalleled capabilities. Access to the media, and influence on the advertisement and entertainment establishments, are primary means of control, and through this control, the symbols of patriotism are easily maintained and manipulated (see Cohen, 1989, chap. 5). Melvin Small demonstrates the ability of the media to manipulate mass perceptions of a "national threat" by examining the changing public opinion regarding the Soviet Union during World War II and its immediate aftermath, concluding, "The media . . . probably play an unwitting supportive role for official policy makers as they help to prepare a country for rapprochement or enmity with some other power" (1974:478). William Gamson and Andre Modigliani (1989) document a similar role of media in shaping opinions toward nuclear energy.

Although there is little operational research linking mass media and advertising with the socialization to issues of war, peace, and patriotism, there are some theoretical arguments postulating the relevant connections. Some evidence points to a substantial relationship between television violence and aggression in children; unfortunately, little points to a *direct* causal sequence. In a laboratory setting, the mass media's impact on behavior has been fairly well demonstrated, though extrapolating this cause and effect to the larger social setting is more problematic (see Schramm, 1980:332). But maintaining and reinforcing the symbols that convey a heightened degree of threat and that help to generate public support for the policies of continued mobilization requires some socialization mechanism.

In addressing the question of how an elite can maintain control over the attitudes of the public, and the symbols necessary to manipulate those attitudes, Robin Luckham points to four instruments of control: (1) through direct state ownership or operation of the educational system and the media; (2) through advertisements on privately held means of "cultural production," such as TV, radio, newspapers, and publishing houses; (3) through the self-censorship and the constraints of professional communities, such as the tendencies toward the lack of criticism within these communities; and (4) through the entertainment outlets that market toys, movies, and video games, through which images of war and destruction are manipulated and conveyed (1984:16-19).

For our purposes, the role of the schools in creating and reinforcing the symbols of and attitudes toward the nation has been sufficiently discussed. Moreover, the evidence appears to be strong enough that these arguments cannot be readily dismissed. The other three mechanisms of control raised by Luckham also appear to have some role in the mobilization of society yet have received little empirical attention. Of these remaining three, the role of the media and entertainment will be dealt with systematically.

The Media

As far back as 1926, Philip Noel-Baker argued that there was an undue influence exerted on the media through the "private manufacture of arms." According to him, news is the commodity that the press has to sell to the public and "war-news sells a paper better than anything else" (229). Therefore, he argued, the press is more likely to evade issues that pertain to disarmament or peace and focus on stories serving the interests of the nation as viewed from the War Department. While there is a nominally free press in both the United States and Great Britain, the mainstream media outlets in both countries are generally large corporations that operate under the dictates of the economic system in which they are imbedded. An unprofitable newspaper or television network will not survive in these fiercely competitive markets. Advertising revenues make up a great proportion of the operating budget of the normal newspaper or television industry,[1] and the largest source of advertising dollars is the major corporate sponsors. This can result in a considerable degree of influence over news and entertainment on the part of these major donors. Advertisements not only directly affect what is considered to be in vogue, socially acceptable, and in the "national interest" but also shape what we see and hear as news and watch as entertainment.

Furthermore, advertising revenues play such a large role in the profitability of major newspapers that the content of the reporting is potentially held hostage to advertising dollars. Although theoretically there is a direct relationship between circulation and advertising, in practice content also plays a role in determining where the advertising revenues flow. In addition, corporate sponsors influence the content of television programing, with the results being a form of de facto censorship (Herman and Chomsky, 1988; Lee and Solomon, 1990; Whitfield, 1991). Probably the most glaring examples of corporate control over mass media can be found during the McCarthy period in the United States, though more recent censorship has been chronicled by Edward Herman and Noam Chomsky, as well as Martin Lee and Norman Solomon. This influence can be felt not only in the content of "news" that gets disseminated but also in the form and content of what is generally considered entertainment. Stephen Whitfield demonstrates that the "culture of the Cold War" had such a grip over the American public and its institutions that not only did a form of self-censorship emerge, but the media and the movie industries rushed to denounce the Communists and put themselves squarely on the side of the dominant political ideology. There was little effort by these media to play a countervailing role against the rising tide of McCarthyism.

A more rigorous specification of how the form and content of news is "manipulated" has been put forward by Herman and Chomsky. They articulate what they call a "propaganda model" of media penetration into society, with five "filters" through which the media "marginalize[s] dissent, and allow[s] the government and dominant private interests to get their messages across to the public" (1988:2). These filters serve to ensure that the information that does reach the mass public conforms to the elite view of the world. According to their model, the operative filters are (1) the size and economic clout of the mass-media firms, (2) "advertising as the primary source of income of the mass media," (3) the reliance on official sources for information, primarily government officials and corporate experts, (4) "flak," or the negative response to media reports from either government or business, and (5) "anticommunism as a national religion and control mechanism"(2). Furthermore, they posit that these filters function so efficiently because they are ingrained in the system to such a degree that "alternative bases of news choices are hardly imaginable" (2). Such an argument follows very closely with Benjamin Ginsberg's observation that the freedom of press--the absence of state interference--that exists in the minds of many Westerners is in fact a chimera. "The freedom of opinion found in the western democracies . . . is not the unbridled freedom of some state of nature. It is rather the structured freedom of a public forum constructed and maintained by the state" (1986:87).

If the print and television media were benign agents of socialization, this tailoring of information would pose only minor problems. But according to Steven Chaffee et al., the mass media constitute the principal source of political information for young people. They argue that the television and print media are the dominant forces in political learning and that the mass media play a large role in shaping the political opinions of young people (1977:227-28). The relative influence of newspapers and television fluctuates with age, though television remains the dominant medium for the poor. The work of Petra Hesse and John Mack suggests that television cartoons have some impact on the child's identification of an enemy and that "most of the cartoon shows . . . implicitly introduce children to the superpower struggle between virtuous and righteous Americans and godless, evil communists" (1991:148).

Entertainment Outlets

Although there is little direct evidence tying forms of entertainment to military socialization, some inconclusive findings relate media violence to political passivity and antisocial behavior (see Schramm, 1980; Luckham, 1984; Dworetz, 1987; Renshon, 1977). A preliminary report by the U.S. surgeon general concluded that there "is a significant connection between television violence and aggressive behavior," though the public conclusions to the report were watered down for reasons of political expediency (Dworetz, 1987:197). Steven Dworetz goes on to argue that heavy television viewing "cultivates . . . the essential psychological condition for political passivity and obedience"(198). If there is a causal relationship between violence on television and in the movies on the one hand and antisocial behavior on the other, it would be suggestive of the potential impact of various forms of entertainment on social development.

Changing the message from one of antisocial violence to one of a social norm depicting the patriotic duty of the citizenry could have a powerful impact on public attitudes toward the policies of the security elite.

William Gamson and Andre Modigliani posit that culture can be thought of as a toolkit of symbols, stories, rituals, and worldviews, which people use to solve different kinds of problems. One such problem is to make sense of public affairs, and mass media, they argue, provide many of the essential tools for this task. Their model, however, does not posit a direct causal relationship between media discourse and public opinion; rather, that "packages and their elements are essential tools" in an individual's ability to decipher public policy. Furthermore, they argue, "making sense of the world requires an effort, and those tools that are developed, spotlighted, and made readily accessible have a higher probability of being used" (1989:10).

Robin Luckham would take this argument a step further and postulate a direct causal relationship between the "tools and packages" of the entertainment and media outlets and the attitudes and opinions regarding war and the preparations for war. According to Luckham, movies, games, toys, and clothing with a military theme help to condition the public to accept the production and accumulation of armaments, for it is "above all as consumers of manufactured mass culture that men and women are lulled into accepting the warfare system" (1984:20). One could argue that markets for these cultural products only reinforce preexisting public attitudes, though Luckham points to the "organization of [these] markets by monopoly interests and the shaping of consumer tastes by advertising" as an indication that the causal arrows point from the cultural production to the acquiescent attitudes (19).

Wilbur Schramm has outlined a "process model" by which mass media can be used to motivate behavior (1980:302). The necessary components, according to Schramm, are that "the message must be delivered, it must be accepted and internalized, and it must be perceived as a path toward some desirable action, and a person must be put into position to take this action" (304). He argues that the effect of mass media on shaping attitudes and beliefs, as well as motivating behavior, is ubiquitous. "When the media are used in an attempt to manipulate our decisions . . . they are undeniably effective in informing us . . . and they are most potent in a package of communication where they draw on and supplement personal influence and group support" (334-35).

If Schramm's model is correct--as well as the argument that the elite frequently manipulate the perceptions of threat in order to maintain support for policies of military mobilization, as might be found in literature on the Military-Industrial Complex--then we would expect to find: (1) evidence that a cognitive map toward nationalism and patriotism would develop early; (2) that a clear goal is embedded in this cognitive structure; (3) that mechanisms for action must be available; and (4) that the appropriate message is delivered at the appropriate time. There is sufficient empirical evidence to suggest that values of nationalism and patriotism are instilled in children at an early age, that these values are tightly held, and that they are resistant to change. The development of a clear goal--defending freedom, resisting communism--also appears evident (Elder and Cobb, 1983; Hess and Torney, 1967). The existence of behavioral outlets is less clear, but the notion of participation in the political system--voting, supporting a candidate--actively rallying support during a "national crisis" (as was plainly evident during the recent Persian Gulf war), or directly participating in the production or preparations for war are three avenues readily available to give meaning to the "call to action." The remaining component of Schramm's model is the delivery of the message. The "manipulation" of the media and the ubiquitousness of entertainment outlets that portray military themes make this an achievable objective. The marketing of war toys and war movies is one mechanism that might contribute to not only the development of cognitive patterns but also the ease with which the message can be delivered; combined with "news" that reflects an elite worldview, this combination may serve as an extremely effective form of maintaining perceptions and shaping attitudes.

In tying this all together, we would expect to find that the "symbols" of patriotism and the "manipulation" of the perception of a threat become an endemic part of a highly militarized society; little conscious effort or blame can be attributed to any specific core elite. But toys, movies, and the education system help to form mental images of the dominant norms within the society. If a theme common to each of these forms of communication revolves around patriotism, the military, and defending "our" way of life, then we would expect that cognitive maps (or "toolkits") would be drawn that look remarkably similar to an elite view of the world. We should see that periods of high militarization coincide with highly visible symbols that convey a heightened sense of patriotism. Coupling this symbolic influence with an increase in the extent to which the perception of a threat is maintained could generate the support of the general public that is necessary for the extraction of resources--as Lasswell termed it, voluntarily postponing consumption. The mass media contributes to this latter function quite nicely. Moreover, members of the press need not be part of a "conspiracy" but merely acquiescent. In effect they are both victims of the socialization process and unwitting participants in it.

While I will offer no definitive test of a putative causal relationship between sources of entertainment and news on the one hand and the development of promilitary values within the population on the other, I do argue that avenues for entertainment and information form pieces of the links in Schramm's process model. As such, toys, movies, and television programs can have the effect of developing and maintaining the symbols of patriotism so necessary in the generation of support for policies of military mobilization. If the relationship is not directly causal, modes of entertainment must at least play a contributing role in the formation of the symbols and attitudes necessary for the maintenance of a militarized society. In essence, toys and movies with patriotic or war themes contribute to the "psychological numbing" (Lifton, 1982) of the masses that leads to the political passivity and obedience alluded to by Steven Dworetz. Ultimately these symbols will be manipulated to generate public support for the mobilization policies of the power elite. None of this, of course, challenges the argument that war toys and movies are simply a response to market forces and that producers of these forms of entertainment are merely capitalizing on public attitudes, not shaping them. Nor do I think that it is necessary to enter into such a debate. Whether or not there is some identifiable entity that is marshaling the effort to produce and distribute war toys or movies is less important than the fact that symbols that help sanctify elite foreign policy become part of the societal landscape just at the time when public support is needed most. The more often the public is subjected to images and ideas that condone or even reify the elite view of the world, the easier will be the task of generating the support of the public for those elite policies.

SOME TESTABLE HYPOTHESES

Three hypotheses emerge from the preceding discussion: (1) that the number of stories in the popular press conveying a sense of threat will covary with the extent to which a society is militarized; (2) that the proportion of "war" toys and movies in society will covary with changing levels of militarization; and (3) that public attitudes toward the military will be reflected in both press stories about the military, war, or a national threat and the proliferation of toys and movies with patriotic or war themes. Each of these hypotheses will be tested below. As with the earlier analyses, this component involves data from the United States and Great Britain from the turn of the century until 1985.

IN SEARCH OF RIGOR:
THE OPERATIONALIZATION OF VARIABLES

The indicators and measurement for two new variables need to be introduced at this time. One is societal symbols that convey a sense of efficacy on the military; the other is survey data on the public's attitudes toward issues of military preparedness and the threat of war. A discussion of the measurement of the extent to which a perception of a threat is maintained in the public eye and the index of militarization can be found in chapter 2.

Symbols of Patriotism

Two indicators of the societal mechanisms that help to create and maintain a sense of patriotism and the efficacy of the military as an instrument of state policy are used in this study: war toys and war movies. Both are measured as a percent of the total population of toys or movies released in each particular year. Data on war toys in the United States were derived through a "toy count" in the *Sears Catalog*, using the "Christmas Wish List" from 1935 to 1985 and the fall-and-winter edition in the earlier years. For Great Britain, data were taken from *Freeman's Catalog*, fall and winter editions if they were available. Although somewhat smaller than Sears, Freeman's was the only comparable catalog outlet from which data were readily accessible. In both instances the total number of toys offered for sale was counted, as was that subcategory of toys classified as war toys.[2] Likewise, the number of war movies released in each particular year was generated in a similar manner. The data source in this instance was the Magill's Cinema Survey. The total number of films released in each particular year and country was calculated, and then that proportion of films that had the words *military*, *war*, or *patriotism* in the descriptor was excised from the larger pool. The ratios of war toys/movies to total toys and movies are the measures used in this study.[3]

Public Attitudes toward the Military

Obtaining data on public attitudes toward the military was slightly more problematic, at least covering the entire longitudinal dimension of this study. Results of annual Gallup polls are available for the United States as far back as 1939, though inconsistencies in the questions asked posed some difficulties. Other survey data, such as the *Monitoring the Future* project, show consistency in their questioning, though the time span is rather short (starting date 1975). Data on British attitudes are even less consistent, though the international Gallup polls do ask questions regarding the need for a military draft from the mid-1940s to the mid-1950s. Validity and reliability would be threatened by combining responses to related, albeit significantly different questions in surveys conducted over these periods. However, plotting these data over time will afford some insight into the relationship between public attitudes and the symbolic politics of military mobilization, even though patterns across the entire longitudinal dimension cannot be discerned.

METHODOLOGY

The techniques used to uncover patterns in the relationship among the variables were confined to simple bivariate correlations, though in the case of public attitudes toward the military, time-series graphs were used to display the data. While more sophisticated statistical techniques do not in themselves impute causality, by setting up a statistical model that uses various regression-type estimators, the researcher imputes a causal order to the theoretical model. My argument is *not* that the creation and manipulation of symbols causes militarization but rather that symbols are an integral part of the process in the militarization of society. As such, the more accessible are particular symbols to the general public, the more likely that the public will respond positively to attempts to manipulate those symbols. We would expect to see, therefore, that periods of high military mobilization would coincide with the high visibility of symbols that condone--or even reify--such behavior.

WHAT THE DATA TELL US: THE FINDINGS

Correlations between Variables

A correlation matrix of the prevalence of war toys and war movies, the index of press reporting on promilitary themes, and the measure of the extent to which the United States was militarized is presented in table 5.1. The most notable feature of these correlations is the strong relationship between war toys and movies on the one hand and the measure of militarization on the other. For the United States, the correlations are .74 and .83 respectively, over an eighty five year period. The relationship between war toys and movies and the number of weekly stories in the press with a promilitary theme is less startling, though still strong enough to take notice. The respective correlations are .53 and .42. As a first cut, this evidence lends strong support to the theoretical argument, at least with regard to the United States. The strength of the correlations between symbols of war and the militarization of the United States is such that the symbolic politics argument rests on quite strong footings.

Movies, however, were not accessible to the mass public throughout the entire time frame covered in this analysis; Magill's survey, for instance, does not start cataloging films in the United States until 1930.[4] Removing the years before 1930 from the analysis increases the strength of the relationship between media coverage of military-related issues and war movies to .62, though at the same time it slightly diminishes the relationship between militarization and movies (.71). Even with the changes that resulted from deleting the years when movies were irrelevant, these findings are consistent with what was expected theoretically and in fact offer very strong evidence that these relationships cannot be attributed solely to the vagaries of time. If the variables are not directly causally related, their systematic covariation suggests that they are somehow interrelated in the process of militarizing a society.

Table 5.2 is a comparable matrix for data on Great Britain. As is evident from this table, the relationships among some variables show a significant deviation from the pattern established using data from the United States. Most pronounced is the negative correlation between war toys on the one hand and each of the other indicators on the other. War movies, however, are correlated fairly strongly with both the extent to which Britain was militarized (.65) and the number of stories in the press with a positive characterization of the military

(.77). Likewise, my measure of British militarization is highly correlated with the number of press stories conveying a heightened sense of threat (.82). With the exception of the weak finding pertaining to war toys, data from Britain also lend considerable support to the theoretical argument. A partial explanation for the negative relationship between the number of war toys offered for sale in Britain and the other indicators that are allegedly associated with militarization might be found by looking at two areas. First, the records kept by *Freeman's* were incomplete. All of the catalogs for the years before 1927 were missing, as was the catalog for the year 1932. This "missing data" problem means that most of the strength and direction in the relationship is the result of the post-World War II period, a time of substantial retrenchment in the British military. Second, at the height of World War II, not only were no war toys offered for sale but *no toys* were offered in the catalogs. In the year 1940 nearly 7 percent of the toys offered for sale were war toys; by 1942 toys were no longer available for purchase. And it is not until 1950 that war toys appear on the scene again. One interpretation is that Britons were mobilized for the survival of their state, and under such circumstances toys became not only a luxury but also "symbols" of the threat were ubiquitous and did not need to be reinforced.

Table 5.1
Bivariate Correlations between Societal Symbols and Militarization, Unlagged Models (U.S.)

Militarization	1.000			
War Movies	.83	1.00		
	p=.000			
War Toys	.74	.64	1.00	
	p=.000	p=.000		
Threat Manip	.44	.42	.53	1.00
	p=.004	p=.005	p=.000	
	Militarization	War Movies	War Toys	Threat Manip

All significance tests are one-tailed

The next step is to take a purely exploratory turn and introduce lags into the analysis. I introduce lags to see if there is any clear indication of the direction to the unfolding sequence (tables 5.3 and 5.4). While this is far from any attempt at demonstrating causality, the results can be enlightening; what I am looking for is a drastic change in either the strength or the direction of the coefficient of correlation. The most striking finding with the lagged models for the United

Table 5.2
Bivariate Correlations between Societal Symbols and Militarization, Unlagged Models (U.K.)

Militarization	1.000			
War Movies	.65 p=.000	1.00		
War Toys	-.38 p=.035	-.35 p=.052	1.00	
Threat Manip	.82 p=.000	.77 p=.000	-.41 p=.023	1.00
	Militarization	War Movies	War Toys	Threat Manip

All significance tests are one-tailed

States is that the correlation between lagged press reporting and the measure of militarization jumps from .44 to .59, suggesting that the chronicling of the perception of a threat might precede mobilization. Lagging toys and movies does not greatly affect the strength of the relationship with militarization (.62 and .86 respectively), though it significantly diminishes the strength of the relationship with press reporting on issues relating to the military (.19 and .29 respectively). Previous press reporting does not, however, seem to appreciably alter its association with the prevalence of either war toys or war movies. The measure of militarization in the previous period has a substantially lower correlation with toys, movies, and press reporting than the unlagged models, though the

Table 5.3
Bivariate Correlations between Societal Symbols and Militarization, Lagged Models (U.S.)

Lagged Militarization	.76 p=.000	.61 p=.000	.40 p=.009	.08 p=.311
Lagged Movies	.86 p=.000	.75 p=.000	.57 p=.000	.29 p=.048
Lagged Toys	.62 p=.000	.47 p=.002	.50 p=.001	.19 p=.135
Lagged Threat Manip	.59 p=.000	.40 p=.008	.49 p=.001	.51 p=.001
	Militarization	Movies	Toys	Threat Manip

All significance tests are one-tailed

coefficient associated with news reporting on military issues is statistically insignificant, even in a one-tailed test. These latter findings might indicate that interest in war toys and movies does not follow increased mobilization, as some might argue, though any interpretation is clearly just suggestive.

Introducing lags to the British data does little to change the substantive findings from the unlagged correlations (table 5.4). Lagged war toys remain either negatively correlated with each other variable or statistically indistinguishable from random; lagging the index of militarization significantly diminishes the relationship to press reporting on military issues (from .82 to .60), though the coefficient is still relatively robust and positive. Likewise, lagging war movies does not dramatically change the strength or direction of the correlation with either press reporting or the level of militarization (.57 and .56, respectively). However, as mentioned at the outset of this discussion on lagging, this was undertaken as an exploratory exercise, and of course any conclusions must be tempered by its primitive nature. This exploration does, however, point to areas for further research, where more precise model specification might contribute to the argument of whether this is indeed "manipulation" and, if so, how and to what effect it is carried out.

Table 5.4
Bivariate Correlations between Societal Symbols
and Militarization, Lagged Models (U.K.)

Lagged Militarization	.66	.44	-.52	.60
	p=.000	p=.012	p=.004	p=.000
Lagged Movies	.56	.33	-.43	.57
	p=.002	p=.063	p=.022	p=.002
Lagged Toys	.008	.04	.44	-.11
	p=.485	p=.430	p=.020	p=.302
Lagged Threat Manip	.56	.26	-.46	.58
	p=.000	p=.098	p=.012	p=.000
	Militarization	Movies	Toys	Threat Manip

All significance tests are one-tailed

A couple of points might be raised to account for the variation in the findings between the United States and Britain, particularly with regard to the prevalence of war toys offered for sale. First, this could reflect a cultural difference between the two societies, where toys in general take on different levels of importance and where the objects used to create symbols of political community in the two societies differ. Second, the lack of any toys for sale during the World War II period may suggest that the use of symbols to generate support may be irrelevant when national survival is at stake. Finally, the data problem alluded to earlier may be seriously confounding the analysis or the sources for data on toys may not have been reliable. For the United States I was able to check the reliability of the Sears catalog as an indicator of the volume and mix of toys offered for sale in each year by performing a "toy count" in the J. C. Penney and the Montgomery Ward catalogs, so there is some relief here. But for British data I had to rely solely on the Freeman's outlet. It could be that Freeman's was not representative of the British society.

War Toys, War Movies, and Public Attitudes toward the Military

Public attitudes in the United States toward the military also appear to fluctuate with changes in the prevalence of symbols of war or the military within society. Although reliable statistical patterns cannot be generated with the available data, trends are evident to the casual reader. For instance, in the United States during the period 1975 to 1985, the fear among high school students of nuclear war climbed in a fairly steady progression from 40 percent saying they feared a nuclear war in 1975 to 64 percent worrying about such a cataclysmic

Figure 5.1
Militarization and Societal Symbols with
Patriotic Themes, United States, 1900-1985

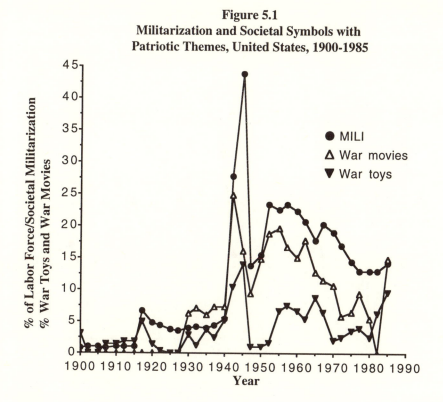

event by 1985. During the same period, war movies went from nearly the lowest recorded percentage (6 percent of total movies) in 1975 to a level obtained only during times of U.S. involvement in a war or at the height of the Cold War (15 percent of total movies). War toys follow a similar path, climbing from 3.5 percent of total toys in 1975 to the highest ratio of war toys outside of the World War II period by 1985 (9.5 percent of total toys). The number of press articles reporting on war, threats of war, or issues of military spending moves from an average of 2.2 articles per week in 1975 to a point in 1977 where stories with an antimilitary theme predominate, before climbing again to over 2 articles per week by 1985. The press, it might seem, played a less obvious role in shaping students' attitudes regarding nuclear war. The level of militarization during this period saw a fairly steady decline from the height of the Vietnam War and remained stable until 1982. From 1982 to 1985 there was a rather sharp increase as a result of President Ronald Reagan's arms buildup. The increased prevalence of war toys and movies, in this instance, appears to precede the increases in military mobilization and is somewhat congruent with the fears of the high school students (see figures 5.1-5.4).

Figure 5.2
Maintenance of the Perception of a Threat (U.S.)

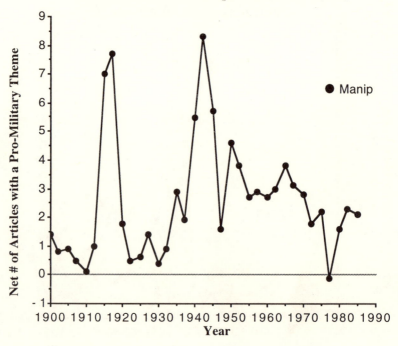

During the middle part of the century the trends are more difficult to detect, though to the careful observer they do appear evident. At the end of World War II nearly 70 percent of respondents to a Gallup poll expressed fear of another major war in the foreseeable future; by 1950 those harboring such fears had dropped to about 40 percent of respondents. The trend climbs again with the onset of the Korean War to reach a peak of 70 percent and then drops to a trough of 34 percent by 1960. As unrest in Southeast Asia began to heat up, it appears that the fear of a world war again followed suit, though data from the Gallup organization stops at this point. Samuel Fitch, however, reports that the percent of respondents saying that the United States is spending too little on the military "drops from an average of 30% during the late 1950s and early 60s to less than 10% by 1969" (1985:35). This marked decline in support for military spending

Figure 5.3
U.S. Attitudes Regarding Future Wars and
Societal Symbols with a Patriotic Theme

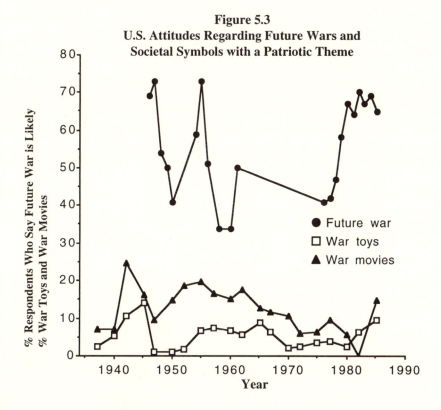

experienced a sharp turnaround in the latter part of the 1970s and early 1980s, apparently related to increased Cold War tensions. Closely examining the data presented by Ted Goertzel (1987) indicates that public attitudes toward military spending are related to the amount of media exposure given to issues of military expansion or threats, at least until the dissension over the Vietnam War gathered momentum (see figures 5.1 and 5.2). While data on public attitudes seem remarkably intuitive when viewed in isolation, comparing fluctuations in attitudes with changes in the prevalence of the symbols associated with a threatening environment is somewhat more revealing. In figure 5.3 we can see that the symbols conferring a heightened degree of efficacy on the military follow a trend similar to that of public attitudes regarding the fear of global or nuclear war.

Data on British attitudes are even less comprehensive than data from the United States, in terms of both substantive questions and longitudinal completeness. Most of what is accessible on British attitudes deals with issues of the military draft. However, what appears evident from these surveys is that support for compulsory military service increased significantly as World War II began to heat up but then dropped to prewar levels after the cessation of hostilities. Although one should be extremely hesitant to draw conclusions from such limited data, the pattern roughly follows the data on war toys and war movies in the immediate postwar period. Furthermore, a cursory glance at the

Figure 5.4
U.S. Attitudes toward Military Spending

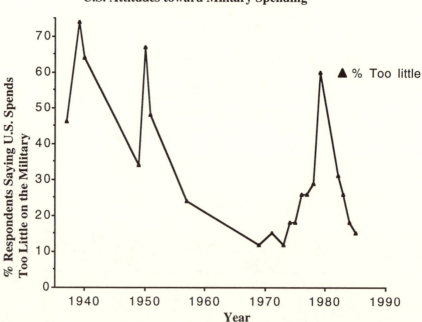

data on war toys and movies and the extent to which British society was militarized from 1930 to 1985 gives some grounds for insightful speculation and investigation (figure 5.5). However, because of the limited nature of this data on British attitudes and symbols, it is more prudent to leave this part of the analysis as a topic for further research. Any inferences at this stage are mere speculation, and it is best not to indulge.

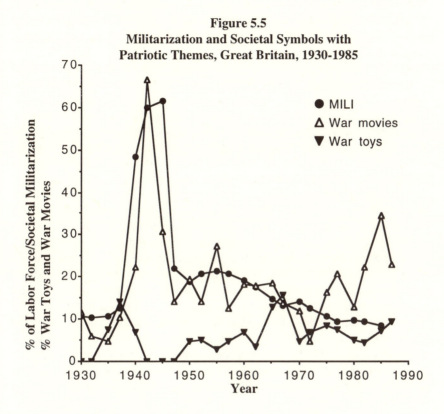

Figure 5.5
Militarization and Societal Symbols with
Patriotic Themes, Great Britain, 1930-1985

SYMBOLIC POLITICS AND MILITARIZATION: INTERPRETING THE FINDINGS

The interpretation of these findings may prove to be more problematic than the discovery of the longitudinal trends, though it would seem that inferences can be drawn that could help advance our understanding of the militarization of societies. Again, the direction of causality is far from clear, in terms of both the theoretical argument and the data analysis, but the results presented do illustrate a potential role for symbols in the creation and maintenance of favorable public attitudes toward the military and the subsequent extension of military-based organization into the civil sector of society.

To demonstrate that Harold Lasswell's "garrison state" construct has some degree of empirical validity, it would be necessary to substantiate his claim that the socialization of the general public to the worldview of the elite is carried out, in large part, through the creation and manipulation of symbols. Likewise, Wilbur Schramm (1980) suggests that for propaganda efforts to be successful, cognitive maps must be created, the appropriate message must be delivered, and the public must have an outlet for action. The thorough nature of modern-day military penetration into the civil aspects of society would require that the use of symbols appear as just a normal part of daily life--almost subliminal in nature. Again according to Lasswell: "from the earliest years youth will be trained to subdue--to disavow, to struggle against--any specific opposition to the ruling code. . . . The conscience imposes feelings of guilt and anxiety upon the individual whenever his impulses are aroused, ever so slightly, to break the code" (1941:460). This reliance on social conformity and the acceptance of the elite view of the world must be a result of either coercive violence or the subtle manipulation of symbols. In both the United States and Great Britain, widespread coercion can for the most part be ruled out.

The findings presented above, however, suggest that symbolic meaning can be imputed to some of the ubiquitous forms of entertainment and that the prevalence of these symbols has some empirical relationship to both public attitudes toward the military and the extent to which the society is militarized. These findings, however, are much more robust for the United States than for Great Britain. As with Gamson and Modigliani's analysis of the media "toolkit" that helps shape public images regarding nuclear energy, the consistent exposure to forms of entertainment that glorify the military and espouse the virtues of unwavering support for elite views of "national security" must affect the development of the cognitive maps in individuals. This, coupled with a steady stream of news articles that convey a sense of national peril and imminent threat or, at a minimum, detail the need for a strong military, would very likely result in a toolkit that appears remarkably similar to those carried by the "national security elite."

Under these circumstances we might expect the development of an "armament culture" and possibly even a society more predisposed to encourage--or desire-- entertainment outlets that maintain themes extolling the virtues of the military. As Fred Milano (1988) pointed out, it might not be in the state's interests to take steps to reduce the prevalence of symbols that reify the military, because an elite that relies on such violent methods in both its domestic and its foreign policy needs to promote the acceptance of such values in the populace. While far from confirming the thesis that symbols and attitudes are "manipulated" by the security elite, the findings for the United States do point to a fairly strong relationship among the creation and maintenance of symbols in society, the maintenance of the perception of a threat in the media, public attitudes toward the military, and the extent to which the United States can be considered militarized. And while the empirical relationships are somewhat weaker for Britain than for the United States, a similar underlying trend does appear evident. One of the inferences that can be drawn from this analysis is that a crucial impediment to disentangling the civil sector of society from its military counterpart might be the role of entertainment and media networks. As we have seen in light of the recent Persian Gulf war, many forces in society are actively resisting the movement toward demilitarization. The sales of "Desert Storm toys" and the flag in the United States and the increased media hype regarding the successes of technology and soldiers all presage the forthcoming political battles to be waged over military reductions. The tentative results of this analysis should point toward reductions in the symbolic glorification of the military if there is to be a hope that current military reductions are more than an ephemeral event.

6

In Search of Generalizations: The Case of Brazil

A historical description of the evolution in the Brazilian military's influence over, and coordination of, the civil sector of society should serve as a good point of departure for an examination of the militarization process in a country that is lower on the developmental spectrum. As I will argue below, Brazil is clearly not highly militarized, and in fact, recent events might presage a movement in the opposite direction. The military in Brazil, however, has taken on an increasingly prominent role not only in Brazilian politics but also in the economic organization of the society. As Brazil has moved from a loosely organized country into a more unified society, with many of the resources required of a major actor on the international scene, its military bureaucracy has played a central role. By 1985, although facing almost no serious international or domestic threat to their security, Brazilians were one of the world's major exporters of weapons systems, ranking first in the export of tracked military vehicles. As we shall see, Brazil used the production of military hardware as a platform to develop the industrial infrastructure necessary to become a world-class producer in heavy manufacturing and steel production and, in doing so, has begun to blur the boundary between the civil and the military sectors of society. The use of the military as an industrial platform could be justified in terms of "national security" and therefore helped to coalesce the various domestic actors behind a somewhat unified economic strategy.

This chapter will recount the evolution of civil-military relations in Brazil. I will start with the organization of the military and civilian sectors of society at the turn of the century, moving on to discuss the role of internal and external threats to the security of the ruling elites, arms purchases and production, the economic ties between industry and the military, the role of schools and institutes of higher education in inculcating military values in the minds of the general public, and finally, the use of coercion by the state. This analysis will demonstrate that during the early part of the century there were two distinct sectors of society, civil and military. Internal and external threats--not always as real as the elite might have been led to believe--forced the development of a more centralized military, and with it came a much larger domestic constituency. Prolonged military rule helped to solidify a central unifying role for the military and subsequently the development of a relatively vast and sophisticated military infrastructure, not only fielding a sizable armed force but also producing advanced weaponry. By the latter part of the century the Brazilian military could claim control over a sizable education system, training engineers and scientists to build the next generation of weapons, and an industrial sector capable of producing some of the world's best military equipment. In the process, the boundary between the civil and the military sectors of Brazilian society has become much more hazy. Up until 1985, Brazil had taken many of the steps characteristic of a society set on the path toward a high degree of dependence on the military sector for economic and political vitality, yet as we will see, the effect of this societal militarization has not shown up in the amount of violence evident in Brazilian foreign policy.

It should also be clear what this chapter will *not* do. First and foremost, this exegesis is intended only to illustrate and should not be considered a formal test of any of the hypotheses outlined in earlier chapters. Although I suspect that a more formal test would be enlightening, time, resources, and data prevent such an effort at this time. Second, this historical description relies primarily on secondary sources, so inferences or conclusions should, of course, be drawn accordingly. And, finally, the treatment of some of the variables in my theoretical model has been less systematic in this description than in the empirical chapters pertaining to the United States and Great Britain, most specifically the issues of existential and manipulated threats. Two factors mitigate the impact of this slippage: (1) the evidence seems clear that Brazil is not a highly militarized society, suggesting that it should be less prone to manipulate perceptions of a threat and that the hypothesized feedback should be much less pronounced; and (2) in a descriptive analysis such as this it is less important that every detail be chronicled than that the roles of various actors and variables be made explicit.

THE MILITARY AS AN ORGANIZATION, 1900-1985

As Brazil neared the turn of the century, the military as an institution was loosely organized and racked by internal dissent. State militia and local police were the dominant forces at their respective levels of government, while no policy existed for implementing a program of compulsory military service. The annual report of the Minister of War in 1900 "admitted that the army did not have a national character" (McCann, 1984:739). A state-based national guard existed, but control of the guard fell under the Ministry of Justice. Recruits for the guard generally came from the upper classes of society, leaving the army to recruit from the working class (740). The result of this class-based pool for recruiting meant that the young men from the rural upper classes could serve in their local areas, while those from the poorer classes had to leave their homes for the squalid barracks of the Brazilian army. This served another, more political purpose, however. By staffing the state militia with people from the local area-- who have a decided interest in maintaining local autonomy--while building a national army from a widely dispersed pool of recruits with few ties to either the central authority or the town in which they are barracked, it set up a confrontation between the rural oligarchies in the states and the central government.

While the military was aware of the consequences of this decentralization of authority, the process of integrating and centralizing the forces of coercion was destined to meet with resistance. The first step had to be the transfer of control of the state-based national guard from the Ministry of Justice to the Ministry of War; the second was to implement a program of compulsory military service. It was apparent to those in the military hierarchy that national security was tied to the existence of a well-organized and centralized military establishment; a unified military bureaucracy was in turn contingent on adequate training and the development of a sense of national pride in the minds of the population. In 1905 a Brazilian army officer, Augusto Sa', offered a five-point plan that would move the military in the direction of this desired professionalism. This plan proposed obligatory public education, an increase in the ranks of the officers corps, and the incorporation of local police into the military hierarchy (McCann, 1984:744).

By 1906 legislation had been introduced in the Chamber of Deputies requiring compulsory military service and the reorganization of the military bureaucracy, but it was not until some fifteen months later that the bill was finally passed. Frank McCann points out, "That there was less than complete political support for army reforms can be noted in the fact that it took until 1908 to get the obligatory service bill through the Congress and then another eight years to get it enforced" (1984:742).

The military leadership saw itself and its institution as the only force within society capable of transforming Brazil from a sleeping giant into an industrial power. According to an editorial in a 1913 edition of a Brazilian defense journal, *A Defeza Nacional*: "A well-organized army was one of the most perfect creations of the human spirit, because in it narrow individual interests must be abandoned in the name of the great collective interests. . . . If such influence could be noted in the old, cultured societies of Europe, in a country like Brazil it will be an even more powerful factor in the modification of a retarded and shapeless society" (quoted in McCann, 1984:749). There was little doubt in the minds of the military elite that if there was to be a unifying force in Brazilian society, the military would have to take on such a role.

World War I helped to move Brazil in the direction envisioned by the military elite. The threat of war not only spurred on the enforcement of compulsory military service but also justified the reorganization of the army and the national guard. Control of the latter was finally moved from the Justice Ministry to the Minister of War, which subsequently "remodeled the hated guard out of existence" (McCann, 1984:758). Although the war facilitated the centralization of the coercive forces in Brazil, as an institution the military was far from cohesive; as a society Brazil was a long way from the road to industrialization.

Although Brazil did not commit troops to battle and lost only a small number of ships to German torpedoes, its experience during the war served as a catalyst to move the political elite in the direction espoused by the military. During the war Brazil was cut off from the weapons it had purchased from Germany, making painfully clear the need for domestic production of armaments. At the same time, the size of the army nearly tripled, from 18,000 to 50,000 (McCann, 1981:174). So while the increased number of soldiers heightened the sense of national capability, the inability to adequately equip the forces increased the sense of foreign dependence, fostering a nationalistic drive within the military and beginning the process of developing an indigenous arms industry. The first step would have to be the creation of a Brazilian steel industry, an idea that captured the attention of the political elites (761).

The interwar period was also a time of rebellion within the ranks of the military. The divisions among the officer corps were as much ideological as they were status-driven. Relatively low pay and close proximity to the civilian sector of society gave the officers a standard by which to judge their quality of life; many were disgruntled by what they saw. But equally important were the ideological schisms that had surfaced within the ranks of the officer corps. One group, the reformers, viewed the proper role of the military as the tool to shape the political institutions of society; the other group was more conservative and opposed the military's involvement in politics (Murilo de Carvalho, 1982:198). This divisiveness boiled over on a number of occasions during the 1920s and 1930s, leading eventually to civil war in 1932. Besides the São Paulo rebellion in 1932 that led to the civil war, there were rebellions within the military in 1922 and 1924 and again in 1930. According to Jose Murilo de Carvalho: "Such revolts occurred in 1931, when sergeants and enlisted men seized control of the 25th Infantry Battalion of Teresina and of the 21st Battalion of Recife, and in 1932 with the 18th IB of Campo Grande. In Teresina, the rebels went so far as to overthrow the interim governor and name a corporal to replace him. Plans for a major revolt led by sergeants developed in São Paulo between 1933 and 1934" (197).

It was not until the Getúlio Vargas dictatorship and the establishment of the *Estado Novo* in 1937 that the military began to function as one unified institution--and even then the predominant actor was the army. An alliance between the reformers within the armed forces and those whose focus was on the professional role of the military permitted the military to take an activist position in the development of the political institutions of Brazil. The professionals "accepted interventionism, provided it was done under the control of the hierarchy; the [reformers] accepted hierarchical control, provided the hierarchy agreed to intervention" (Murilo de Carvalho, 1982:200). The Vargas dictatorship was the culmination of years of military infighting and, by some measures, was a turning point in the institutional development of the Brazilian armed forces. Again according to Murilo de Carvalho: "During the period 1930-45 important transformations took place inside the Brazilian armed forces and in their relationships with the Brazilian state and society. From a weak and poorly organized institution, and a rather marginal social and political actor, the armed forces, particularly the army, became a respected fighting force and more powerful both socially and politically. The changes affected the structure of the military institution, the conception of its political role and the role itself"(193).

The Vargas dictatorship (1937-1945) not only ushered in a new era within the military bureaucracy but also fostered a greater coordination between the civil bureaucracy and its military counterpart. President Vargas was a civilian who ruled with the consent of the military. The Vargas period also changed the relationship between the rural oligarchies and the central government, as well as between the working class and the state. According to Youssef Cohen, "Under the leadership of Vargas, [the] state elite transformed the country from a loose federation of states ruled by rural oligarchies into a highly centralized national state that curbed even the power of the great landowners" (1989:86). A system of corporatist-interest representation was instituted by the Vargas regime that helped coalesce the working class around the interests of state. This system of state control over labor and industry would have lasting effects on Brazilian society.

Although the military retreated from the front lines of running the affairs of state and although civilian control of the bureaucracy returned to an electoral format, the soldiers were never far from the palace. When Getúlio Vargas was elected president in 1950, the military was suspicious that he was on his way to becoming Brazil's Juan Perón. In 1954 he committed suicide on the eve of the coup that was to overthrow him. From 1954 until a military coup in 1964, any civilian leader had to keep a close eye on the Ministry of War, lest the latter get agitated and intervene in politics. In 1955 the leadership of the army revolted in response to a disagreement with an interim president's policy on disciplining a military officer. In the aftermath, the army had removed the acting president and shelled the navy cruiser taking him into exile (Dulles, 1970:43). Later in the same month, the army forced the Congress to depose the convalescing president when he tried to return to office. Though much of this activity on the part of the military was designed to ensure the succession of the democratically elected president and vice president, its effect was to highlight the influence of the military over civilian affairs (30-60).

The military elite continued to play an active role in Brazilian politics up until the coup of 1964, when they began the process of redefining Brazilian political life. Under a succession of army generals, the military ruled with an iron fist until the elections of 1985. In the interim period they reshaped the political landscape by the use of "institutional acts" that served to outlaw political parties, ban certain politicians from participating in Brazilian politics, censor the media, repress political dissent, and change the multiparty system in place before the coup into a two-party system dominated by the military bureaucracy (Skidmore, 1988). By the mid-1970s, the military dictators were beginning to make the transition back toward civilian rule, but it would not be until the election of 1985 that the transition would be completed. In the intervening period, from when the military first began to exercise political control during the 1930s until they relinquished the direct governing of the affairs of state in 1985, they profoundly shaped the Brazilian society.

As we have seen above, in the early days of the Brazilian republic, the military was an actor, but neither a strong nor a unified actor. There were also very few backward and forward linkages between the civilian and the military sectors of Brazilian society. "The first [backward linkages] indicated the inflow of people from society into the army, the second [forward linkages] the outflow of people from the army into society." In the early years of the republic, "both linkages were weak and the Brazilian army was very much isolated from important sectors of society" (Murilo de Carvalho, 1982:201). By the end of the *Estado Novo* period, however, these linkages were greatly enhanced, in part by the strict enforcement of the draft laws. The integration of society was also bolstered by the proliferation of "Escolas de Instrucao Militar, devised to provide initial military training to high school students" (202). As we will see below, this increased coordination between the civilian and the military sectors of society greatly affected the development of an industrial infrastructure and, eventually, the production of indigenously designed and manufactured weapons systems. In the process, the legitimacy accorded the military was greatly enhanced, and a constituency began to develop around continued funding of the bureaucracy.

CIVILIAN ATTITUDES TOWARD THE MILITARY

Like relationships and attitudes within the military itself, the attitudes of the civilian population toward the military also evolved over time. As noted above, there were strong animosities between the rural oligarchies and the military hierarchy, dating back to the early days of the republic. These feelings ran so deep that Brazilian society was virtually polarized between two organized forces of coercion: the state-based national guards, administered and staffed by the sons of the rural elites, and the national army, staffed by recruits taken from the lower classes of society. Attempts to eliminate this source of division met with severe resistance in the Congress, taking a year and a half of negotiations and eight years of procrastination before the onset of World War I would compel the enforcement of compulsory draft legislation.

That the Brazilian public was not excited about the prospects of compulsory military service can be seen in the following passage by Frank McCann:

Militarized shooting clubs, commonly known as Tiros, sprouted around the country so rapidly that by mid-1910 there were more than 10,000 members; excited officers regarded the uniformed marksmen as reservists. Many secondary schools had requested army instructors, while short-term volunteers signed up for field maneuvers. Even the little-heard national anthem was sung in public! In their enthusiasm, officers perhaps missed the obvious: the Tiros, military instruction in the schools, and volunteering for field exercises were ways, under the obligatory service law, of avoiding being called up for a year of training. Brazilians had not suddenly become fascinated with things military; rather, they were seeking a way (*jeito*) to avoid the more onerous experience of the barracks. Once the public realized that the law would not be enforced beyond the compilation of lists of eligible men, the Tiro societies began to decline and the volunteer rate fell sharply. (1984:746)

Transforming Brazilian society was bound to meet severe obstacles along the way. The civilian distrust of the military, visible in the response to the obligatory draft legislation, had very deep roots. "Those advocating a popular army had their problems: such an army would be very difficult to organize. For one thing, the most aggressive sectors of the working class had a long tradition of antimilitarism attributable to anarchist influences going back to the beginning of the century" (Murilo de Carvalho, 1982:200). According to McCann's analysis, it was clear that Brazilians would not serve in the military unless they were forced to do so. "The tradition of forced recruitment of lower-class men and the harsh life of the soldiers created a lasting image of a distasteful institution that the 'better' families wanted their sons to avoid" (1984:747).

This distrust was not confined to those who faced the threat of serving in the armed forces; it permeated throughout the entire social fabric. The poor did not want to serve because of the low image of military life; the upper classes did not want to serve because of the harsh conditions in the barracks and because their interests were more regional than national; and the workers did not want to serve because of long-held antimilitarist traditions. But a centralized military also posed a threat to the political domination of the civilian elites. According to Murilo de Carvalho:

The armed forces as an *institution* had interests that conflicted with those of the civilian elites as a *politically dominant class*; these interests called for changes in the regime to allow for greater centralization of the political system, less power to the regional oligarchies, control of the military police forces by the army, greater state intervention in the economy, and so forth. The leftist sectors of the armed forces, on the other side, had a reform program that challenged the interests of the civilian elites as a socially dominant class and, potentially, that of the state itself. (1982:215)

But all of this was to change with the implementation of reforms during the dictatorship of Getúlio Vargas. As noted above, the reformers and the professionals within the ranks of the officer corps agreed on how their intervention in political life could best be achieved. This paved the way for a strong military influence in any ruling coalition. The implementation of the compulsory draft law greatly increased the "forward-backward" flow within society; improvements in the quality of army life increased the attractiveness of military service as a career. "The new visibility and increased political importance of the military positively affected the image of the military as a career among members of the middle and upper classes" (Murilo de Carvalho, 1982:203). The implementation of the draft laws meant that literally thousands of citizens moved in and out of the army on a yearly basis, with the result that the emerging national army greatly increased the penetration of the civil society by the military sector (203).

The evolution of Brazilian society went deeper than merely a reorganization of the armed forces and increased backward-forward linkages. A corporatist system of interest representation was also implemented during the Vargas dictatorship. This new system of representation helped foster the identification of the interests of the working class with those of the state. The interest of the state, in the meantime, had been transformed into the interest of the military elite. A fundamental change swept over Brazilian society, affecting the relationship among the military, the political elites, and the civilian population. Youssef Cohen argues that the attitudes and interests shaped during the Vargas dictatorship carried over into the period of democratic civilian rule, 1954-64, and on into the two decades of the subsequent military dictatorship. Surveys taken in 1972 and 1973 consistently show that the working class in Brazil had more trust in the military than in the civilian politicians (1989, chap. 3; Skidmore, 1988:157).

Part of the military's rationale for directly intervening in politics was tied to a perceived internal threat to state security, but midway through the military dictatorship (1964-1985) any element of internal threat to the viability of the regime had been put down, however the internal security apparatus continued to operate. The Brazilian "economic miracle" helped to focus attention away from the fact that the military was running the state and, in fact, lent credibility to the military leadership (Skidmore, 1988, chap. 5). As we will see later on, the late 1970s and the 1980s saw a marked increase in the level of military production within Brazil. Both the range of weapons produced and their technological sophistication brought the interests of the civilian population much closer to the interests of the military. At the beginning of the century there was a great deal of mistrust between the civilian sector of society and its military counterpart; by the time the military relinquished direct control over most political and economic aspects of Brazilian society in 1985, civilian attitudes toward the institutions of the military were generally positive, and in fact a sizable portion of the population had direct ties to the military.

Up to this point we have focused on the evolution of the institution of the military within Brazilian society. The threads of the military as a centralizing force within society have thus become fairly evident. The military appears to have been a critical factor in the unification of a loosely organized country into something akin to a coherent whole. As such, the military not only increased in size and influence but also developed a sense of national legitimacy, as well as a considerable constituency. To help inform the theoretical argument that is guiding this analysis, we must now turn to the role of threats as a motivating force behind the development of the Brazilian military as a national institution.

THE MOTIVATING FORCE: THREAT

Trying to discern the extent to which a threat faced by any particular country is "real" or "manipulated" is tricky under the best of circumstances; when using a descriptive form of analysis, it is infinitely more difficult. In the case of Brazil there appears to be an even greater confounding factor, for as we shall see, in the 1980s Brazil produced weapons mainly for export. External threat as justification for the continued production of the weapons of war was stressed only minimally. Having the capability to indigenously produce the material necessary to equip its armed forces in the event of war does underlie much of the weapons-production strategy of the country, but it seems that economics and not military concerns drove the weapons-manufacturing industries.

Even early in the century, when World War I served as a catalyst for centralizing the military, Brazil faced at most a minimal threat to its territorial or political sovereignty. Throughout the duration of the war, Brazil neither sent troops into combat nor contributed much to the global war effort. It will become clear, however, that threats--or the perception thereof--were central to efforts to mobilize the population behind the efforts of the military, but as the twentieth century comes to a close, economics has taken on the leading role. This is entirely consistent with the theoretical model outlined earlier and is highly convergent with the expectations of a country at this stage of political and economic development pursuing an industrialization strategy closely tied to military production. Furthermore, if Brazil were to continue along the militarization path we would expect to see the nature of the threat change somewhat, from something quite tangible to a threat that would appear to be more ephemeral.

Although a recent assessment of the level of external threat faced by the Brazilian state rates it as quite low (Franko-Jones, 1986, and 1987-88), a glance back through the history of Brazilian politics suggests that there was a time when the actual threat may have been quite high. And during the inter- and postwar periods, even if the objective determination of an external threat was not high, the perception of hostile international forces was clearly on the minds of the military elite.

The Brazilian-Paraguayan war ended in 1870, but the end of the war did not see the end of Brazilian border disputes or threats from the unstable nature of South American politics. In the early part of the twentieth century, Chile and Argentina were at constant loggerheads; Brazil was justifiably concerned that this would break out into full-scale war. Civil disorder in Paraguay prompted Brazil to send a naval fleet into the area to protect its interests in both 1905 and 1910. There was constant tension between Bolivia and Paraguay during the 1920s, and there was a flow of Uruguayan rebels across the Brazilian border during the first decade of the century (Hilton, 1984:630). All of these incidents are symptomatic of the concerns that needed to be addressed by the relatively decentralized Brazilian state. According to Stanley Hilton:

Underlying the whole problem of continental instability was Brazil's historic rivalry with Argentina. Brazil's victory in the arbitration of the Missions dispute in 1895 set the stage for a marked revival of tensions in the 20th century. The two adversaries engaged in an intense naval race in the early 1900's and border alarms were common. Senator Ruy Barbosa in 1908 warned President Afonso Pena that Argentina might attack without warning, and the two countries in fact approached the brink of war that year. (1984: 631)

While the external situation was keeping military planners on the alert, internally the turn of the century was rife with insurrection and challenges to the domination of the ruling coalition. During the 1890s there was a a civil war in Rio Grande do Sul, along with a naval revolt in Rio de Janeiro. In the latter incident foreign warships intervened against both the government and the rebel forces (Hilton, 1984:632). In 1897 a "band of rebellious backland fanatics" was put down by the army, though at a cost of five thousand lives. The Canudos affair, as it is known, was quite an embarrassment to the government, taking more than one year and the help of the state government to triumph over the rebels. A similar incident erupted in 1914-1915 in Santa Catarin-Parana, when six thousand troops and several expeditions were required to again subdue a band of religious fanatics (632).

This continuous internal and external unrest served as the backdrop for the evolution of the Brazilian armed forces up to the onset of World War I. That the military elite saw their role as preserving the integrity of the Brazilian state from both internal and external forces is evident in a 1913 editorial in the military journal A Defeza Nacional (AND). "Without wishing the unjustified incursion of the military elements in the internal business of the country, the army needs, however, to be prepared for its conservative and stabilizing function over the social elements in motion--and prepared to correct the internal disturbances so common in the tumultuous life of societies in formation" (quoted in McCann, 1984:750). The same edition of AND also spoke of the threat to the frontiers of Brazil's "vast, fertile, opulent, and beautiful country" from either land or sea (750). Clearly the early years of the new century presented the Brazilian elite with persistent challenges to its national security (defined in the narrow interests of the elite). As we have seen, World War I highlighted the vulnerability of the Brazilian military to the vagaries of foreign suppliers of weapons and field equipment. But it also facilitated the implementation of military reforms and the enforcement of compulsory-service legislation. So it was the early threat to the sovereignty of the Brazilian state, coupled with the potential for a continued disruption in the supply of arms, that propelled Brazil toward an increasing role of its military sector in Brazilian society. As we have seen, this required not only a unified and centralized military bureaucracy but also an indigenous weapons-production program.

The period between the two world wars was a time marked more by internal unrest than any threat from an external foe. But that, of course, does not mean that the Brazilian military was oriented solely toward maintaining domestic order. Again, in the influential journal *A Defeza Nacional*, the inspector general of the artillery forces argued, "With the end of the war in Europe conquerors and conquered . . . will not hesitate to develop imperialist policies, and South America, principally Brazil whose riches had already stirred the greed of several (foreign) syndicates, will be the objective of the conqueror's claws" (quoted in McCann, 1984:175). The conclusions that he draws from his perception of the threat are that Brazil must be strong and that strength entails a national steel and defense industry. The bulk of any external threat at this time, however, came from Brazil's southern neighbor, Argentina. Throughout the 1920s "military planners made frequent comparative studies of Brazilian and Argentine strength and invariably found Brazil wanting, a realistic judgment that foreign experts shared" (Hilton, 1982: 633).

On the domestic front the Brazilian hierarchy faced a much more immediate threat to its security from forces operating within Brazilian society. In the 1920s and 1930s, Brazil struggled through a series of military revolts. As Frank McCann put it, "For most of the decade (1920's) [Brazil] had to deal with internal dissension, conspiracy, and rebellion" (1981:180). There was an uprising at Fort Copacabana, Rio de Janeiro, in 1922, a rebellion in São Paulo in 1924, and the roving lieutenants' revolt, which roamed the backlands for two years until finally brought under control in 1927 (180). The latter episode was an embarrassment to the central government and highlighted its military weakness (Hilton, 1982:633). This period culminated in the civil war of 1932, which led to the eventual centralization of authority under the Vargas dictatorship.

The heightening tensions that led up to World War II were naturally of great concern to the Brazilian leadership. There was a fear that the aggressiveness exhibited by Japan, Italy, and Germany on the Asian, African, and European continents would spread to South America. And although the United States viewed Brazil as a strategic asset susceptible to German interference, any real threat to Brazil at this time still rested with its southern neighbor, Argentina. With the end of World War II and the onset of the Cold War, elite perceptions of a hostile external environment resided in the East-West confrontation that was taking shape. But in light of any potential for external conflict, Brazil has remained free from major participation in an international war since the Paraguayan war of 1865-1870.

The level of threat perceived by the Brazilian military to be emanating from the domestic front, however, had increased since the end of World War II. As we have seen above, the military has had continued involvement in the civilian affairs of state since the consolidation of the *Estado Novo* period. The military intervened in the office of the presidency on at least three occasions between 1954 and 1964, with the last intervention culminating in a twenty-year military dictatorship. Presumably each instance of the military's direct role in the policies of the president was based on a perceived threat to the security of the Brazilian state (Skidmore, 1988; Dulles, 1970). From 1968 to 1974 the military waged a war of repression against what it viewed as subversive elements within the civilian population. The alleged threat that drove this internal war was based on a fear of communist subversion (Skidmore, 1988). There is little to suggest that during this period there was any threat from external sources or that the internal insurgency was much more than a nuisance than an actual threat to domestic security.

By 1985 it could be argued that the perception by Brazilian elites of either an internal or an external threat to their security was more imagined than real (Franko-Jones, 1987-88). This is not to deny that military planners will understandably develop scenarios based on potential threats but rather to point out that the drive for such high levels of military production do not appear to be rooted in an external threat to the survivability of the Brazilian state. We must look elsewhere for the mechanisms that drive the high levels of military production and organization seen in Brazil today. As we will see shortly, the political and economic forces behind a burgeoning Military-Industrial Complex will take us a long way.

Weapons Procurement:
The Involvement of the Civil Society

At the beginning of the twentieth century, the Brazilian military not only was less than cohesive as an institution but also relied on foreign suppliers for nearly all its equipment. "When Brazil entered the century, there were army arsenals in Rio de Janeiro, Porto Alegre and Cuiaba, naval arsenals in the federal capital, Belem, and Mato Grosso, and three munitions plants--one in Ralengo, a suburb of the capital, for cartridges; one at Estrela, in the state of Rio de Janeiro, for manufacturing powder; and a moribund powder plant in Mato Grosso" (Hilton, 1982:639). The Ministry of War appeared content with its dependence on foreign sources for military wares, and the army was apparently happy enough with its role in maintaining arsenals that functioned as repair facilities. In the early 1900s the Minister of War noted, "For our limited army three arsenals . . . are more than sufficient" (McCann, 1981:171). These facilities, however, were in a ghastly state of repair, and the "military workers and craftsmen probably spent as much time repairing the buildings as they did arms"

(172). As we will see, Brazil moved from a near total dependence on foreign sources for military hardware at the beginning of the twentieth century to virtual self-sufficiency and major exporter status as the century comes to a close.

In the early 1900s, Brazil was dependent on Britain and Italy for naval vessels and on Britain for the munitions necessary to equip its meager fleet. Germany was the Brazilian supplier of cannons, carbines, pistols, powder, and optical equipment. Denmark supplied rifles, and even the canvas used to make field equipment was imported from England (Hilton, 1982:634). The problems associated with a reliance on foreign sources for weapons and field supplies were painfully evident to Brazilian military officers and can be seen in the following passage by Stanley Hilton:

Ships hastily ordered from the US during the naval revolt in 1893, for example, were said to be in pathetic condition. At the turn of the century, the Ministry of War bought almost 750,000 Mauser cartridges that turned out to be defective; smokeless powder that arrived for its Krupp artillery also proved unsuitable and had to be exchanged. Military technicians in 1906 discovered an extremely high percentage of cracked shells among a consignment for testing weapons, and in 1911 tests conducted on 145,000 recently purchased Mauser rifles showed the barrels to be structurally weak.(1982:636)

Although the Brazilian military was not heavily involved in producing the weapons required to outfit the soldiers, some of the more basic necessities of military life were being supplied domestically. In the early part of the twentieth century, according to Hilton,

the extent of civilian participation in defense work is not clear. Since the backbone of manufacturing activity during the era was the textile sector, logically the major civilian role would be that of supplying clothing, bedding, and the like. The minister of war reported in 1900 that, when he opened public bidding for a contract to furnish uniforms, there had been a huge number of respondents. But in addition, there was a vast array of light manufactures that the armed forces obtained from local industry. In the early 1900's, for example, the army bought shoes, dishes, building materials, and paper from domestic companies. The navy, for its part, was doing business on the eve of WWI with more than sixty firms, excluding shipbuilders, that provided scores of products, from acids, inks, and soap to carbon paper and wire. (1982:645)

The experience of World War I made clear the costs associated with a near total dependence on foreign suppliers for military hardware. Brazil had ordered artillery equipment and machine guns from Germany just before the outbreak of hostilities, only to have them sit in Hamburg throughout the war (McCann, 1981:174). A chorus of voices proclaimed the need to develop domestic production facilities if such a precarious dependency was to be avoided in the future. A spokesman for the Army General Staff put it very succinctly in 1917 when he argued, "We need to manufacture our explosives and powders, our rifles and machine guns; cast our cannon and battleships; build our vessels, our airplanes and dirigibles, our submarines and minesweepers; make our canned goods and fodder; weave our cloth, [and produce our] gear and utensils, from the raw material to the delicate finishing touch" (quoted in Hilton, 1982:638). The key to achieving these goals was the development of an indigenous steel-production capability.

In 1919 the acting president, Delfim Moreira da Costa Ribeiro, declared to the Congress: "The organization of our military industry will be the greatest patriotic achievement of the generation that accomplishes it" (quoted in McCann, 1981:178). According to Frank McCann: "A year later his successor repeated these sentiments and . . . linked arms production to the necessity for local sources of steel. And he observed that until a national steel industry existed, Brazilians would be kept in complete dependence" (178). Although the vision of a national steel-production capability and the independence from foreign military supplies was widely held at the time, moving the nation in the direction espoused by the elites was not readily attainable. "The goal of independent iron, steel, and arms production involved more than a few factories. The country had to be mapped. Roads and railroads had to be built; mines and mineral processing developed; and telegraph and telephone networks laid out. Managers and workers had to be educated and trained, a host of subsidiary supply industries had to come into being, and somehow money had to be found to pay for it all" (178). It would not be until the Vargas regime, when authority became centralized enough to marshal the resources necessary to take on this challenge, that any hope for a national steel industry would materialize (Hilton, 1982:646). And it would not be until after World War II that the obstacles in the path of national development would be sufficiently overcome to permit large-scale iron and steel production, not the least of which was the technical skills required for the engineering and manufacturing processes. The first Brazilian university was not even inaugurated until 1931.

During the interwar period, Brazil again turned to foreign sources to equip its military, and again, the hostilities that culminated in World War II interrupted that supply network. In 1938 the Brazilians signed a $55-million agreement with Krupp of Germany for artillery and accessories, only to have the war interfere with delivery. As a result, the Brazilians reluctantly turned to the United States for the needed weaponry. This agreement, however, required that Brazil allow the United States access to naval and air bases and the commitment of Brazilian air and ground forces to the European theater (McCann, 1981:184). The need for domestic production of military material continued to be of paramount concern to the military elite, though by the beginning of World War II, Brazilian industry had begun to supply the military with many of the accessories and components required of a fully equipped armed forces.

By 1940, civilian industries were supplying copper items and aluminum, small amounts of steel, cellulose products, components for weapons and ammunition, machine tools, textiles, semimanufactured parts, electrical equipment, and parachutes. This supporting cast of supplier firms consisted of more than sixteen production facilities in over a half dozen cities (Hilton, 1982:660). These manufactured items indicate an increasing level of sophistication over the textiles, shoes, and dishes supplied by civilian industry during the early years of the century. But they also suggest a greater degree of coordination between the civilian and military sectors of Brazilian society, a glimpse of what the future would hold.

The war played a significant role in increasing domestic production of military supplies. In 1942 Vargas decreed a series of measures designed to discipline the economy according to military requirements. Government support for industries involved in production for the military took the form of tax exemptions, special freight rates, guaranteed orders, and bank loans. The Ministry of War offered a contract for the establishment of an arms industry; the army pushed for loans to establish chrome, zinc, copper, and aluminum facilities; long-term contracts for artillery shells, detonators, shell casings, and grenade casings were advocated; the army devised a plan for the domestic production of machine guns; and the Ministry of War initiated the development of an optical factory through its interest in binoculars and range-finders. "Activity in federal war plants was substantial, as output reached an all-time high in 1942 and then increased another 60% the next year" (Hilton, 1982:661-62).

In the postwar period, the Brazilian military continued to purchase arms abroad, mainly surpluses from U.S. stocks, while working with civilian industry to develop the indigenous capability to produce sophisticated weaponry. Brazil moved toward an independent arms-production capability within the context of an economic-development plan in which the military became increasingly influential (McCann, 1981). Plans were made for the development of a domestic steel industry with the technical assistance of the United States. After a rather slow start due to wartime priorities, a steel mill at Volta Redonda began production in 1946. The initial capacity was 270,000 tons but grew to 1.2 million tons by 1965 and by 1979 totaled 13.9 million tons, making Brazil the world's thirteenth-largest steel producer (McCann, 1981:185). As an indication of the amount of organization required to produce at this level, the president of the Venezuelan Metallurgy and Mining Industry Association noted that producing fifteen million tons of steel entailed extensive training. "48,000 workers . . . will work directly in the industry; that industry generates indirect employment for 960,000 workers and . . . therefore, concrete plans must be devised to provide housing, water, energy, education, sanitation and transportation" (quoted in Howell et al., 1988:252). By 1986 Brazil consumed approximately fourteen million tons of domestically produced steel, not all of which was affiliated with military-based production, but without the military consumption and organization, the Brazilian steel industry might not have had such a successful beginning.

The Volta Redonda steel mill was part of a concerted effort by Brazilian elites to develop the industrial infrastructure of the country, using national security as the motivating force. The need to develop the industrial infrastructure of Brazilian society closely followed the need for a relaxation of the dependence on foreign sources to equip the military forces. The domestic production of weapons would serve as the stimulant for the demand of the fledgling industries. "By the end of 1945 the army . . . had improved and expanded existing arsenals and munitions works and added new ones; it had a growing number of well-trained technicians; it looked with pride on Brazil's new steel mill then coming on line; and oil production and exploration were going forward. Moreover, the military had firm links with civilian industrialists and politicians" (Howell et al., 186).

The developments in the Brazilian arms industry moved slowly but steadily in the early postwar period. Inroads continued to be made in the production of small arms and ammunition, but private investors seemed unwilling to take the risks necessary to embark on the initial startup of weapon-production facilities. In 1949 Brazil still needed to import 30,000 semiautomatic rifles from Belgium, but the contract was contingent on the transfer of the technological blueprints necessary to permit local manufacture. It was not until 1954 that the arsenal at Rio de Janerio produced its first cannon; before the year was out, "three great industrial establishments were working on the initial order of fifty guns" (Hilton, 1982:668). A national motor factory established during the war began to convert from the production and repair of aircraft engines to include the production of agricultural equipment, truck motors, and auto parts in its repertoire, eventually producing Alfa-Romeo trucks (669). An industry started with military applications in mind soon began to produce vehicles for civilian consumption while maintaining--and even expanding--the military component of the manufacturing process. The lessons learned were not lost on Brazilian industrialists.

The coordination between civilian manufacturers and the military greatly benefited civilian industry. According to Stanley Hilton:

Contacts between the military and industry were continuously broadened. . . . Military and industrial representatives worked closely together on various agencies and councils involved in promoting general economic development. . . . It was a subcommittee headed by Commander Lucio Meira that drew up the plan in 1952 for creating an automobile industry by imposing progressive restrictions on imports of automotive parts and banning after July 1953 the importation of complete vehicles (1982:670).

By the mid-1950s, a vast array of civilian companies was producing for the military, and industrial projects "such as the automotive industry were under way that would open up new dimensions for military production" (673).

Brazil utilized a two-pronged approach to the development of an indigenous arms-production capability. The first entailed the creation of technical institutes that could train the engineers and scientists necessary for the domestic design of weapon systems and the capability for technological innovation. Originally two such facilities were organized around the needs of the defense industry: the Aerospace Technical Center (CTA) and the Technical Center of the Army (CTEX). Both eventually played an integral part in the development of the Brazilian aviation and armored-vehicle industries. The second approach was to import the technology from the major arms producers, using this imported technology as the platform from which to expand domestic production. The development of the Brazilian tank industry is illustrative of how the importation of technology led to the domestic design and production of a broad range of tracked military vehicles; the aircraft industry is a clear example of the two approaches working in unison.

In the 1950s Brazil acquired most of its tanks from the surplus stocks of the United States. Approximately eighty M3A1 light tanks and over three hundred M-41 Walker Bulldog tanks were delivered to Brazil through U.S. military aid programs. But by the early 1970s these tanks needed complete overhauls; the Bernardini company of São Paulo was awarded the contract to rebuild the tanks. The engine and turret were replaced, along with a new 90mm gun and an indigenously produced fire-control system. The next step was for Bernardini to produce a modified version of the M3A1 tank, using imported engines and guns but a domestically produced chassis. This led to a contract to build an entirely new Brazilian tank, still dependent on foreign components but of indigenous design (Louscher and Schwarz, 1989). By 1985 Brazil was one of the world's largest producers of armored vehicles, and Bernardini, who had initiated Brazil's move into tank production, was far outflanked as a tank producer by the ENGESA group. Bernardini, however, had more meager beginnings, far removed from the world of tank production. It started out as a manufacturer of safes and office furniture and in 1982 was listed as one of the largest enterprises in the furniture and decoration sector of Brazilian industry. At that time it was listed as having 365 employees (Lock, 1986:93).

The aircraft industry in Brazil went through a somewhat similar developmental history. Although the Brazilian military tinkered with the idea of domestically produced aircraft as early as 1932 and, by 1939, had tendered a contract for an aircraft factory, this resulted in only a small number of relatively unsophisticated planes being produced (Hilton, 1982:655). Thirty years later EMBRAER, a mixed public-private company started by engineers from the CTA, burst onto the market with a mix of civilian and military aircraft. Acquiring technology from both Piper Aircraft of the United States and Aermacchi of Italy, as well as designs developed by engineers at the CTA, EMBRAER acquired a full line of military and civilian aircraft. With its own niche in the world market, EMBRAER grew to a company of 12,000 employees (*Aviation Week and Space Technology*, "Embraer Moves", 1987). In 1985 it was the fourth-largest Brazilian investor in research and development, and today it has produced and delivered nearly four thousand aircraft worldwide (Franko-

Jones, 1987-88:52). In 1979 EMBRAER relied on the military market for 20 percent of its sales (McCann, 1981:191); by 1983 that figure had risen to nearly one-third, with expectations of a higher proportion going to the military in the years to come (Franko-Jones, 1986:152-57). In 1987 EMBRAER had generated approximately $400 million in sales from exports and had advanced to the stage of being an exporter of technology rather than just the manufactured product (Franko-Jones, 1987-88:58).

As we have seen, Brazil has evolved from a being a country totally reliant on foreign sources for its military hardware at the turn of the century to being one of the ten largest exporters of conventional weapons. In the early 1900s Brazil even had to import the canvas with which to make field supplies; today it exports sophisticated jet fighters and various missile systems. According to Frank McCann,

Beginning in 1975 . . . the army and civilian manufacturers found that they could lessen costs and simplify supply by using civilian components rather than turning out special military ones. And using the army's relatively modest orders to cover basic costs, civilian companies turned to the international arms market to achieve economy of scale. [By 1979] some fifty-five companies are involved in arms production, while about three hundred more supply uniforms and other quartermaster items. Altogether these enterprises employ some one-hundred thousand workers, and so their impact on the internal labor market is being felt . . . their sales, which in 1979 earned $400 million, are producing revenues that will help the government pay off the country's reported $50 million debt. . . . At the end of 1979, arms figured fifth on the list of exported manufactures. (1981:190)

But the export strategy had another purpose that served the narrow needs of the military. While the revenues generated from the sale of weapons abroad were important to the Brazilian economy, the exports also relieved the military from the need to stockpile large supplies of domestically produced weapons. The Brazilian army has an adequate supply of *Cascaveis* (tanks) for training purposes, so with the supplier at hand, it need not spend scarce cash on stockpiling.

By 1985 the Brazilian military had entrenched itself even deeper into the industrial sector of society. Three large manufacturers of weapon systems accounted for approximately 4 percent of Brazilian exports: EMBRAER, ENGESA, and AVIBRAS. Collectively these three companies directly employed more than 25,000 people, with each maintaining a supplier network consisting of hundreds of firms. According to one source, the Brazilian navy oversees the operation of twenty five shipyards employing nearly 100,000 workers. These facilities produce supertankers, radar, sonar, naval engines, propellers, and anchors, along with modern submarines and missile-launching corvettes (Young, 1982:213). In 1973 there were 356 suppliers to the fledgling EMBRAER group, producing such accessories as "electrical and steel cables, metal plates and molds, instruments, tires, special dyes, plastics for the windows, antennae, and brakes" (Franko-Jones, 1986:80). Likewise the armored-vehicle industry has strong forward-backward linkages to the industrial sector. According to Patrice Franko-Jones, ENGESA currently "draws from 850 of the 1,500 domestic auto parts factories with approximately 400 of the suppliers on permanent contract" (1986:37).

Although no exact figures are available for the number of people employed by the state-run holding company for the production of small arms and ammunition, IMBEL, Jordan Young suggests that the company employed 100,000 people in 1980 (1982:90). All told, the number of Brazilians directly involved in the manufacture of defense-related materials quickly climbs into the hundreds of thousands.[1] Alfred Stepan, one of the more notable scholars on Brazilian civil-military relations, comes to a similar conclusion regarding the extent and penetration of military production into Brazilian society. According to Stepan: "a key point that needs to be recognized is that nonmilitary industrialists, both domestic and foreign, are a major component in the military-industrial complex. Clovis Brigagao estimates that 50 Brazilian firms directly produce military equipment . . . and that 200,000 people are involved in the arms industry" (1988:83). Regardless of whose figure is closest to the actual number of Brazilians employed in military production, it is clear that by 1985 the Brazilian military accounted for a substantial portion of Brazilian employment. The number of people directly and indirectly employed in steel production, the size of the manufacturing sector dependent on the military, the size of the military bureaucracy required to organize such a large-scale effort, and the number of active-duty personnel all attest to the depth of military penetration into civil society. A military-industrial-complex has clearly developed within Brazilian society.

As we have seen in the above discussion, Brazil has evolved from a country with a near total dependence on foreign sources for equipping its armed forces to a country that is one of the world's top exporters of military equipment. The size of the work force and the amount of industrial infrastructure devoted to military production showed a slow but steady increase from the turn of the century until the late 1960s. A myriad of forces coalesced behind an industrial strategy based on the development of a viable and competitive arms industry. As military production began to take root within the Brazilian society, the growth curve changed from geometric to exponential. Today Brazil is a major player in the world of arms production. Its weapons have performed remarkably well in a number of international conflicts, including the Iran-Iraq, the Malvina-Falkland, and the Lybian-Egyptian wars. The organization of civil society around the production of the tools of the military has become more complete through the eighty five years covered in this study. Brazilians have moved from the simple manufacture of shoes, uniforms, dishes, and soaps by the civilian sector--along with the assembly of shells by the military ordnance department--to the production of sophisticated jet aircraft, tanks, air-to-air missile systems, and naval vessels. To achieve this transformation from rudimentary military supplies to high-technology weapons, Brazil developed the requisite iron and steel industries, railroad networks, and communication facilities, all employing hundreds of people. The education system also played the handmaiden to the military sector. Before Brazil could move along the cycle from an importer of hardware to a modifier of hardware and from there to an importer of technology and eventually a creator of technology (Franko-Jones, 1986:197), it had to develop a system of higher education that could train capable engineers. The army and the air force readily obliged. Since 1950, the Aerospace Technical Institute (ITA) of the CTA has "graduated over 72,000 engineers and granted 300 postgraduate degrees" (Franko-Jones, 1987-88:51). While the penetration of civil society by military organization has been quite substantial over the past eighty five years, the real test of the entrenchment of the Brazilian military will come in the near future, when the market for military exports is predicted to drop precipitously. Two paths appear plausible. The first would be to convert military manufacturing facilities to the production of civilian products; the second would be for the Brazilian armed forces to guarantee a market for the continued production of weapons. If Brazil adopts the latter course, it may very likely require an external threat to justify its choices.

COERCION AS A FOREIGN POLICY
TOOL AND THE FEEDBACK LINK

The final place to turn in this historical treatment is to examine the extent to which violent foreign policy has taken on a more central role in Brazilian international diplomacy, as well as any evidence of the hypothesized feedback. What would be expected, in terms of the theoretical argument, is that as the level of societal militarization increased, so too would the propensity of the state to become embroiled in foreign conflicts. But the evidence suggests otherwise. Furthermore, the theoretical argument posits that as a society becomes more militarized, the perception of an external threat will be more visible to the general public. As mentioned at the outset, this latter issue cannot be addressed sufficiently at this juncture and must await more systematic treatment. By any account, however, there is no support for the thesis that that an increase in societal militarization and the violent foreign policy of the state are part of a self-amplifying process in Brazil. The path toward a more highly militarized society appeared to follow a pattern consistent with the theoretical model, but Brazil has yet to reach a stage where it manifests itself in the use of international coercion.

As we have seen above, Brazil was involved in a few military confrontations with its neighbors during the early part of the century and did commit some troops to the Allied effort in World War II, but in general it has been able to remain fairly aloof from much of the international violence. The two world wars were clearly seen as a threat to Brazilian sovereignty and as such were used to mobilize societal resources behind an expanded role of the military. But the development of a burgeoning Military-Industrial Complex has not led to the increased use of violence in Brazil's foreign policy. However, a more systematic examination is warranted.

Using Correlates of War data, we get a much clearer indication of the extent to which the Brazilian elite relied on force to achieve its foreign-policy objectives. What it is evident from a perusal of the data is that the Brazilians were no more prone to entanglement in foreign disputes in the latter part of the century than they were when their economy was less tied to the production of military hardware. Brazil was involved in only a handful of militarized disputes in the post-World War II period, and between the early 1970s and 1985, when Brazilian industry surged ahead in the production of armored vehicles and military aircraft, there was no more than one ongoing dispute at any one time. This is in stark contrast to the use of coercion by a country such as the United States, although it is to be expected somewhat, given the different roles each country plays in the international arena. The theoretical model that has been articulated would have led us to predict that as the Brazilian society became more tied to the institutions of the military, the elite would have taken on a much more aggressive foreign-policy posture. This does not seem to have happened.

While this anecdotal evidence fails to demonstrate a self-amplifying feedback between societal militarization and the coercive behavior of the state, the result was not totally unexpected. Although Brazil has taken great strides in the development of a domestic arms-manufacturing industry, the society cannot be considered highly militarized. As we saw with the United States, the strength of the relationship between militarization and violent foreign policy appears to be in large part a function of the crossing of a threshold in the extent of militarization. It is unlikely that Brazil has even approached such a threshold.

SUMMARY

As a test of the hypotheses outlined earlier, this historical treatment is far from complete. But as a glimpse of the evolution in the coordination between the civil sector of the Brazilian society and its military counterpart, this analysis has been enlightening, particularly in terms of the developmental aspects of the theoretical model. Brazil clearly shows signs of responding to a perceived threat to "national security" by resorting to the development of a military infrastructure. This focus on the military, furthermore, has contributed to the centralization of the Brazilian state, to the development of an industrial sector capable of competing on a global scale, and to the laying of the structural infrastructure on which this political and economic expansion could occur. At least this aspect of Brazil's development is consistent with the theoretical model.

As we have seen, Brazil has evolved from a decentralized country often waging war against itself to a country with a centralized state with a well-developed Military-Industrial Complex. As a result of this "complex," the number of jobs directly tied to the production of military hardware is quite substantial, and the military hierarchy plays a decisive role in the day-to-day operation of the political affairs of the state. Civilian attitudes toward the military have also shifted as the military has taken on a greater role in the society. In the early stages of nation-building there was clearly a barrier between the military and the civilians. Today Brazil maintains an armed force of nearly 300,000 people, with recruitment based on voluntary enlistment.[2] And by some estimates, an equal number of civilians are involved in the production of weapons and material to equip this formidable military. While no mention has been made of the size or influence of the civilian bureaucracy that supports the military, a reasonable estimate would suggest that it is a considerable fraction of those on active duty. All told, the Brazilian military directly accounts for probably at least one million jobs, which as a percent of the labor force is quite small. However, in a developing country that suffers from severe problems of underemployment, hunger and malnutrition, and vast income disparities, this segment of the population could wield a disproportionate amount of political and economic influence. The ramifications of this could prove ominous.

The theoretical argument that I have spelled out postulates that the increased penetration of the military into the civil sector of society will have implications for the behavior of the state in the international arena. More specifically, there will be a self-amplifying feedback between societal militarization and the violent behavior of the state. And although the descriptive evidence presented above does little to support the feedback hypothesis, it does seem to support some of the evolutionary components of the hypothesized militarization process. Threats were originally the motivating force for the development of a centralized military, though threats appear to have taken a backseat to economic issues in the later part of the century. Whether the extent to which the Brazilian society is militarized can influence the state's use of force in the global arena is difficult to determine, though it is apparent that the emphasis on the production of military hardware has, in part, shaped foreign economic and political relations. If in no other way, this can be seen in the policies that guide the sale of Brazilian weapons to foreign clients.

The key to the evolution of Brazilian society may turn on whether or not its military-based industrialization strategy begins to feed on itself, in the end becoming a means of economic strength. From the perspective of a political and economic development stratagem, the Brazilian experience has been quite successful. The nation has a more unified state, a stronger economy, and a greater sense of nationalism, and on many dimensions it is approaching the ranks of the major powers. But whether this path to success will begin to "require" the manipulation of perceptions and the level of coercion in foreign diplomacy remains to be seen. Expectations of a shrinking market for weapons may pose an unenviable choice for Brazilians: either to demilitarize that portion of their industrial sector producing weapons by converting to the production of civilian products (which could have severe short-term costs), or to absorb a substantial portion of the weapons they produce into their own force structures. The latter may be more costly in the long run. Recent events, however, seem to suggest that Brazil *may* be opting for the retooling strategy.

7

Conclusion

In the preceding chapters I have outlined a theoretical model, discussed operational indicators, measurements, and analytical techniques, and presented the findings from the analyses. Though some of the results are quite tentative, others are fairly robust and, in all, remarkably convergent with the theoretical argument outlined in the introductory chapter. This final chapter will attempt to tie the whole story together and, in the end, offer tentative generalizations from what we know about the militarization process and the relationship between the internal organization of society and the external behavior of the state. I will start with a brief recapitulation of the model and my findings, moving on to broaden the scope to which my argument and findings are potentially generalizable.

SUMMARY OF THE THEORETICAL ARGUMENT

My central thesis was that militarization is a process that unfolds through time and that involves interactions among attributes and behaviors of the society, the state, interstate relations, and the global system. My conception of militarization focused on how thoroughly the civil sector of society was organized around the production and preparations for war and the effect of this societal momentum on the use of force by the state. The theoretical model presented in the opening chapter argued that militarization can play a pivotal role in political and economic development, serving to build the political and institutional infrastructure in the early stages of nation-building. At some intermediate point, militarization can act as an engine for technological or industrial growth, thereby bolstering a fledgling economic infrastructure. Yet at a more advanced stage, as the military sector begins to consume vast amounts of resources--both human and capital--militarization often works as an engine for political and economic decline.

At the forefront of my theoretical argument was the notion that the militarization of society and the violent external behavior of the state were part of a self-amplifying feedback mechanism. The more thoroughly the society became involved in the preparations for war, the more predisposed the state would be to employ violence in pursuit of foreign-policy objectives. A number of factors appeared to contribute to the self-amplifying nature of this hypothesized feedback, including domestic political and economic pressures as well as heightened international tensions that result from parabellum-type behaviors.

Organizing a society around the military is, of course, not a straightforward task. Extracting resources from the civil sector and allocating them to the military is unlikely to be the preferred policy of the general public, given their other needs and preferences. One way to help ensure voluntary compliance with such a transfer of resources is to cultivate the perception that the international environment poses a threat to domestic tranquility. As Harold Lasswell pointed out quite some time ago, the public must be socialized to accept the condition of the continued expectation of violence, lest they resist the transfer of resources from civilian to military consumption. The perception of a threat is a necessary condition for this diversion of resources, though the threat need not be existential in nature. The manipulation of the perception of a threat can suffice. This "manipulation," furthermore, requires the socialization of the general public to the worldview of the elite, not in the sense of a "false consciousness" but rather a conceptual understanding of the world as a violent, dangerous, and threatening place. There is an enemy out there, but it surely does not come from within and is oftentimes ephemeral. If the socialization of the public is one component in the militarization of society, then there must be agents of socialization that maintain both a positive image of the military and the notion of a society embattled by some international evil.

I posited that a variety of variables, ranging from the substate to the system level, contributed to a feedback in which the militarization of society and the violent behavior of the state were locked into a self-amplifying cycle. This cycle was fed by the political use of symbols that convey a heightened sense of efficacy on the military and emphasize its role in defending society from the ravages of the international environment. In an attempt to verify this scholarly hunch, I embarked on a quest for empirical evidence.

SUMMARY OF FINDINGS

The analytical approach to testing for the hypothesized feedback was broken down into four separate components; linear regression models were used on data generated from the United States and Great Britain, 1900-1985, and a historical case study of the evolution of the Brazilian military was presented. As an initial step I divided the feedback model into two separate sets of analyses, one examining factors that predict changes in the extent to which society is militarized and the other examining the domestic and international conditions that predict the violent behavior of the state. The two halves of the model were then reunited, and the impact of the hypothesized feedback was subjected to a direct test. The symbolic-politics component of the argument was then put to the test by examining the relationships between societal symbols that help contribute to the perception of a hostile global arena and the extent to which the United States and Great Britain were militarized. And finally, a historical analysis of the evolution of the Brazilian military as an institution was used to provide insight into the potential for generalizing the theoretical argument beyond the highly industrial, major-power categories.

Two points might help to put the summary of my findings into perspective: (1) the data for the United States fit the models much better than that of Great Britain, holding across all sets of empirical analyses; and (2) there is a remarkable convergence between the findings from both countries. The magnitude of the substantive impact of a particular variable on another may vary, but the *direction* of that impact--as determined by the sign of the coefficients--is quite often the same. In general the empirical analyses offer strong support for most of the theoretical arguments, however, this interpretation is neither universal nor definitive.

In chapter 2, I attempted to model the process by which societies militarize, with predictor variables ranging from the number of ongoing disputes to the level of technological development in each country. One of the more interesting findings was that the violent foreign policy of the state affects the level of militarization differently when it is above or below a threshold of the extent to which that society was militarized. Violent foreign policy in general was negatively associated with militarization, though in a more highly militarized society violent foreign policy appears to contribute to increased militarization. Thus, in a more highly militarized society, involvement in international disputes leads to a greater entrenchment of the military. This result is highly consistent with my theoretical model, as well as those models articulated by Ted Gurr (1988), J. David Singer (1970), and others. During less militarized periods, however, international violence tends to facilitate the demilitarization of the society, a finding that runs counter to my theoretical argument. A further result of the first segment of this analysis suggests that increased militarization in the previous period is associated with increases in the current year, which is consistent with a bureaucratic politics argument. Interestingly enough, in the more fully specified feedback model, this bureaucratic politics argument did not stand up to empirical testing. The extent to which the perception of a threat is maintained in the mass media appears to strongly influence the level of militarization, which not only confirms the thesis that I have postulated but also is consistent with a body of work emanating from the field of sociology. Furthermore, it was hypothesized that technological development would play a role in the military's penetration into society, though the evidence was mixed.

Overall, the findings gave encouraging signs that the more fully specified self-amplifying feedback process might stand the test of empirical scrutiny.

The third chapter approached the other side of this hypothesized feedback, attempting to model those factors that will predict the use of violence by the state in the international arena. Much of the theoretical reasoning and the empirical evidence to date posits that system-level variables should account for a considerable amount of the variation in the violent behavior of a state. Using two system-level variables as predictors--capability concentration and system leadership--as well one domestic variable--societal militarization--I was able to demonstrate that militarization in either Britain or the United States is a strong predictor of state-led international violence. Systemic-level variables, however, were less consistent across cases. For example, system leadership appears to come at a cost to the United States of an increase in the resort to force to achieve foreign-policy objectives, whereas in Great Britain system leadership is associated with a reduction in the amount of international violence in which it was a participant. This result appears to lend support to advocates and evidence identifying a hegemonic actor as a critical component in patterns of global violence (see Boswell and Sweat, 1992). The effect of system leadership, for instance, suggests that the decline of one hegemonic leader and the rise of the successor may be evident. Likewise, the system concentration findings are also consistent with arguments about the role of hegemonic actors in international politics. The evidence suggests that the more concentrated the distribution of capabilities the less violent will be the central members of the system. This latter finding lends some credence to those who argue that the fewer the number of poles, the more stable will be the system (Waltz, 1979), though this is somewhat incongruent with the findings of Paul Huth, Christopher Gelpi, and Scott Bennett (1992) and Ted Hopf (1991).

One problem remained, however. If the data used in this analysis were produced as a result of a feedback between societal militarization and the violent foreign policy of the state, then the results just summarized would be suspect due to an egregious violation of one of the central assumptions of least squares estimating. To get unbiased and consistent estimates of the various hypothesized relationships, we needed to specify the statistical model as a system of equations; this would also allow for a more direct test of the feedback hypothesis, as illustrated in Chapter 4.

With the model specified as a system of equations, there was little change in the substantive impact of the predictor on the outcome variables. The marginal effect of most variables in the model did change--relative to the unidirectional models--reflecting the increased consistency in the parameter estimates obtained with a more fully specified model. But in nearly all instances, the signs of the coefficients were fairly constant, suggesting that the effect of the predictor variables is quite robust across model specifications. This was for the most part expected. However, the effect of previous militarization on current levels did reverse direction under the more rigorous model specification. The bureaucratic politics argument apparently does not hold up when taking into account system-level explanations. The most glaring result of the test for a self-amplifying feedback among societal militarization and the use of violence by the state was that at first glance it apparently is not self-amplifying in the United States. In fact, the findings suggest that these two behaviors run at crosscurrents. The immediate inference is that the theoretical model needs to be revisited, but a closer examination should give pause to the notion of revamping the theoretical model before strengthening the empirical tests. First of all, there was evidence of a self-amplifying feedback in Great Britain, so the theoretical argument is not without merit. But in light of the evidence, in chapter 2, that the impact of militarization works differently above and below a threshold, the disconfirmation of the feedback hypothesis is somewhat suspect. A further complicating factor in the inability to empirically demonstrate a self-amplifying feedback in the United States can be laid at the doorstep of indicator construction. Let me try to clarify this position.

The theoretical argument postulated that in a more highly militarized society, the state would be more prone to resort to the use of force to achieve foreign-policy objectives. But the range of options available to the state that relies on violence in pursuit of policy is much broader than the overt use of military force--or threat to use force--against another state, the indicator used in this analysis. Military intervention on behalf of another state, the covert use of force against a foreign actor, and military aid in support of insurgency or counterinsurgency are examples of the use of force in pursuit of foreign-policy objectives that are not captured by this indicator. Each of these alternative uses of force, moreover, not only is consistent with the theoretical argument but also, under certain circumstances, would be the expected behavior of the state. For example, as the leader of an alliance organized predominantly around an ideological dimension, the United States has been "obligated" to defend that ideology from encroachments by counter-ideological forces--in this instance, defending the "free world" from Communists. But in light of the enormous costs of directly confronting the progenitor of those challenges, a more covert approach to interventionism was integrated into the foreign-policy process. So it seems that the extent to which violence is a central component of foreign policy initiatives does not necessarily change, but the form it takes may well do so.

Although analyzing the type of violence used in pursuit of these policy objectives is beyond the scope of this project, the analytical framework appears to support my findings. The demonstrated self-amplifying feedback in Great Britain is partially determined by this nation's place in the international system. A nonleader of an alliance would be predisposed to let the dominant member take the brunt of responsibility for maintaining alliance integrity. Therefore, Britain would mobilize to fight, though only in circumstances when a more traditional use of force was appropriate. The British would have little interest in, and limited capability for the projection of force through more covert methods. Expanding the range of the indicators used in this analysis is central to a more complete understanding of the militarization/foreign-policy feedback, though that task will have to await further research.

But before moving on, we must not be to hasty in dismissing alternative explanations. The democratic process may offer a reasonable counter proposition for why there is an overall trend for increased international violence to be associated with decreased militarization, though neither is this straightforward. One way to interpret these findings may be that the public becomes weary of the costs associated with foreign conflicts and demands a retrenchment in the size and scope of the military. But once a society becomes more highly militarized, this restraining effect changes roles--in effect, even the democratic process gets subverted by the persistent influence of the military sector. This argument is quite consistent with Harold Lasswell's revised version of his "garrison state" (1962). Such an interpretation of the relationship among democracy, militarization, and international violence is also consistent with the difference in the results between U.S. and British data, as well as the threshold finding for the United States. The democratic process had yet to be subverted in the pre-Cold War United States and had long ago succumbed in Great Britain. What this might suggest, therefore, is that the increased use of force as a policy tool is associated with an increase in the influence of the military, but only when there is not a strong democratic tradition to keep it in check. The indicator may be adequate, but the theoretical postulates need to be more fully explored.

The final place to turn in this summary is to the role of societal symbols in helping to ensure the support of the general public for the policies of the security elite. If spending for military, as opposed to civilian, consumption is economically inefficient, then presumably the general public would be reluctant to support this diversion of resources, absent a perceived threat. And if public support is to be maintained in light of conflicting evidence regarding that threat, then the public needs to be conditioned to accept and condone the policies of the elite through the political socialization of public attitudes and beliefs. To a large extent this is an argument that is central to the literature on the Military-Industrial Complex and models of a garrison state.

The prevalence of war toys and war movies--as determined by the numbers offered for sale in each year--was used as an indicator of the symbols available to the various agents of socialization; their relationships with public attitudes toward the military and trends in militarization were tracked over time. While no causal argument could be made--either theoretically or empirically--regarding the effect of, say, the availability of war toys on attitudes toward the military, the evidence presented was suggestive of an underlying relationship. The bivariate correlations between trends in the number of war toys offered for sale in any one year and the extent to which the United States was militarized were remarkably strong; this was true for war movies as well. In Great Britain the findings were not as robust, and in fact, the availability of war toys was weakly and negatively associated with societal militarization, though this too appeared to be largely a data problem related to the inability to generate "toy counts" throughout the entire temporal period. In both countries there was also a fairly strong empirical relationship between the extent to which promilitary themes were reported in the mass media and the level of societal militarization. Again, these findings are only suggestive, but they do point to a potentially influential role for symbolic politics in the organizing of a society around the preparations for war. Much more systematic research is in order here.

SOCIETAL ATTRIBUTES AND STATE BEHAVIOR: SOME GENERALIZATIONS

Taken by themselves, the findings presented in this study are quite revealing, though the broader implications may prove to be more central to our understanding of the interactions among the society, the state, and interstate relations. Generally, the evidence in the previous chapters confirms much of the theoretical reasoning behind the militarization process. But when taking the feedback between the organization of society and the external behavior of the state to a more general plateau, some very interesting implications emerge. To demonstrate this, I need to generalize these findings to that broader category of cases where the society and the state interact and where that interaction has implications for interstate relations. What becomes apparent is that distinct forms of societal organization may generate enough momentum to force the state elite to act in a manner consistent with a narrowly defined view of "national security." Two examples should make this point clear.

Before launching into the examples, however, let me first try to put at ease concerns that I cannot generalize about a feedback among societal attributes and state behaviors when the empirical support for such a thesis is mixed. Although a self-amplifying feedback was only demonstrated with the most rigorous test for Great Britain, there is some empirical support for the hypothesized self-amplifying process in the United States. Recall that originally the number of ongoing disputes in the United States was associated with the demilitarization of society, though when I controlled for the number of disputes during periods of relatively high military mobilization, there was a strong positive association. The inference I drew was that the hypothesized feedback operates differently above and below some threshold in the level of militarization, at least in the United States.[1] This finding supports the theoretical argument and, when viewed in conjunction with the narrow scope of the indicator used to tap into the violent foreign policy of the state, gives good reason to stay the course.

The first example is the U.S. automobile industry. For the most part, those who run the three automotive giants, as well as those who make the foreign-trade policies that directly affect the fortunes of these companies, are advocates of free trade. Almost without exception, these political and economic leaders make the philosophical argument that it is the market that should determine supply, demand, and price. Furthermore, these three companies create employment, either directly or indirectly, for hundreds of thousands of U.S. citizens. The constituency group composed of those who derive their livelihood from the continued economic viability of the U.S. automotive industry is quite substantial. In 1987, for example, nearly three-quarters of a million people worked directly in the automotive or automotive parts industries (M.V.M.A., 1990); this figure excludes those indirectly involved in the auto manufacturing process or those providing services for the auto industry and its employees. If there is a city that epitomizes a localized "society" organized around the auto industry, it is Detroit, Michigan.

Generalizing the results of my analysis on militarizing a society, one might predict that organizing a large portion of society around a particular industry would lead to hostile international rhetoric, if not policy, on the part of the political and economic elite. This hostile behavior, furthermore, would not only increase the fervor with which the public would identify with that industry, but the hostility would appear to run counter to the principles around which the automobile market is organized. Following the predictions of the model, as the American automobile industry becomes less competitive in world markets, the response is not to reassess the long-term prospects for maintaining competitiveness in this increasingly deconcentrating industrial sector but rather to respond with language and policies reminiscent of warlike behavior. The domestic automotive constituency is too large and too vocal to permit a drastic reduction in the reliance on this industry, which a market-based analysis might suggest. Instead, in language that betrays their belief in market forces, the political and economic leaders wage preemptive or punitive war on the most aggressive competitors. Japan-bashing, import restrictions, and threats of "retaliation" become the hallmark of the foreign economic policy-making process. All are fed, furthermore, by media blitzes that challenge the public to "buy American." The greater the feverish pitch to wage economic war against alleged Japanese abuses of the American market, the more tightly the society becomes wrapped around maintaining a dominant position in an industry rapidly becoming obsolete for a highly industrial society. Symbolic politics play a crucial role in marshaling public support for policies and pronouncements that cater to this rather narrow constituency, by--inter alia--portraying the American economy as embattled by unfair Japanese marketing practices. This patriotic fervor to support the American worker penetrates much of the economic spectrum and is exacerbated by advertising blitzes and media complacency.

The degree of "violence" evident in the foreign economic policy appears to be only indirectly tied to the decline in competitiveness of the U.S. automobile industry. The harsh economic policies, it might seem, are also related to the size of the constituency that is associated with this industry. A declining industry itself is not a sufficient reason to invoke the verbal and economic violence, but coupled with the extent to which society is organized around the manufacture and sale of automobiles, this might be a sufficient condition to lead the political leadership to adopt such a course of action. Again, this is an area that deserves further exploration.

The second example is religious fundamentalism. A theocratic state that uses its "divine guidance" to organize society around its religious doctrine can also end up with its foreign policy and the organization of the society feeding on one another. If the organizing concept is the "holy scripture," the infidel is often the tool used for maintaining religious cohesiveness at a feverish pitch. Iran is the most obvious example in contemporary times. The leadership that came to power after the fall of the Shah professed the need to remake the society based on the teachings of the Koran. To achieve this task meant throwing off the yoke of Western materialism and ridding the society of any vestiges of the secular ways of life. The infidel became the United States, symbolized as the "great Satan." But it seemed that words alone were insufficient to ensure the ascendency of the fundamentalist coalition, as well as the transformation of society. Deeds were required, though in this case the deeds centered on the international behavior of the state. Foreign embassies were sacked, hostages were taken, terrorist activities were supported, and war was waged, all in defense of the holy scripture. As the range of tolerant activity became more constricted, nearly all members of society became active adherents. And as the number of "true believers" multiplied, so too did the extremes to which the state elite would go. The takeover of the U.S. embassy, for instance, was initiated by students who in essence compelled the acquiescence, and later the support, of the state. Without any firm evidence, it appears that the more pervasive the influence of the fundamentalist traditions, the more violent became the state's foreign policy. And as might be expected, the more violent the foreign policy, the more entrenched became the organizing concept, religious fundamentalism.

Although neither example has been sufficiently developed to be anything more than anecdotal evidence of a societal organization/foreign-policy feedback, both are suggestive of where further research might prove fruitful. Combined with the empirical evidence regarding the organization of society around the military, and its relationship to the violent foreign policy of the state, this evidence supports assertions that scholars of world politics need to adopt a broader approach in pursuit of that elusive "theory of politics" (Ferguson and Mansbach, 1991).

The empirical analysis, as well as my attempts to generalize about the impact of the society/state nexus on elite foreign policy, leads to two basic questions. First, at what level of societal organization does the feedback mechanism begin to operate? And second, is it possible to demilitarize--or deorganize--a society once it is highly militarized? An answer to the first question can only be a matter of speculation, though there are tentative guidelines that might be supported by the data. And while history tells us that the answer to the second question is very definitely "yes," the results of my analysis point to a few concrete steps that might help ease the pain of the process.

THE ELUSIVE THRESHOLD

The threshold at which the organization of society and the external behavior of the state begin to operate in a feedback must be determined in large part by the issue around which the society is organized. Obviously, specifying such a threshold is a key factor in more fully understanding this relationship between societal organization and the foreign policy of the state. The quest, moreover, is an empirical exercise, to which the findings of my analyses may give some indication of where to look for boundaries. In chapter 2, I demonstrated the effect of a threshold in the extent to which the societies were militarized; the somewhat arbitrarily derived threshold in each case was the mean level of societal militarization. In the United States this mean level of militarization was 12 percent of the labor force participating in the preparations for war. And although I did not vary that cutoff point to test for the sensitivity of this threshold on the impact of the postulated relationship, it was reasonably similar to the mean for Great Britain, as was the result of the effect of breaching the threshold on the relationship between militarization and violent foreign policy. Furthermore, the Motor Vehicle Manufacturers Association (MVMA) has estimated that in 1987 nearly 15 percent of the U.S. labor force worked in motor vehicle and related industries (1990). The group of industries that is used to arrive at this figure is quite broad, and many of those who fall into this compilation will be affiliated with imported motor vehicles, but the size of the constituency is substantial and its effect on policy plainly evident. Even reducing the size of this constituency by the percentage of the domestic market made up of imported vehicles-- approximately 30 percent--still leaves 10 percent of the work force tied to the domestic motor vehicle industry, at least in terms of the potency of the force behind lobbying efforts. Though still speculation, it appears that about 10 percent of the labor force constitutes a political and economic lobby strong enough to influence the conduct of foreign policy, although that threshold could very well be considerably lower.

We might have hoped that the historical study of Brazil would have shed some light on this question and, in doing so, betray a sense of where the threshold might be found. To some extent the rather vague data from Brazil does tell us that the threshold is not very low. With only about 1 percent of the Brazilian labor force tied to the military--though still quite a substantial number in absolute terms--the elite there seem to be under no pressure to resort to the use of violence as a foreign-policy tool. Nor do they appear to be much of a target for international violence. If a critical range exists, it is probably closer to the 10 percent figure than anywhere near the 1 percent mark.

PROSPECTS FOR DEMILITARIZATION

Having taken us from a specific model to the generalization of that model to a broader category of events, let me move back toward the specifics. In the introductory chapter I briefly alluded to two approaches to demilitarizing a society. Both approximated an uncontrolled free-fall rather than a well-designed strategy to remake the economic, social, and institutional bonds of society. The first was total defeat in a war. Nazi Germany and Imperial Japan epitomize this method of demilitarization, and the costs involved possibly far outweighed those associated with the militarization of society. The other avenue was the confluence of a severe economic crisis with a crisis of political leadership. The former Soviet Union portends to be the model for this process, though neither is this the ideal. I will conclude this research effort by attempting to link my empirical findings to policies that might facilitate the demilitarization process, at least in the United States and Great Britain. And although my comments will be directed toward these specific countries, they may well be more widely applicable.

Some of the factors that appear to be strongly associated with the militarization of society--such as system leadership and the concentration of material capabilities--are virtually nonmanipulable in the short term. There would seem to be little mileage, therefore, in attempting to couch demilitarization efforts in terms of the state's role in the global arena. It would appear that structural conditions would have to be taken as a given and domestic policies or initiatives orchestrated from within those structural constraints. Manipulating these systemic variables, moreover, is akin to the free-fall approach to demilitarization experienced by Germany and Japan--clearly not a desirable strategy, though possibly quite effective. Focusing on domestic and interstate opportunities, as well as reining in the propensity by the elite to resort to the use of force, should provide some guidelines for designing a strategy to achieve fairly deep and institutionalized cuts in the level of military preparedness.

The first point to be raised when articulating the components of a strategy to demilitarize society runs counter to much of the anecdotal and empirical evidence regarding the influence of the military bureaucracy. The findings from my analysis suggest that the trend over the past forty years is toward demilitarization, and it is the occasional reversals in that trend that need to be controlled. Granted, the extent of militarization in the United States reached a plateau well into the post-World War II period, but on the whole the trend is to gradually reduce military mobilization. This, however, does not imply that sitting back and waiting will eventually result in a virtually demilitarized society. The all-too-frequent tendency to reverse that trend needs to be short-circuited. This follows the theoretical reasoning which argues that the perception by the general public that they live in a hostile international environment will suffice to maintain relatively high levels of mobilization but that this perception cannot be maintained indefinitely without some actual bloodletting. In the

United States a few international crises have worked to buck the post-World War II trend--the Korean and Vietnam wars and Ronald Reagan's period of the "Evil Empire"--though the most recent one did not involve a direct military confrontation. British data also confirm that the long-term pattern is toward demilitarization.

In spite of the overall trends in militarization, by 1985 Britain had only recently dropped back to interwar levels of mobilization, with approximately 9 percent of its labor force still tied to continued funding of the military. At the same time, the extent to which the United States was militarized was about 300 percent above pre-World War II levels. It seems clear that the elite in the United States were not overly determined to demilitarize their forces, trends not withstanding. So if time alone will not reduce tendencies to remilitarize, then we must find other mechanisms for assisting the momentum of that trend.

My evidence suggests that there is a role to be played by the mass media, in terms of both popularizing societal symbols and helping to maintain the perception of an international threat. These findings buttress earlier work by Melvin Small (1974) and William Gamson and Andre Modigliani (1989), who demonstrated that press reporting can have an impact on the way the public perceives issues and adversaries. If efforts to demobilize are to be moderately successful, forms of entertainment available to the mass public need to emphasize the role of cooperation in the international environment, forgo the propensity to create a "bad guy," and highlight the effect of civil technology on societal development. These steps would help reduce the tendency toward creating enemies of society. The print and television media, furthermore, could facilitate the demilitarization process not only by returning to a more traditional countervailing force in society but also by resisting the temptation to bestow praise on nearly all things military. This does not imply that the media needs to adopt a distinctly antimilitary stance but rather to be more critical of the official position and give equal time to such topics as the benefits of conversion. A reduction in the extent to which the prowess of the military is portrayed in a positive light should contribute to the formation of cognitive maps that leave the public with alternatives other than support for the military. Revamping the "toolkit" with which the general public understands the foreign policy of the elite will go a long way toward relaxing the grip of the military over the social structure of society. But this will not be enough to ensure sustained demilitarization.

The evidence clearly points to interstate relations as a key factor in the maintenance of a large military establishment. An existential threat was a strong predictor of increases in the extent to which either the British or the U.S. society was militarized, as was the amount of international violence when the society was more highly militarized. One of the obvious implications of these findings is that the state needs to temper its reliance on the use of force as a policy tool and rely on peaceful diplomatic initiatives in an attempt to keep military challenges in check. This, however, might not be so easy. In light of the rather strong theoretical arguments that the state will use force in an effort to maintain public support for the continued diversion of resources from civil to military purposes, a simple change in policy could be difficult to achieve. To make this an obtainable goal, public attitudes and interests must not constrain the options available to the elite. This is apparently a two-edged sword, with the military and much of the civil sector of society having short-term interests in maintaining the status quo while the civil sector, at least, also has a long-term interest in reinvesting in a civilian-based economy (Melman, 1980, 1985; Dumas, 1988). As the historical record of Brazil has shown, the military need not work at crosscurrents with the civilian sector of the economy; in fact, an adequate defensive posture can be maintained without increasing the external threat and while minimizing the use of international violence as a form of diplomacy. In short, the elite cannot feel that they have a free hand in the projection of military force, lest they incur the wrath of the electorate, though enforcing constraints on the political and economic elite is not an easy task given the disparity in access to information and resources. However, since there is support for the hypothesized feedback between the violent foreign policy of the state and societal militarization, breaking the links at one point might help turn a self-amplifying process into a self-suppressing one.

No component of a demilitarization strategy is independent of the others; therefore, successfully addressing one component will not by itself ensure that the size or the reach of the military is greatly reduced. But movement in one quarter will most likely have an impact on efforts in other quarters. Eliminating the prevalence of societal symbols that extol the virtues of the military should help diminish the amount of public support that can be generated by the elite for foreign adventurism or for the diversion of limited resources from civil projects to the military. Likewise, the more rare becomes the projection of forces overseas, and the less visible the military as an institution, the more likely that we would see a diminished role for symbolic politics. It is in these ways that the self-amplifying feedback might help reinforce efforts to reduce the influence of the military, and the evidence from a number of research projects suggests that the impact will be felt not only by the domestic economy but also in the welfare of the entire global village (Leontief and Duchin, 1983).

DEMILITARIZATION AND GLOBAL WELFARE

I began this thesis by arguing that militarization has costs that are borne at the expense of the social, political, and economic fabric of society. These costs are particularly harsh when put into perspective of the tens of millions of people who suffer daily from malnutrition, when tens of thousands of people in the wealthiest countries are homeless, and when the global population of refugees is greater than the total population of many of the countries of the world. Those who have for years been advocating the retooling of the U.S. industrial base--

from an undue emphasis on military production to that of a more civilian nature-
-have often detailed the industrial and infrastructural dimensions of these
conversion efforts (Dumas, 1988; Melman, 1980, 1985; Gordon and McFadden,
1984). When the problem is viewed from a sociopolitical perspective, however,
there is little wonder that not much headway has been made .

In many ways issues of global militarization, particularly in Third World
countries, appear to be a mirror image of the problems faced by the United States
and Great Britain. The developmental aspects of militarization, furthermore,
might fuel policy debates that weight the costs of arming against the perceived
benefits of centralizing control, developing an industrial infrastructure, and
fostering a "unified" society. This was clearly evident in Brazil. The evidence of
a feedback between the militarization of society and the foreign policy of the
state may also be applicable to states that are not members of the major-power
system and, if so, may point to strategies that simultaneously reduce global
tensions and increase the social, political, and economic development of many of
the world's poorer nations.

If only a small portion of the resources freed up from demilitarization could
be transferred into programs designed to address issues of hunger,
unemployment, and homelessness, then the more humane global village that
could result might also be less conflict-prone. If there is a feedback between the
organization of society and the violent behavior of the state, then it may also
operate at levels other than that of the nation-state. Demilitarizing the global
community might contribute to the amelioration of some of the violence evident
throughout the system, be it intra- or inter-state. But even when the scope of the
potential benefits is restricted to the level of the nation-state, there is some
encouragement in the fact that the structural factors generally assumed to be non-
manipulable in the short run may be less rigid in the present international
climate, possibly facilitating efforts to "experiment" with some of the societal-
level variables. In any event, there seems to be adequate evidence to suggest that
the unique opportunities presented by today's international environment ought
not to be squandered needlessly.

Appendix 1

Coding Rules for the Manipluation
of the Perception of a Threat

Measuring the manipulation of a threat is not an easy task. Not only does one have to confront the issue that the decision-makers may truly believe that there is some objective threat motivating their behavior and, therefore, that their public pronouncements are offered in good faith, but it also becomes the obligation of the researcher to discriminate between an "actual," or objective, threat and one that is much more subjective. In spite of these difficulties, an attempt was made to make these distinctions and to measure traces of them in a fairly systematic fashion. In pursuit of a valid and reliable measure of the extent to which the perception of a threat was maintained in the public eye, a simple set of coding rules was outlined, a coding form created, and the task undertaken.

Four basic areas were used to organize articles that conveyed a promilitary theme: (1) articles that dealt with issues of military size, makeup, reorganization, deployment of forces outside of territorial boundaries, training, or budget in a manner that is either "objective" or supportive of such policies; (2) articles that addressed issues of emerging military technology or the introduction of new technology into the armed forces; (3) articles that identified a clear international military threat, reported on a war or threat of war, or relayed the remarks of a foreign leader who spoke disparagingly about the specific country; and (4) articles that conveyed a sense of patriotism or an imminent threat by reporting on such themes as the perils or threat of communism, freedom, democracy, service to the motherland, the "evils" associated with various actors or systems in the world, and a catchall category of patriotism. This latter heading is meant to incorporate such topics as war heros, military parades, and voluntary service in support of a war. The antimilitary themes were divided into two categories: (1) articles that discussed issues of disarmament, reductions in the size or scope of the military, arms control, or peace negotiations in a positive fashion; and (2) articles that were distinctly critical of the military, policies of military expansion, or a particular war or the threat of war, or that reported positively on the actions of antiwar or antimilitary activists. Book or movie reviews were excluded from the article counts, as were letters to the editor, though these restrictions apply only to the coding of British data.

Though the categories themselves might appear to be straightforward, strict coding rules that can guide the categorization of each of the hundreds of articles analyzed are a bit more problematic. Any coding procedure on a topic such as this is bound to be more subjective than a researcher might want, though most of the possible errors would be confined to which of the four promilitary or two antimilitary categories a particular story might fit into. Rarely would there be a question of whether or not an article reported on a militarily related theme, and usually one can readily discern which of the two broad categories should guide the reading of the article. Therefore, reliability might be less robust within each of the organizing categories than it is across categories or on the net article count in general. With these caveats in mind, I will outline the rules that did guide the measurement of the extent to which a perception of a threat was manipulated.

PROMILITARY THEMES

1) Articles that reported on the size, makeup, reorganization, training, or budget of the military forces or the need to deploy forces outside the territorial boundaries of either the United States or Great Britain, respectively. The intent here is obviously to take account of the number of articles that address issues relating to the expansion of either military forces or the military bureaucracy. This category counted only those articles that were either positive or "neutral" toward increases in the military or its budget. Articles that reported on military reductions were counted in the appropriate category and subsequently subtracted from those articles conveying a positive image of military mobilization. Articles detailing the reshuffling of forces or commanders, negotiations or legislative fights over the military budget, and training programs for soldiers or officers are examples of articles that fall into this category.

2) Articles that reported on emerging weapons technology or the introduction of new weapons into the force structure. Because of the role played by weapons production in the political battles over budgeting, the reporting on new weapons technology and its potential role in "defending the interests of the nation" forms an integral part of maintaining the perception of an external threat. As such, any article that describes a new or potential weapon technology, discusses the research, development, or production of a weapon, or reports on the introduction of a new weapon into the standing force structure is counted in this category.

3) Articles that reported on a war or threat of war. This seems to be an intuitive category, and it generally is. Any story that describes or reports on a

war that is currently in progress, whether or not the country under examination is a participant, is to be counted. A report on an ongoing civil war in a country in which it is made clear that this conflict falls into the "security interests" of either the United States or Great Britain, respectively, is to be counted. When an article reports on or identifies a clear threat to international peace or the stability of the international order, it is to be counted. And when an article reports on a speech, or the remarks of an international leader who threatens or speaks threateningly about either the United States or Great Britain, respectively, it is to be counted. The intent of this category is to capture reporting that conveys the sense that the United States or Great Britain exists in a threatening environment.

4) Articles that conveyed the sense of a threatening international environment through the use of words or topics that imply--or explicitly state-- the need for vigilance, employ patriotic buzzwords, or denounce an enemy. There are many ways to maintain the perception that a country or its organizing principles face imminent peril without directly referring to the military or a military threat. Invoking the theme of patriotism, chronicling the destructive potential of internal subversion, and identifying a potential adversary in terms designed to heighten the perception of international tensions can all have the effect of rallying the public behind the policies of the state. Patriotism can be invoked in a myriad of ways, such as reporting on military parades, the display of war weapons, stories about war heros, events that motivate the public to support a war effort or restrict consumption in response to the need for critical materials, or simply the sanctity of symbols of the nation, such as the flag. Similarly, reporting on espionage, or the attempt by an adversary to subvert internal dissident groups, should be counted. Attempts by national leaders to identify a foreign actor--or its political-economic system--as evil or inimical to the interest of either the United States or Great Britain, respectively, were also counted in this category.

ANTIMILITARY THEMES

1) Articles that reported on arms control, disarmament, or peace negotiations. Presumably, stories that discuss ongoing negotiations to reduce international tensions, or the levels of armaments, will serve to reduce the perception of a foreign threat. Any articles that report on multilateral or bilateral negotiations or treaties to reduce or control armament levels are counted in this category. Likewise, stories that discuss ongoing or successful peace negotiations also tend to create the perception of a less threatening environment and should be noted here. But not all articles about arms control or peace negotiations refer to these events in "positive" terms, and in fact, disparaging remarks about ongoing negotiations may serve to increase the perception of a hostile international adversary. In this category only those articles that convey a "positive" or "neutral" perspective on the negotiations should be counted; "negatively" oriented articles should be counted as a threat in one of the earlier categories.

2) Articles that were distinctly critical of the military, military expansion, or a particular war or the threat of war or reported positively on antimilitary or antiwar activists. Articles with a clear antimilitary theme may help to embolden those working to curtail the spending or expansion of the military and may therefore diminish popular support for continued military spending. Reports on the activities of antimilitary activists written in a "positive" or "neutral" light should be counted, as should those stories that report on the high costs of continued military expansion or its deleterious consequences for the economy. Articles that are critical of U.S. or British involvement in a particular war should also be counted. As with the previous category, a story that portrays a negative image of an antiwar group may serve more to chronicle a threat than to diminish such perceptions; they should not be counted in this category but rather in the appropriate "promilitary" grouping, if at all.

Appendix 2

Coding Rules for Counting War Toys

The general theme of this "toy count" was to determine the prevalence of war toys in each of the two countries under examination; thus determining the ratio of war toys to total toys offered for sale in merchandise catalogs was the objective of this coding procedure. For this purpose, a "war toy" was defined quite narrowly as any toy that is a replica of a military-issue weapon or supporting equipment, that depicts war scenes, or that is designed to elicit mental images of war or engage a person in war playing. Not all toys that depict violence necessarily fall into the category of a "war toy." Guns, for instance, are not intrinsically "war" guns and thus not all should be counted in the "war toy" category. A gun used by a cowboy, a hunter, a police officer, or a robber is not a war toy. On the other hand, modern "war" scenes--at least as they pertain to toys--do not necessarily involve human-looking men in green uniforms, but the toys that portray this new image of a warrior are no less war toys.

Each individual toy is to be counted--with categorical exceptions that will be discussed below--that is found on a page in the catalog that is identified in the index as a page with toys on it. For example, each doll is to be counted, even if the dolls are simply variations on one another (size included). Likewise, each model car, each individual toy soldier that is not part of a set, and each train set is to be counted as a toy. Two tabulations are to be kept: one for the total number of toys offered for sale; the other for that subgroup that can be considered war toys.

The exceptions to the toy count are fairly straightforward. Bicycles, sporting equipment, and board games--electronic or otherwise--are not to be counted. Games that require some human participation other than rolling dice and moving pieces should not be excluded as a board game. Two other exceptions to the general rule are doll clothing and individual pieces of train equipment--for example, stop signs, road crossing, single pieces of track, etc. A train car, a bridge, or a depot, for instance, is to be counted as a toy.

These rules could obviously be subject to much debate, with divisions turning in large part on the perception of the role of violence in society. I have no interest in entering into that debate and thus have made the coding rules as restrictive as possible. If a toy passes these criteria, there should be little doubt that it is a toy that depicts war or is designed to stimulate war playing. Additionally, by counting every toy offered for sale, I did everything possible to minimize the ratio of war toys to total toys (for example, the same doll generally comes in various sizes--twelve, fifteen, nineteen, and twenty four inches--and each of these was counted as a toy). I hoped that this would make the test of my thesis more demanding.

Appendix 3

Coding Rules for Counting War Movies

Data on the ratio of war movies to total movies released in each country during each particular year were derived through an on-line service with access to Magill's Cinema Survey. The procedure involved determining the total number of movies with a release date in the year under observation and with the country of origin being either the United States or Great Britain, respectively. A second search was requested for the existence of either *war*, *military*, or *patriotism* as a root term in the descriptor section of the survey's report. The number of movies falling into the latter category was then divided by the total number of movies released in that year.

There are some obvious problems with this coding procedure. First, using key words in the descriptor to discriminate war movies from "other" movies leaves room for both type I and type II errors. An antiwar film, for instance, may show up as a war film; conversely, the descriptor of a film with a military or war theme might not actually use any of these three words. Second, the coding rules employed by Magill's do not seem to be terribly systematic, and the actual coding appears to be highly subjective. An example found through random sampling involved two *Rambo* films: one was clearly described as a war film, whereas another was described as an "adventure" film with plenty of action. While these problems are potentially serious, they pose only minor concern for two reasons: (1) the distribution of errors is likely to be random and normally distributed, and therefore type I and type II errors should be equally likely to occur; and (2) a casual perusal of the descriptors suggests that the number of antiwar films is quite low relative to war films. The cost of rectifying these problems--in terms of both time and money--was prohibitive, and therefore the measure was, and should be, taken as an approximation.

Appendix 4

Notes on the Coding of Data for the Militarization Index

As mentioned in the body of the text, the bulk of the data that compose the militarization index was taken from official government documents. For most of the six indicators and each of the years, this was a fairly straightforward task, and data were readily available. The exceptions, however, are numerous and need to be spelled out as explicitly as possible. The following is a description of the procedures used to estimate data points when official sources failed to provide adequate estimates. The procedure was at times somewhat complicated, using, for example, Input-Output tables, though many of the estimated points were derived through simple extrapolation. Since the estimated points were just one part of a composite index, the crude estimations are not overly troubling. In each case where a data point was not accessible, an attempt was made to make a conservative estimate, even if it meant that the estimate appeared to be unreasonably low. For those indicators that were not applicable in a particular year--for instance, ROTC programs between 1900 and 1920--the index simply comprised the five other indicators.

GREAT BRITAIN

Military Reserves

Data for reserve military forces for the years 1967 and 1972 were not available, so to estimate them I simply found the number of reserve forces immediately before and immediately after the missing data, took the difference between those two, and divided that figure in half. The resultant figure was either subtracted or added to the previous year, depending on the direction of the trend. In effect, this was an extrapolation.

Data for British Cadet Forces were estimated for the years 1902, 1905, 1925, 1935, 1937, 1947 through 1955, 1960, 1972, 1977, and 1982, though for many of the years for which data were available, they were composed of only one or two of the Cadet programs (for which there was a total of four). They too could be considered estimates, albeit low ones. The only years for which good data were available were after 1965, and even here there were gaping holes. Remarkably enough, the Cadet organizations themselves kept complete records only during the latter part of the century, even though at times the number of enrollees was in the tens of thousands.

The missing Cadet data were derived as follows: for the pre-1945 years, I simply carried forward the number of Cadets from the preceding period for which I had data. For instance, 1902 and 1905 were estimated to have six hundred members because that is the figure for the year 1900. In the post-1945 period, I estimated the data by extrapolating a trend line based on the procedure outlined for reserve data above.

Employment in Weapons Industries

Defense employment data were derived in four ways: (1) by using the percentage of shipbuilding devoted to the military to extrapolate to the larger population of munitions industries, when the appropriate data on shipbuilding were available (1900-1939, with the exception of the years 1915, 1917, and 1920); (2) by using Input-Output tables for the years for which tables were compiled (1955, 1965, 1967, 1970, 1972, 1975, and 1982). The percentage of the output from "munition industries" that was consumed by the military was used to calculate the percent of the labor force in those industries that were producing military-related equipment (a list of those industries considered part of the "munitions" complex can be obtained from the author, though in various years between thirteen and seventeen SIC classifications were used; for an example of the industries considered critical to national defense, see the Statement of Defence Estimates, Command Paper 8212II, 1980-1981); (3) in the pre-World War II period, when shipbuilding data were not available, by taking the ratio of defense employees to active-duty forces in the years immediately preceding and following the point to be estimated, taking the average of those ratios, and then multiplying the number of active-duty forces by the derived ratio to come up with a defense employment figure; and (4) in the post-World War II period for which Input-Output tables were not appropriate, by simply developing a trend line between periods of missing data and calculating a smooth line between points, again an interpolation procedure.

The number of civilian personnel working for the Ministry of Defense was estimated for the years 1902, 1905, 1907, and 1912. Here I simply used the value for the years immediately preceding the missing data. In this instance, the figure for the years 1902, 1905, and 1907 was the value for the year 1900, which was garnered from official documents.

UNITED STATES

The data that needed to be estimated for the United States consisted mainly of employment in defense industries in the pre-World War II period and civilian employees of the Department of Defense in the years 1900, 1902, 1905.

Estimates on employment in defense industries were derived by taking the ratio of defense employment to active-duty personnel for each year bordering on a year with missing data. The mean of those two ratios was then multiplied by the number of active-duty forces during the year for which data were missing. This is the same procedure used to estimate British data when either shipbuilding or Input-Output data were not accessible. Reasonably accurate data were available for the years 1900, 1905, 1910, 1915, 1917, and 1922. Data for the remaining years before World War II had to be estimated.

During the period from 1922 to 1937, I used .65 as the multiplier to calculate defense employment. This figure was simply the mean of the ratio of defense employees to active-duty personnel in the years 1920 and 1940. Since there appeared to be very little fluctuation in either the number of active-duty personnel during this period or the number of defense employees just before and immediately following these years, this seemed a reasonable alternative to simply smoothing the line. In 1920 there were 214,000 defense industry employees; in 1940 there were 314,000.

Data for the number of civilian personnel working for the Department of War during the years 1900, 1902, and 1905 were unavailable. Rather than trying to extrapolate without a reference for the earlier period, I used the percentage change in the number of active-duty personnel for each period as a benchmark and worked backward from 1907.

The only other data point that was estimated was the number of ROTC students in 1957. Here I simply took one-half of the difference between the two adjacent points; in this case, I subtracted 10,000 from the number for the year 1955, which had 337,000 enrollees.

Notes

CHAPTER 1

1. The security sector is broadly conceived in this instance, including those aspects of the political and economic elite concerned with physical as opposed to economic security. In the United States, for instance, the security sector includes the Department of Defense, portions of the Department of State, the National Security Council, portions of NASA, and the planning commissions organized in the event of war. To some extent the leadership of many of the largest corporations are also part of the security elite even though their loyalties are split between company profits and national sovereignty, two aspects of corporate life that are often commingled.

2. Also see Ted Gurr, *War, Revolution, and the Growth of the Coercive State* (1988). Gurr's definition of a militarized state is very similar to the one I adopt here, though his focus is on the state elite rather than the organization of society. He defines the militarized state as one that "maintains a large military establishment and is ruled by an elite whose policy agenda is dominated by preparations for war and national defense"(51).

3. Van Evera never develops clears or operational definitions of the terms *militarism* and *militarization* and at times appears to use them interchangeably. When discussing the role of industrialization in the militarization process, he often employs the term *militarism* in a manner consistent with my use of the term *militarization*.

4. For an interesting historical description of the role of organizing and equipping a country's armed forces in the development of the political and economic institutions of a society, see W. H. McNeil, *The Pursuit of Power* (1982).

5. The state in many of these countries may be under the direct control of the military, or at best under the watchful eye of those in uniform, but this does not imply that the masses are any more organized into the structure of military dominance than in a civilian-led state.

CHAPTER 2

1. The nonregular intervals between data points are generally not a problem in time series analysis and in fact are quite common in the physical and earth sciences (for example, ocean temperatures measured from the surface of the ocean; and seasonal variations in various geological measurements are two examples). Where there is the potential for a problem is in the effect and interpretation of lagged variables, in this case militarization lagged for one period. However, tests for the effect of a differential in the lagged periods demonstrated that the nonregular data intervals are not a problem for this analysis. The interpretation of the results to follow throughout this manuscript should be rather straightforward. (see C. W. Granger, 1980:36 for a discussion of using data with non-regular intervals).

2. See Merit Roe Smith, *Military Enterprise and Technological Change* (1987), for a discussion about the hierarchical nature of weapons production.

3. The role of employees as active lobbyists can be seen in the recent example of the efforts to generate support for the B2 Stealth Bomber, where Northrop Corp. had enlisted the help of its employees in lobbying Congress for continued funding for the craft. See *Detroit Free Press,* May 17, 1991.

4. Veteran membership for Great Britain was not available, even within the country (in fact, membership data beyond the period of the 1980s are not even known by the administrators of the Royal British Legion). As a surrogate I used the number of people receiving war pensions. The latter figure generally appears to be considerably lower than the sketchy veteran data that were available. The basic theme behind war pensioners is quite similar to that of organized veterans. The intent is to measure the size of political and economic constituencies that support and lobby for continued funding of the military. Data on war pensioners were taken from the *Annual Abstract of Statistics.*

5. These figures for induced employment are actually derived from base-related expenditures--much of which entail spending at government-subsidized stores--and comparable figures for induced employment from weapons production would be substantially higher. In the latter instance, personal spending would filter more directly into the surrounding community and subsequently increase the economic multiplier attributable to military spending (Department of Defense, 1983). However, I will use the lower estimates in order to reduce the probability of overestimation or bias in my calculations.

6. For the *New York Times,* only the front page of each Sunday paper was used, though for the *Sunday Times* the entire paper was subjected to an article count. Furthermore, only two months were used in the coding of British data--March and May. Unfortunately, the *Sunday Times* did not present a "front page" in the usual sense of the term until some time in the latter part of the century. Until that point, the front page is something akin to a marquee, advertising theaters and restaurants. The indicator used when analyzing British data is the average number of articles per page per week, rather than the average number of articles per week on the front page of the Sunday paper, as was used for the United States.

7. For Great Britain, this threshold was calculated at 18 percent.

CHAPTER 3

1. For example see: Garnham (1976), Leng (1983), and Huth, Gelpi and Bennett (1992) who focus on the role of contiguity, bargaining, and enduring rivalries, respectively. Empirical evidence demonstrating the role of systemic attributes on the propensity of the state to resort to violence short of war is quite scanty. There is, however, a fair number of theoretical exegeses that link system characteristics to the use of force in the international environment (Deutsch and Singer, 1969; Waltz, 1979, 1969; Singer, 1990).

2. Although many would argue that Great Britain was no longer the system leader by the turn of the century, Wallerstein, Thompson, and Gilpin all seem to suggest that this is a period of the deconcentration of British domination (see Boswell and Sweat, 1991), and although the US was in the ascendancy, Britain was still the dominant actor in the global arena.

CHAPTER 4

1. Endogenous variables are those that are determined *within* the system--or could be thought of as the outcome variables in the model. Exogenous variables are those that are determined *outside* the system--in a sense the predictor variables. For example, militarization is in part determined by the extent of violent foreign policy, and vice versa, while system concentration is assumed to be a function of things other than the dispute behavior of the state. *Included* variables are those included in both equations; *excluded* variables are those that are in one equation but not the other. In this model system concentration is included in the equation that has disputes as the outcome variable, but is excluded from the other equation.

2. The British model was corrected for a rather strong presence of autocorrelation. This involved transforming the entire matrix by the value of *rho* associated with the residuals at time "t-1". For a discussion of the correction procedure see Kelejian and Oates, 1989:296-299. The presence of autocorrelation was only minimal in US data, and therefore no correction was made.

3. How, for example, do changes in dispute behavior at time "t" influence decisions regarding military allocations at time "t"? As mentioned earlier in the text, to test the validity of this finding I expanded the statistical model to include three endogenous variables (DELTAMILI, DELTAMILI @ t+1, and # ongoing disputes). This would allow me to test the effect of disputes at time "t" on militarization at time "t + 1". There was little substantive change between models, with disputes still showing a negative relationship to militarization at time "t + 1", though the strength of the finding is reduced somewhat--beta (-2.49). Because the expanded model did not appear to offer any substantive benefits, and might simply make the analysis appear unnecessarily complicated, I have not reported these findings.

CHAPTER 5

1. In the United States T.V. and radio receive nearly 100 percent of their revenues from advertisements, newspapers 75 percent, and magazines 50 percent(Lee and Solomon, 1990:59).

2. A description of the coding rules can be found in the appendices, but in summary not all violent toys were considered war toys. Guns, for instance, were not necessarily counted as war toys unless they were specifically military-type guns. To be counted as a war toy the toy had to evoke images of the military, battle situations, or war in general. Toys depicting hunting, cowboy and Indian scenes, criminals or crime fighting, or life in the "wild west" did not constitute war toys. The population from which this ratio was derived included, for example, every doll, every stuffed animal and every model car offered for sale in each particular year. In order to minimize error the coding criteria for war toys were made as strict as possible, while those for toys in general were made as inclusive as possible.

3. Because war movie data was generated through an "on line" service, a descriptor search for keywords has room for error, both type I and type II. For instance the reviewer for one "Rambo-type" film may use words such as those that I have identified, while another reviewer might choose an entirely different set of descriptor words. In this instance I would pick up one war-type film and not the other. The opposite may also happen, for instance, where the theme of the film is distinctly anti-war yet the word war gets used in the descriptor. In this case it would unfortunately be included in my sample. Although resources prevented a visual examination of each review, it is assumed that the number of type II errors relative to type I was rather small, and therefore not greatly effecting the results.

4. The year 1982 was also removed from the analysis at this point because the McGill's survey reports only seven movies released during that year; none of them fit the descriptors for inclusion as a war film. Suspecting that this reflects a data problem, rather than a true indication of the number of films released in 1982, I deleted the year.

CHAPTER 6

1. This figure requires a patchwork of sources, most of which are mentioned in the text. No comprehensive figure is available in any one source. Peter Lock(1986) suggests that the figure of 100,000 for total employment in the Brazilian arms industry is too high. His figures, however, explicitly omit IMBEL and he seems to refute the magnitude of naval construction suggested by Jordan Young.

2. Correlates of War National Capabilities data set.

CHAPTER 7

1. Because of difficulties in incorporating the threshold concept into a model using a system of equations, this more rigorous specification was not carried forward.

References

Allison, Graham T. "What Fuels the Arms Race?" In John F. Reichart, and Steven R. Sturm, eds., *American Defense Policy*, 5th Ed., Baltimore: Johns Hopkins University Press, 1983.

Aron, Raymond, "Remarks on Lasswell's The Garrison State." *Armed Forces and Society* 5, #3 (Spring 1979):347-59.

___. "War and Industrial Society." In Leon Bramson and George W. Goethals, eds., *War: Studies from Psychology, Sociology, Anthropology*. New York: Basic Books, 1964.

Aviation Week and Space Technology. "Avibras Emerges as Major Exporter for Brazilian Aerospace Industry," August 17, 1987, 49.

___. "Brasilia Transport, Tucano Trainer Form Backbone of Embraer Product Line." August 17, 1987, 42.

___. "Brazil Forms High-Technology Venture To Develop Advanced Weapon Systems." August 17, 1987, 52.

___. "Brazilian Air Force to Accept First Production AMX in August." March 20, 1989, 87.

___. "Brazilian Army to Buy 260 Helicopters for Airmobile Battalions." August 17, 1987, 47.

___. "Embraer Developing Stretched Brasilia for Regional Market." June 19, 1989, 158.

___. "Embraer Moves to Solidify Role as Leading Aircraft Manufacturer." August 17, 1987, 40.

Axelrod, Robert. *The Evolution of Cooperation*. New York: Basic Books, 1984.

Bachman, Jerald G., Lee Sigelman, and Greg Diamond. "Self-Selection, Socialization, and Distinctive Military Values: Attitudes of High School Seniors." *Armed Forces and Society* 13 #2 (Winter 1987):169-87.

Bachrach, Peter and Morton S. Baratz. *Power and Poverty: Theory and Practice*. New York: Oxford University Press, 1970.

Baek, Kwang-il, Ronald D. McLaurin, and Chung-in Moon, eds. *The Dilemma of Third World Defense Industries*, Boulder, CO: Westview Press, 1989.

Ball, Nicole. *Security and Economy in the Third World.* Princeton: Princeton
    University Press, 1988.
Beck, Paul Allen. "The Role of Agents in Political Socialization." In Stanley A.
    Renshon, ed., *Handbook of Political Socialization: Theory and Research.* New
    York: Free Press, 1977.
Benoit, Emile. *Defense and Economic Growth in Developing Countries.* Lexington,
    Mass.: Lexington Books 1973.
Berghahn, V. R. *Militarism: The History of an International Debate, 1861-1979.*
    Cambridge: Cambridge University Press, 1981.
Boswell, Terry, and Mike Sweat, "Hegemony, Long Waves, and Major Wars: A Time
    Series Analysis of Systemic Dynamics, 1496-1967." *International Studies
    Quarterly* 35, no. 2 (June 1991):123-49.
Bramson, Leon, and George W. Goethals, eds. *War: Studies from Psychology,
    Sociology, Anthropology.* New York: Basic Books 1964.
Brunton, Bruce G. "Institutional Origins of the Military-Industrial Complex." *Journal
    of Economic Issues,* 22, no 2 (June 1988):599-606.
Brzoska, Michael, & Thomas Ohlson, eds. *Arms Production in the Third World.*
    Stockholm: Stockholm International Peace Research Institute, 1986.
Bueno de Mesquita, Bruce. "Systemic Polarization and the Occurrence and Duration of
    War." *Journal of Conflict Resolution.* 22, no. 2 (June 1978):241-67.
___. "Risk, Power Distributions, and the Likelihood of War." *International Studies
    Quarterly,* 25, no. 4 (December 1981):541-68.
Bueno de Mesquita, and David Lalman. "Empirical Support for Systemic and Dyadic
    Explanations of Conflict." *World Politics,* 26 no. 1 (October 1988):1-20.
Chaffee, Steven H., et al. "Mass Communication in Political Socialization." In
    Stanley A. Renshon, ed. *Handbook of Political Socialization: Theory and
    Research.* New York: Free Press, 1977.
Cohen, Youssef. "Democracy From Above: The Political Origins of Military
    Dictatorship in Brazil." *World Politics* 40 (1986):30-54.
___. *Manipulation of Consent: The State and Working-Class Consciousness in
    Brazil.* Pittsburgh: University of Pittsburgh Press, 1989.
Crawford, Neta C. "MEAN State Syndrome: An Ir/Rational Theory of Force-Prone
    foreign Policy." Presented at the annual meeting of the American Political
    Science Association, San Francisco, August 30-Sept. 2, 1990.
Cypher, James M. "Military Spending, Technical Change, and Economic Growth: A
    Disguised Form of Industrial Policy?" *Journal of Economic Issues* 21, no. 1
    (March 1987):33-59.
DeGrasse, Robert W. *Military Expansion Economic Decline.* New York: Council on
    Economic Priorities, 1983.
De Tocqueville, Alexis. "On War, Society, and the Military," In Leon Bramson and
    George W. Goethals, eds., *War: Studies from Psychology, Sociology,
    Anthropology.* New York: Basic Books, 1964.
Deutsch, Karl, and J. David Singer, "Multipolar Power Systems and International
    Stability." In James Rosenau, ed., *International Politics and Foreign Policy.* New
    York: Free Press of Glenco, 1969
Dibble, Vernon. "The Garrison Society." *New University Thought* 5, nos. 1, 2
    (1966-67):106-15.

Diehl, Paul F. "Arms Races and Escalation: A Closer Look." *Journal of Peace Research*. 20, no. 3 (1983):205-12.

___. "Arms Races To War: Testing Some Empirical Linkages." *The Sociological Quarterly*. 26, no. 3 (Fall 1985):331-49.

Diehl, Paul F., and Jean Kingston. "Messenger or Message?: Military Buildups and the Initiation of Conflict." *The Journal of Politics*. 49 (1987):801-13.

Disabled American Veterans. *The DAV: Who We Are and What We Do*. March 1989.

Dogan, Mattei, and Dominique Pelassy. *How to Compare Nations*. Chatham, N.J.: Chatham House, 1984.

Doran, Charles, and Wes Parsons. "War and the Cycle of Relative Power." *American Political Science Review*. 74 (1980):947-65.

Dulles, John W. F. *Unrest in Brazil: Political-Military Crises 1955-64*. Austin, Tex.: University of Texas Press, 1970.

Dumas, Lloyd J. "Economic Conversion: The Critical Link." *Bulletin of Peace Proposals*. 19, no. 1 (1988):1-10.

Dunne, J. P. "The Employment consequences of Military Expenditure: A Comparative Assessment." *World Employment Programme Research, Working Paper #5*. New York: United Nations, 1986

Dworetz, Steven M. "Before the Age or Reason: Liberalism and the Media Socialization of Children." *Social Theory and Practice*, 13, no. 2 (1987):187-218.

Elder, Charles D., and Roger W. Cobb. *The Political Uses of Symbols*. New York: Longman, 1983.

Evans, Robert Dervel. *Brazil: The Road Back from Terrorism*. London: Institute for Conflict Studies, 1974.

Falk, Richard A. "Militarization and Human Rights in the Third World." *Bulletin of Peace Proposals*. 8, no. 3 (1977):220-32.

Fasano-Filho, Bernhard Fischer, and Peter Nunnenkamp. *On the Determinants of Brazil's Manufactured Exports: An Empirical Analysis*. Tubingen: J.C.B. Mohr Publishers, 1987.

Ferguson, R. Brian. "Anthropology and War: Theory, Politics, Ethics." In Paul R. Turner and David Pitt, eds. *The Anthropology of War and Peace: Perspectives on the Nuclear Age*. Granby, Mass.: Bergin and Garvey Publishers, 1989.

Ferguson, Yale H., and Richard W. Mansbach. "Between Celebration and Despair: Constructive Suggestions for Future International Theory." *International Studies Quarterly*. 35, no. 4 (December 1991):363-86.

Finer, S. E. *The Man on Horseback*. Boulder, Colo.: Westview Press, 1988.

___. "The Role of the Military." In Charles Tilly, ed., *The Formation of National States in Western Europe*. Princeton: Princeton University Press, 1975.

Fitch, Samuel J. "The Garrison State in America: A Content Analysis of Trends in the Expectation of Violence." *Journal of Peace Research*. 22, no. 1 (1985):31-45.

Franko-Jones, Patrice. *The Brazilian Defense Industry: A Case Study in Public-Private Collaboration*. Ph.D. Dissertation, University of Notre Dame, Department of Economics, 1986.

___. "Public Private Partnership: Lessons From the Brazilian Armaments Industry." *Journal of Interamerican Studies and World Affairs*. (Winter 1987-88):41-68.

Fulbright, J. W. *The Pentagon Propaganda Machine*. New York: Liveright, 1970.

Funkhouser, G. Ray. "The Issues of the Sixties: An Exploratory Study in the Dynamics of Public Opinion." *Public Opinion Quarterly.* 37 (Spring, 1973):62-75.

Galbraith, John Kenneth. *How to Control the Military.* New York: Signet Books, 1969.

___. *The Anatomy of Power.* Boston: Houghton Mifflin Co., 1983.

Gamson, William A., and Andre Modigliani. "Media Discourse and Public Opinion on Nuclear Power: A Constructionist Approach." *American Journal of Sociology.* 95, no. 1 (July 1989):1-37.

Garnham, David. "Power Parity and lethal International Violence, 1969-73." *Journal of Conflict Resolution.* 20, no. 3 (September 1976):279-89.

Geller, Daniel S. "Nuclear Weapons, Deterrence, and Crisis Escalation." *Journal of Conflict Resolution.* 34 (June 1990):291-310.

Geyer, Michael. "The Militarization of Europe, 1914-1945." In John Gillis, ed., *The Militarization of the Western World.* New Brunswick, N.J.: Rutgers University Press, 1989.

Gilbert, Felix. *The Historical Essays of Otto Hintze.* London: Oxford University Press, 1975.

Gillis, John R., ed. *The Militarization of the Western World.* Brunswick, N.J.: Rutgers University Press, 1989.

Gilpin, Robert. *War and Change in World Politics.* New York: Cambridge University Press, 1981.

Ginsberg, Benjamin. *The Captive Public: How Mass Opinion Promotes State Power.* New York: Basic Books, 1986.

Gochman, Charles. "Capability Driven Disputes," In Charles S. Gochman and Alan Ned Sabrosky, eds., *Prisoners of War? Nation-States in the Modern Era,* , Lexington, Mass.: Lexington Books, 1990.

Gochman, Charles, and Zeev Maoz. "Militarized Interstate Disputes, 1816-1976." In Melvin Small and J. David Singer, eds., *International War: An Anthology and Study Guide.* Homewood, Ill.: Dorsey Press, 1985.

Goertz, Gary, and Paul F. Diehl. "Measuring Military Allocations: A Comparison of Different Approaches." *Journal of Conflict Resolution.* 30, no. 3 (September 1986):553-81.

Goertzel, Ted. "Public Opinion concerning Military Spending in the United States: 1937-1985." *Journal of Political and Military Sociology.* 15 (Spring 1987):61-72.

Goldschmidt, Walter. "Inducement to Military Participation in Tribal Societies." In Paul R. Turner and David Pitt, eds., *The Anthropology of War and Peace: Perspectives on the Nuclear Age.* Granby, Mass.: Bergin and Garvey Publishers, 1989.

Gordon, Suzanne, and Dave McFadden. *Economic Conversion: Revitalizing America's Economy,* Cambridge, Mass.: Ballinger, 1984.

Gurr, Ted Robert. "War, Revolution, and the Growth of the Coercive State." *Comparative Political Studies.* 21, no.1 (April 1988):45-65.

Hanson, Betty C., and Bruce M. Russett. "Testing Some Economic Interpretations of American Intervention: Korea, Indochina, and the Stock Market." In Rosen, Steven, ed., *Testing the Theory of the Military-Industrial Complex.* Lexington, Mass.: Lexington Books, 1973.

Harris, Robert. *Gotcha!: The Media, The Government, and the Falklands Crisis.* London: Faber and Faber, 1983.

Hartley, Thomas, and Bruce Russett. "Public Opinion and the Common Defense: Who Governs Military Spending in the United States." *American Political Science Review.* 86, no.4 (December, 1992):905-15.

Henderson, Conway. "Military Regimes and Rights in Developing Countries: A Comparative Perspective." *Human Rights Quarterly.* 1982

Herman, Edward S., and Noam Chomsky. *Manufacturing Consent: The Political Economy of the Mass Media.* New York: Pantheon Books, 1988.

Hess, Robert D., and Judith V. Torney. *The Development of Political Attitudes in Children.* Chicago, Ill.: Aldine Publishing Co., 1967.

Hesse, Petra, and John E. Mack. "The World is a Dangerous Place: Images of the Enemy on Children's Television." In Robert W. Rieber, ed., *The Psychology of War and Peace: Images of the Enemy.* New York: Plenum Press, 1991.

Hilton, Stanley. "The Armed Forces and Industrialists in Modern Brazil: The Drive for Military Autonomy (1889-1954)." *Hispanic American Historical Review.* 62 (November 1982):629-73.

Hintze, Otto. "Military Organization and State Organization." In Felix Gilbert, ed., *The Historical Essays of Otto Hintze.* New York: Oxford University Press, 1975.

Howell, Thomas R., William A. Noellert, Jesse G. Kreier, and Allan W. Wolff. *Steel and the State: Government Intervention and Steel's Structural Crisis.* Boulder, Colo.: Westview Press, 1988.

Huntington, Samuel P. *Political Order in Changing Societies.* New Haven: Yale University Press, 1968.

___. *The Soldier and the State: The Theory and Politics of Civil-Military Relations.* New York: Vintage Books, 1957.

Huth, Paul K. *Extended Deterrence and the Prevention of War.* New Haven: Yale University Press, 1989.

Huth, Paul K., Christopher Gelpi, and D. Scott Bennett. "International Conflict Among the Great Powers: Testing the Interactive Effect of Systemic Uncertainty and Risk Propensity." *Journal of Conflict Resolution.* 36, no. 3 (September 1992):478-517.

Interavia. "Embraer Almost at the Top of the Climb." May 1988, 439.

___. "Production-Line AMX." June 1988, 581.

Janowitz, Morris. "Military Elites and the Study of War." In Leon Bramson and George W. Goethals, eds., *War: Studies from Psychology, Sociology, Anthropology.* New York: Basic Books, 1964.

___. *Military Institutions and Coercion in the Developing Nations.* Chicago Ill.: University of Chicago Press, 1977.

Jervis, Robert. *Perception and Misperception in International Politics.* Princeton, N. J.: Princeton University Press, 1976.

Jones, M.E.F. "Regional Employment Multipliers, Regional Policy, and Structural Change in Interwar Britain." *Explorations in Economic History.* 22 (1985):417-39.

Kaldor, Mary, Margaret Sharp, and William Walker. "Industrial Competitiveness and Britain's Defence." *Lloyds Bank Review.* 162 (October 1986):31-49.

Katz, James Everett, ed. *Arms Production in Developing Countries: An Analysis of Decision Making.* Lexington, Mass.: Lexington Books, 1984.

Kegley, Charles W., Jr., Neil Richardson, and Gunter Richter. "Conflict at Home and Abroad: An Empirical Extension." *Journal of Politics* 40, no. 3 (August 1978):742-52.

Kelejian, H. Harry, and Wallace E. Oates. *Introduction to Econometrics: Principles and Applications.* 3d ed. New York: Harper and Row, 1989.

Kennedy, Gavin. *The Military in the Third World.* London: Duckworth Publishing, 1974.

___. *Defense Economics.* New York: St. Martin's Press, 1983.

Kennedy, Paul. *The Rise and Fall of the Great Powers.* New York: Random House, 1987.

Koistinen, Paul A. C. *The Military-Industrial Complex: A Historical Perspective.* New York: Praeger Publishers, 1980.

Kurth, James R. "Aerospace Production Lines and American Defense Spending." In Steven Rosen, ed *Testing the Theory of the Military-Industrial Complex.* Lexington, Mass.: Lexington Books, 1973.

Langton, Kenneth P. "The Influence of Military Service on Social Consciousness and Protest Behavior: A Study of Peruvian Mine Workers." *Comparative Political Studies.* 16, no. 4 (January 1984):479-503.

Lasswell, Harold D. "The Garrison State." *American Journal of Sociology.* 46 (1941):455-67.

___. "The Garrison State Hypothesis Today." In Samuel Huntington, ed. *Changing Patterns of Military in Politics.* New York: Free Press, 1962.

Lebovic, James H., and Ashfaq Ishaq. "Military Burden, Security Needs, and Economic Growth in the Middle East." *Journal of Conflict Resolution.* 31, no. 1 (1987): 106-38.

Lee, Martin A., and Norman Solomon. *Unreliable Sources: A Guide to Detecting Bias in News Media.* New York: Lyle Stuart, 1990.

Leng, Russell. "When Will They Ever Learn?: Coercive Bargaining in Recurrent Crises." *Journal of Conflict Resolution.* 27, no. 3 (September 1983):379-418.

Leontief, Wassily, and Faye Duchin. *Military Spending: Facts and Figures, Worldwide Implications and Future Outlook.* New York: New York University Press, 1983.

Lieberson, Stanley. "An Empirical Study of Military-Industrial Linkages." In Steven Rosen, ed *Testing the Theory of the Military-Industrial Complex.* Lexington, Mass.: Lexington Books, 1973.

Lifton, Robert Jay. "Beyond Psychic Numbing: A Call to Awareness." *American Journal of Orthopsychiatry.* 52, no. 4 (1982):619-29.

Lock, P. "Brazil: Arms for Export." In Michael Brzoska and Thomas Ohlson eds., *Arms Production in the Third World.* Stockholm: Stockholm International Peace Research Institute, 1986.

Looney, Robert E., and P. C. Frederiksen. "Growth in Developing Countries." *Journal of Peace Research.* December 1986: 329-37.

Louscher, David and Anne Naylor Schwarz. "Patterns of Third World Military Technology Acquisition." In Kwang-il Baek, Ronald D. McLaurin, and Chung-in Moon, eds., *The Dilemma of Third World Defense Industries.* Boulder, Colo.: Westview Press, 1989.

Luckham, Robin. "Armaments, Underdevelopment and Demilitarisation in Africa." *Alternatives.* 6 (1980):179-245.

___. "Armament Culture." *Alternatives*. 10 (1984):1-44.

McCann, Frank D. Jr. "The Brazilian Army and the Pursuit of Arms Independence 1899-1979." In Benjamin Franklin Cooling, ed. *War, Business and World Military-Industrial Complexes*. Washington, D.C.: National University Publications, 1981.

___. "The Formative Period of Twentieth Century Brazilian Army Thought, 1900-1922." *Hispanic American Historical Review*. 64, no. 4 (1984):737-65.

McNeil, William H. *The Pursuit of Power: Technology, Armed Force, and Society since A.D. 1000*. Chicago, Ill.: University of Chicago Press, 1982.

Maoz, Zeev. *Paths to Conflict: International Dispute Initiation, 1816-1976*. Boulder, Colo.: Westview Press, 1982.

___. "Some Comments on Defense Expenditures and Weapons Inventories as Indicators of Military Power." mimeo, University of Michigan, n.d.

Markusen, Ann R." Structural Barriers to Converting the U.S. Economy." Paper presented at ECAR Conference, University of Notre Dame, October 1990.

Melman, Seymour. *Pentagon Capitalism: The Political Economy of War*. New York: McGraw Hill, 1970.

___. *Barriers to Conversion in Planned, Market and Developing Economies*. New York: Report to the United Nations Conference on Disarmament and Development, 1980.

___. *Disarmament: Its Politics and Economics*. Boston, Mass.: American Academy of Arts and Sciences, 1985.

Milano, Fred. "The Benefits of a Violent Society." *Transformations*. 3 (1988):20-43.

Mills, C. Wright. *The Power Elite*. New York: Oxford University Press, 1956.

Mintz, Alex and Michael D. Ward. "The Political Economy of Military Spending in Israel." *American Political Science Review*. 83, no 2 (1989):521.

Morrow, James D. "A Twist of Truth: A Re-examination of the Effects of Arms Races on War." *Journal of Conflict Resolution*. 33, no. 1 (1989):500-29.

Mullins, A.F. *Born Arming: Development and Military Power in New States*. Stanford: Stanford University Press, 1987.

Murilo de Carvalho, Jose. "Armed Forces and Politics in Brazil, 1930-45." *Hispanic American Historical Review*. 62, no. 2 (1982):

Nincic, Miroslav. *The Arms Race: The Political Economy of Military Growth*. New York: Praeger Press, 1982.

Nincic, Miroslav, and Thomas Cusack. "The Political Economy of US Military Spending." *Journal of Peace Research*. 10 (1979):101-15.

Noel-Baker, Philip. *The Private Manufacture of Arms*. New York: Oxford University Press, 1937.

Olson, Mancur, and Richard Zeckhauser. "An Economic Theory of Alliances." *Review of Economics and Statistics*. 48 (1966):266-79.

Organski, A.F.K. *Stages of Political Development*. New York: Alfred A. Knopf, 1965.

Organski, A.F.K., Bruce Bueno de Mesquita, and Alan Lamborn. "The Effective Population in International Politics," In A. E. Keir Nash, ed., *Governance and Population: The Governmental Implications of Population Change*. Commission of Population Growth and the American Future, vol. 4, Washington, D.C.: Government Printing Office, 1972.

Organski, A.F.K., and Jacek Kugler. *The War Ledger*. Chicago, Ill.: University of Chicago Press, 1980.

Organski, A.F.K., Jacek Kugler, J. Timothy Johnson, and Youssef Cohen. *Births, Deaths, and Taxes: The Demographic and Political Transitions*. Chicago, Ill.: University of Chicago Press, 1984.

Peterson, Sophia. "International News Selection by the Elite Press: A Case Study." *Public Opinion Quarterly*. 45 (1981):143-63.

Pierre, Andrew J. *The Global Politics of Arms Sales*. Princeton: Princeton University Press, 1982.

Pion-Berlin, David. "The National Security Doctrine, Military Threat Perception, and The "Dirty War" in Argentina." *Comparative Political Studies*. 21, no. 3 (October 1988):382-407.

Raczka, Witt. "Socio-Historical dimensions of the Military Mobilization Process." Mimeo, The Graduate Institute of International Studies, Geneva, Switzerland, 1989.

Ralston, David B. *Importing the European Army: The Introduction of European Military Techniques and Institutions into the Extra-European World, 1600-1914*. Chicago, Ill.: University of Chicago Press, 1990.

Regan, Patrick M. "Political Repression in the Developing World: What Role Does the Military Play?" Working Paper Series, Program in Conflict Management Alternatives, University of Michigan, Ann Arbor, 1990.

Renshon, Stanley A., ed. *Handbook of Political Socialization: Theory and Research*. New York: Free Press, 1977.

Rieber, Robert W., ed. *The Psychology of War and Peace: The Image of the Enemy*. New York: Plenum Press, 1991.

Rieber, Robert W., and Robert J. Kelly. "Substance and Shadow: Images of the Enemy." In Rieber, ed., *The Psychology of War and Peace: The Image of the Enemy*. New York: Plenum Press, 1991.

Rosecrance, Richard. *The Rise of the Trading State: Commerce and Conquest in the Modern World*. New York: Basic Books, 1986.

Rosenberg, Douglas H. "Arms and the American Way: The Ideological Dimension of Military Growth." In Bruce M. Russett and Alfred Stepan, eds., *Military Force and the American Society*. New York: Harper and Row, 1973.

Rosh, Robert M. "Third World Militarization: Security Webs and the States They Ensnare." *Journal of Conflict Resolution*. 32, no. 4 (1988):671-98.

___. "Third World Arms Production and the Evolving Interstate System." *Journal of Conflict Resolution*. 34, no. 1 (March, 1990):57-73.

Russett, Bruce M. *What Price Vigilance?: The Burdens of National Defense*. New Haven: Yale University Press, 1970.

___. *Controlling the Sword: Democratic Governance of National Security*. Cambridge, Mass.: Harvard University Press, 1990.

Sampson, Steven L., and David A. Kideckel. "Anthropologists Going Into the Cold: Research in the Age of Mutually Assured Destruction." In Paul R. Turner and David Pitt, eds., *The Anthropology of War & Peace: Perspectives on the Nuclear Age*. Granby, Mass.: Bergin and Garvey Publishers, 1989.

Sasaki, Kyohei. "Military Expenditures and the Employment Multiplier in Hawaii." *Review of Economic Statistics*. 45 (August 1963):298-304.

Schramm, Wilbur. "The Effects of Mass Media in an Information Era." In Harold
Lasswell, Daniel Lerner, and Hans Speier, eds., *Propaganda and Communication
in World History, Vol. III: A Pluralizing World in Formation.* Honolulu:
University of Hawaii Press, 1980.

Sen, Gautam. *The Military Origins of Industrialization and International Trade
Rivalry.* London: Frances Pinter, 1984.

Silbeger, Sara, L. "Peers and Political Socialization." In Stanley A. Renshon, ed.,
Handbook of Political Socialization: Theory and Research. New York: Free Press,
1977.

Singer, J. David. "Escalation and Control in International Conflict: A Simple
Feedback Model." *General Systems.* 15 (1970):163-73.

___. "System Structure, Decision Processes, and the Incidence of International War."
In J. David Singer, ed., *Models, Methods, and Progress in World Politics: A Peace
Research Odyssey.* Boulder, Colo.: Westview Press, 1990.

___. "Threat-Perception and the Armament-Tension Dilemma." *Journal of Conflict
Resolution.* 2, no. 1 (March 1958):90-105.

Singer, J. David, Stuart Bremer, and John Stuckey. "Capability Distribution,
Uncertainty, and Major Power War, 1820-1965". In Bruce M. Russett, ed., *Peace,
War, and Numbers.* Beverly Hills, Calf.: Sage Publications, 1972.

Singer, J. David, and Michael Wallace, eds., *To Augur Well: Early Warning Indicators
in World Politics.* Beverly Hills, Calf.: Sage Publications, 1979.

Singer, J. David, et al. "From War to War: The Role of Major Power Decline and
Response, 1816-1985." Mimeo, University of Michigan, 1989.

___. "Socio-Political Conversion: Measuring and Monitoring Some Obstacles to
Prudent Foreign Policies." Mimeo, University of Michigan, 1989.

Skidmore, Thomas. *The Politics of Military Rule in Brazil, 1964-1985.* New York:
Oxford University Press, 1988.

Skowronek, Stephen. *Building a New American State: The Expansion of National
Administrative Capacities, 1877-1920.* New York: Cambridge University Press,
1982.

Slater, Jerome, and Terry Nardin. "The Concept of a Military-Industrial Complex." In
Steven Rosen, ed., *Testing the Theory of the Military-Industrial Complex.*
Lexington, Mass.: Lexington Books, 1973.

Slotkin, Richard, *The Fatal Environment: The Myth of the Frontier in the Age of
Industrialization, 1800-1890.* Middletown, CN: Wesleyan University Press,
1986.

Small, Melvin. "How We Learned to Love the Russians: American Media and the
Soviet Union During World War II." *The Historian.* 36, no. 3 (1974):455-478.

Small, Melvin, and J. David Singer. *Resort to Arms,* Beverly Hill, Calf.: Sage Press,
1982.

Smith, Dan, and Ron Smith. *The Economics of Militarism.* London: Pluto Press,
1983.

Smith, Merit Roe. *Military Enterprise and Technological Change: Perspectives on
the American Experience.* Cambridge, Mass.: MIT Press, 1987.

Snyder, Jack. *Myths of Empire: Domestic Politics and International Ambition.*
Ithaca, N.Y.: Cornell University Press, 1991.

Spencer, Herbert. "The Military and the Industrial Society." In Leon Bramson and George W. Goethals, eds., *War: Studies from Psychology, Sociology, Anthropology*. New York: Basic Books, 1964.

Stepan, Alfred C. *The Military in Politics: Changing Patterns in Brazil*. Princeton, N.J.: Princeton University Press, 1971.

____. *Rethinking Military Politics: Brazil and the Southern Cone*. Princeton, N.J.: Princeton University Press, 1988.

Stephens, Mark, and William E. Cole. "The Brazilian Motor Vehicle Industry: A Holistic Approach to Project Evaluation." *Journal of Economic Issues*. 22, no. 1 (March 1988):381-88.

Thompson, William R. "Polarity, the Long Cycle, and Global Power Warfare." *Journal of Conflict Resolution*. 30, no. 4 (December 1986):587-616.

Tillema, Herbert K. "Foreign Overt Military Interventions in the Nuclear Age." *Journal of Peace Research*. 26, no. 2 (May 1989):

Tilly, Charles. *The Formation of Nation States in Western Europe*. Princeton, N.J.: Princeton University Press, 1975.

____. "War and the Power of Warmakers in Western Europe and Elsewhere, 1600-1980." In Peter Wallersteen, Johan Galtung, and Carlos Portales eds., *Global Militarization*. Boulder, Colo.: Westveiw Press, 1985.

Tolley, Howard Jr. *Children and War: Political Socialization to International Conflict*. New York: Teachers College Press, 1973

____. "Childhood Learning About War and Peace: Coming of Age in the Nuclear Era." In Stanley A. Renshon, ed., *Handbook of Political Socialization: Theory and Research*, New York: Free Press, 1977.

United Nations Statistical Yearbook. New York: United Nations, 1948-1985.

United States Department of Defense. *Semiannual Report of the Secretary of Defense, and the Semiannual Reports of the Secretaries of Army, Navy, and Air Force, January 1 to June 30*. Washington D.C.: Government Printing Office, 1950.

United States Department of Labor. *Domestic Employment Requirements Table*. Washington, D.C.: Bureau of Labor Statistics, 1991.

United States Department of Commerce. *Statistical Abstract of the United States*. Washington D.C.: Government Printing Office, annual.

VanBuskirk, Steve. "Backgrounder." *Veterans of Foreign Wars of the United States Magazine*. 78, no. 5 (January 1991).

Van Evera, Stephen W. "Causes of War." Ph.D. dissertation, University of California at Berkeley, 1984.

Veterans of Foreign Wars of the United States Magazine. "Legislative and Security Priority Goals for 1991." 78, no. 5 (January 1991).

Wallace, Michael D. "Arms Races and Escalation: Some New Evidence." *Journal of Conflict Resolution*. 23, no. 1 (March 1979):3-16.

____. "Old Nails in a New Coffin: The Para Bellum Hypothesis Revisited." *Journal of Peace Research*. 18, no. 3 (1981):91-96.

Waltz, Kenneth N. *Theory of International Politics*. Reading, Mass.: Addison-Wesley Publishing, 1979.

Wayman, Frank W. "Bipolarity and War: The Role of Capability Concentration and Alliance Patterns Among Major Powers, 1816-1965." *Journal of Peace Research*. 21, no. 1 (1984):25-42.

Weede, Erich. "Conflict Behavior of States." *Journal of Peace Research.* 3, no.
     (1970):229-37.
Whitfied, Stephen J. *The Culture of the Cold War.* Baltimore: Johns Hopkins
     University Press, 1991.
Whynes, David, K. *The Economics of Third World Military Expenditure.* Austin:
     University of Texas Press, 1979.
Wionczek, Miguel S. "Growth of Military Industries in Developing Countries: Impact
     on the Process of Underdevelopment." *Bulletin of Peace Proposals.* 17, no.1
     (1986):
Yarmolinsky, Adam. *The Military Establishment: Its Impacts on American Society.*
     New York: Harper and Row, 1971.
Young, Jordan M. *Brazil: Emerging World Power.* Malabar, Fla.: Robert E. Krieger
     Publishing Company,   1982.
Zwick, Jim. "Militarism and Repression in the Philippines." In Michael Stohl and
     George Lopez eds., *The State as Terrorist: The Dynamics of Governmental
     Violence and Repression.* Westport, Conn.: Greenwood Press, 1984.

Index

A Defeza Nacional, 122, 129
Aermacchi of Italy, 137
Aerospace Technical Center
    (CTA), 136
Aerospace Technical Institute
    (ITA), 139
Allison, Graham T., 28, 89
American system of
    manufacturing, 32
Angola ,14
Argentina, 18, 129
arms industry, 19
arms races, 62, 63, 68
arms spiral, 61, 63
Augusto Sa', 122
AVIBRAS, 137
Axelrod, Robert, 67

Bachman, Jerald, G., 10, 31
Baek, Kwang-il, 18
Ball, Nicole, 2, 15, 16, 18,
    22, 35
Barbie doll, 11
Beck, Paul Allen, 99
Belem, 131
Bennett, D. Scott, 59, 66,
    146
Benoit, Emile, 3, 15
Berghahn, V.R., 6
Bernardini company, 136
bipolar system, 64

Bismarck's Germany, 5
Bolivia, 129
Boswell, Terry, 66, 69, 87,
    146
Bramson, Leon, 8
Brazil, 12, 17, 19, 121
Brazilian arms industry, 135
Brazilian military, 120
Brazilian steel industry, 123
Bremer, Stuart, 3, 29, 62, 65
Brigagao, 138
Brunton, Bruce G., 32
Brzoska, Michael, 17, 18
Bueno de Mesquita, Bruce, 3,
    41, 66
bureaucratic inertia, 35

Cadet Associations, 44
Cambodia, 14
Cascaveis, 137
Chaffee, Steven H., 102
children's cartoons, 82
children's toys, 82
Chile, 129
Chomsky, Noam, 38, 82, 101
Civil society, 5, 32
Cobb, Roger W., 20, 21,
    98, 104
coercion, state-led, 61
coercive diplomacy, 61
Cohen, Youssef, 100, 124,
    127

Cold War, 14, 101, 111, 113,
    130, 148
colonial system, 14
concentration of capabilities,
    65, 68-69
conscription, 9
Correlates of War, 49, 67,
    140
Crawford, Neta, 5
Cuban Missile Crisis, 38
Cuiaba, 131
cultural production, 100
culture of the cold war, 20
Cypher, James, 32
Czechoslovakia, former, 17

de Tocqueville, Alexis 57
declining relative power, 62,
    79
Delfim Moreira da Costa
    Ribeiro, 133
demilitarization, 20-22, 55,
    92, 152
Denmark, 132
Department of Defense, 34
Desert Storm, 96, 118
Detroit News, 47
Detroit, Michigan, 150
Deutsch, Karl, 64
Diamond, Greg, 10, 31
Dibble, Vernon, 4
Diehl, Paul F., 29, 41, 62, 63
Dogan, Mattei, 24
Doran, Charles, 3, 62
Duchin, Faye, 155
Dulles, John W. F., 124,
    131
Dumas, Lloyd J., 2, 27, 35,
    155, 156
Dworetz, Steven W., 102, 104

economic constraints, 22
Egypt, 14
Eisenhower, Dwight D., 95
Elder, Charles D., 20, 21,
    98, 104
EMBRAER, 136, 137
emnification, 79, 82, 97

employment multiplier, 44
ENGESA, 136, 137
entertainment outlets, 11, 20,
    96, 97, 102
Escolas de Instrucao Militar,
    125
Estado Novo, 123, 125
Ethiopia, 14
Evil Empire, 154
existential threat, 16, 21, 22,
    27, 37, 48, 49
expectation of violence, 11
external belligerency, 78
external threat, 10, 11, 20,
    21, 37

Falk, Richard, 15
feedback relationship, 2, 21,
    29, 78
Ferguson, R. Brian, 82, 151
feudal Europe, 9
Finer, S.E., 6, 12, 15, 16
Fitch, Samuel, 113
Fort Copacabana, 130
Franko-Jones, Patrice, 17,
    19, 128, 137, 139
Frederiksen, P.C., 15
Freeman's Catalog, 106
frontier myth, 20, 82
Fulbright, J.W., 7, 34
Funkhouser, G. Ray, 38

Galbraith, John Kenneth, 2,
    37, 61, 99
Gallup polls, 106, 112
Gamson, William, 38, 57,
    100, 103, 118, 154
garrison state, 2, 5, 29, 95,
    117, 148
Geller, Daniel, 3
Gelpi, Christopher, 59, 66,
    146
Germany, 123, 130, 153
Geyer, Michael, 1, 4-5
Gilbert, Felix, 8
Gillis, John, 1, 4
Gilpin, Robert, 61, 64, 65,
    79, 80

Ginsberg, Benjamin, 82, 102
global hegemon, 61, 66
Gochman, Charles, 24, 28,
    30
Goertz, Gary, 41
Goertzel, Ted,113
Goethals, George W., 8
Goldschmidt, Walter, 82
Gordon, Dave, 156
Grenada, 38, 81
Gurr, Ted Robert, 2, 21, 28,
    29, 53, 60, 77, 78, 145

Hartley, Thomas, 90
hegemonic leader, 65, 68, 87
Henderson, Conway, 62
Herman, Edward S., 38, 82,
    101
Hess, Robert D., 98, 104
Hesse, Petra, 81, 102
Hilton, Stanley, 17, 129,
    130, 131, 132
Hintze, Otto, 8, 36, 57
Hitler, 96
Honduras, 14
Hopf, Ted, 68, 146
Huntington, Samuel, 6, 28
Hussein, Saddam, 96
Huth, Paul, 50, 59, 66, 146

Ideal Types, 9
IMBEL, 138
induced employment, 40, 44
industrial societies, 8
industrialization, 7, 13, 20
institutions of socialization,
    99
internal militarization, 78
internal politics, 78
internal security, 18
International Politics, 73
international conflict, 18,
    28, 30, 50, 68, 139
international system
    structure, 64
international violence, 29,
    38
Iran, 7, 151

Iran, Shah of, 151
Iraq ,7, 14, 81, 96
Ishaq, Ashfaq, 11, 15, 49
isolationism, 52
Israel, 7, 14
Italy, 130

J. C. Penney, 111
Janowitz, Morris, 6, 8, 57
Japan, 22, 130, 153
Japan, Imperial, 153
Japan, pre-Imperial, 8
Jervis, Robert, 62
Jones, M.E.F., 44
JROTC programs, 44

Kegley, Charles, 21, 62
Kelejian, Harry H., 84
Kelly, Robert J.,79
Kennedy, Paul, 2, 27, 61,
    64, 68, 79, 80
Kideckel, David A., 10, 82
Kingston, Jean, 63
Koistinen, Paul A.C., 7, 95
Koran, 151
Krupp, 132, 133
Kugler, Jacek, 3, 62, 64
Kurth, James, 89
Kuwait, 96

Lalman, David ,3, 66
Lamborn, Allan, 41
Langton, Kenneth, 9
Lasswell, Harold, 2, 5, 11,
    18, 21, 23, 29, 37, 53,
    57, 60, 78, 79, 95, 104,
    117, 144, 148
Lebovic, James H., 11, 15,
    49
Lee, Martin A., 38, 82, 101
Lehman, Ronald, 27
Leontief, Wassily, 155
Lifton Robert J., 104
Lock P, 19, 136
logrolling politics, 60
Looney, Robert E., 15
Louscher, David, 136

Luckham, Robin, 62, 100,
    102

Mack, John E., 81, 102
Magill's Cinema Survey, 106-
    107
Malvina-Falkland Islands, 139
manipulation of symbols, 20
Mansbach, Richard, 151
Maoz, Zeev, 24, 65
mass media,11, 20, 100,
    102, 149, 154
mass-circulation newspapers,
    47-48
Mato Grosso, 131
Mauser rifles, 132
McCann, Frank D., Jr., 19,
    121, 122, 123, 125,
    129, 132, 133, 137
McCarthyism, 101
McFadden, Suzzane, 156
McLaurin, Ronald D., 18
McNeil , William, 9, 16, 32
medieval Europe, 13
Melman, Seymour, 2, 7, 22,
    27, 35, 155, 156
Milano, Fred, 118
Militarism, 5, 12
militarist society, 5
militaristic, 6, 12
militarization, 4, 7, 8, 11,
    20, 23, 27, 29, 52, 54,
    55, 60, 62, 69, 71-74,
    79, 82, 92, 97, 107, 152
militarization
    index, 41, 45
    process, 12, 97
    changes in, 71
militarized disputes. see
    international conflict
military allocations, 11
military infrastructure, 15
military socialization, 102
military spending, 40
military training programs, 13
military veterans, 10, 13, 31,
    40

Military-Industrial Complex,
    7, 24, 37, 56, 57, 60,
    72, 78, 82, 95, 96, 99,
    103, 140, 148
militia society, 5
Mills, C Wright, 6, 95
Mintz, Alex, 11, 15, 90
missile gap, 81
Modigliani, Andre, 38, 57,
    100, 103, 118, 154
Monitoring the Future, 106
Montgomery Ward catalog,
    111
Morrow, James, 29, 62, 63
Motor Vehicle Manufacturers
    Association, 152
Mullins, A. F., 11
multipolar, 64
munitions industries, 45
Murilo de Carvalho, Jose,
    123, 125, 126

Nardin, Terry, 7, 38, 95
national prestige, 16
national security, 16, 35, 81,
    118
nationalism, 31, 96, 103
Nazi Germany, 10, 22, 44,
    153
New York Times, 46, 47
newly industrializing
    societies, 16
Nicaragua, 14
Nincic, Miroslav, 3, 11, 27,
    35, 36, 56, 90
Noel-Baker, Phillip, 101
nonindustrial societies, 13
nonmilitarized society, 9
North Korea, 14

Oates, Wallace E., 84
Ohlson, Thomas, 17, 18
Olson, Mancur, 67
Organski, A.F.K., 3, 15, 41,
    62, 64

Panama, 38, 81
Paraguay, 129

Parsons, Wes, 3, 62
patriotic themes, 20
patriotism, 10, 96, 97, 103
Pax Britannia, 58
peacetime draft, 20
Pearl Harbor, 81
Pelassy, Dominique, 24
Peron, Juan, 124
Persian Gulf, 38
Peterson, Sophia, 47
Pion-Berlin, David, 18
Piper Aircraft, 137
political legitimacy, 35
political use of symbols, 79,
    95
politico-centrism, 10, 82
Popular myths, 10
Porto Alegre, 131
power cycle, 3
power elite, 6, 42
power transition, 3
preparations for war, 10, 12,
    18, 28
production of military
    hardware, 13
propaganda model, 101

Raczka, Witt, 29, 36
Ralengo, 131
Ralston, David B., 19, 32
Rambo-type movies, 11
ratchet effect, 39, 57
Reagan, Ronald,112, 154
relative capabilities, 80
religious fundamentalism,
    151
Renshon, Stanley ,102
research and development, 40
Richardson, Neil, 21, 62
Richter, Gunter, 21, 62
Rieber, Robert W., 79, 82
Rio de Janeiro, 129
Rio Grande do Sul, 129
Rosecrance, Richard, 1, 8
Rosen, Steven, 7, 23, 28,
    95, 96
Rosenberg, Douglas H., 82
Rosh, Robert, 11, 15, 28,   49

ROTC program, 44
Russett, Bruce, 23, 27, 35,
    56, 57, 61, 75, 79, 90

Sampson, Steven L., 10, 82
Santa Catarin-Parana, 129
Sao Paulo rebellion, 123,
    130
Sasaki, Kyohei, 44
Saudi Arabia, 96
Schramm, Wilbur, 100, 102,
    103, 104, 117
Schwarz, Anne Naylor, 136
Sears Catalog, 106
security dilemma, 37, 61,
    63, 68, 71
security elite, 95
self-amplifying feedback, 60,
    77, 144
Sen, Guatam, 8, 16, 28, 32
Sigelman, Lee, 10, 31
Silbiger, Sara L., 99
simultaneous equations, 83
Singer, J. David, 3, 29, 50,
    60-65, 78, 145
Skidmore, Thomas, 125,
    127, 131
Skowronek, Stephan, 42
Slater, Jerome, 7, 38, 95
Slotkin, Richard, 20, 82, 97
Small, Melvin, 22, 49, 81,
    100, 154
Smith, Dan, 22, 27
Smith, Merit Roe, 32
Smith, Ron, 22, 27
Snyder, Jack, 60-61
social manipulation, 95
socialization, 19
societal symbols, 56, 148
Solomon, Norman, 38, 82,
    101
South Africa, 14
South Korea, 14, 17
Southeast Asia, 113
Soviet Union, 10, 14, 20, 22,
    100
Spencer, Herbert, 8
Stepan, Alfred C., 19, 138

Stuckey, John, 3, 29, 62, 65
Sudan, 14
Sunday *Times* of London, 46
Sweat, Mike, 66, 69, 87,
    146
Symbolic politics, 79, 96,
    97, 98, 117, 149, 145,
    150
symbols of nationalism, 2,
    10, 31
symbols of patriotism, 97,
    104
Syria, 14
system clarity, 62, 64-65
system concentration, 70,
    73, 87, 89
system leadership, 59, 64,
    67, 69, 70, 73, 87
system of equations, 84

Taiwan, 17
Technical Center of the Army
    (CTEX), 136
technological development,
    13, 27, 32, 39, 41, 45,
    54, 57, 81
Third Reich, 44
Thompson, William, 66
Threats
    existential and
    manipulated, 35
    perception of a threat,
        19, 23, 29, 37, 38,
        39, 46, 48, 56, 97,
        100,144
    manipulation of, 18
Tilly, Charles, 9, 12, 13,
    16, 36
Tolley, Howard Jr., 99
Torney, Judith V., 98, 104
traditional society, 12
TSLS, 85

unipolar system, 65
U.S. automobile industry, 149

Van Evera, Stephan, 2, 8,
    32, 57

Vargas, Getulio, 123, 124,
    127
veteran groups, 40
Vietnam, 14, 81
Vietnam syndrome, 81
violent foreign policy, 2, 22,
    29, 53, 59, 70, 139,
    145
Volta Redonda, 134

Wallace, Michael, 62, 63
Waltz, Kenneth, 64, 89,
    146
war movies, 95, 106, 107,
    108, 109, 111, 148
war toys, 95, 96, 105, 107,
    108, 111, 148
Ward, Michael, 11, 15, 90
war-proneness, 65
wars
    Brazilian-Paraguayan,
        131
    Brazilian-Uruguayan,
        129
    Falkland/Malvina, 38
    Iran-Iraq, 139
    Korean, 112, 154
    Lybian-Egyptian, 139
    Paraguayan, 119
    Persian Gulf, 104, 118
    Vietnam, 38, 43, 112,
        154
Wayman, Frank, 3, 66
weapons industries, 42
weapons procurement, 131
Weede, Erich, 21, 62
Whitfield, Stephen, 20, 81,
    82, 101

Yarmolinsky, Adam, 34
Young, Jordan M., 138

Zeckhauser, Richard, 67
Zimbabwe, 14
Zwick, Jim, 15, 62

About the Author

PATRICK M. REGAN is a Lecturer in Political Science at the University of Canterbury in Christchurch, New Zealand. He received his Ph.D. from the University of Michigan.